PENGUIN BOOKS

Life's What You Make It

Life's What You Make It

The Autobiography

PHILLIP SCHOFIELD

PENGUIN BOOKS

PENGUIN BOOKS

UK | USA | Canada | Ireland | Australia
India | New Zealand | South Africa

Penguin Book is part of the Penguin Random House group of companies
whose addresses can be found at global.penguinrandomhouse.com.

First published by Michael Joseph 2020
Published in Penguin Books 2021
001

Plate section: Plate 1: Page 3, top left image: © TVNZ/Getty; Plate 2: Page 1, middle image:
© Celador Entertainment; Plate 2: Page 4, top two images: © Photographs by David Hartley;
Plate 2: Page 7, bottom image: © Photograph by Nicky Johnston, Camera Press London.
Integrated: 1. P. 92, © TVNZ/Getty; **3.** P. 231 & P. 234, © Photographs by Terry McGough; **4.** P. 267,
© Celador Entertainment; **5.** P. 289 © Freemantle; **6.** P. 309 & P. 314 © ITV/Shutterstock.
Every effort has been made to trace copyright holders and to obtain their permission for the use of copyright
material. The publisher apologizes for any errors or omissions and would be grateful to be notified of any
corrections that should be incorporated in future editions of this book.

Typeset by Jouve (UK), Milton Keynes
Printed and bound in Great Britain by Clays Ltd, Elcograf S.p.A.

The authorized representative in the EEA is Penguin Random House Ireland,
Morrison Chambers, 32 Nassau Street, Dublin D02 YH68

A CIP catalogue record for this book is available from the British Library

ISBN: 978-0-241-50119-1

www.greenpenguin.co.uk

For Steph, Molly and Ruby,

Three remarkable women in my life, who, no matter what,
still continue to love me and who have saved me more
times than they will ever know. I love you
all so very, very much.

Writing this book has been a fascinating experience for me, a sort of controlled unravelling of my head, in some ways a reboot, remembering things I didn't realize I'd forgotten. I didn't think for a second, as I sat with my fingers poised over my laptop keyboard at the start of this adventure, that I'd learn anything new about myself. As it turns out, I have. I've always documented my life in one way or another, keeping diaries and even jotting down lines that I imagined would go in my autobiography one day if I was to ever write one. I even wrote what I thought would be the first line, a line that ended up in this very book, when I was just fourteen. My diaries have helped me as I've written, and this 1986 diary has 'Life's What You Make It' written on the front. It rang true then, and it rings true still.

Prologue

On 7 February 2020 at 9.45 a.m. my thumb hesitated briefly over my phone. I looked nervously at those around me, then pressed send and posted these words (and some others) on Instagram:

> You never know what's going on in someone's seemingly perfect life . . .

The response was instantaneous and huge, a massive wave of surprised attention. In my life, I like to think I've been honest and open, mostly. Now, hopefully, I can add some detail to that statement and tell you who I am, the real person behind the bloke you know from the telly and the life that led up to those words, long before they were even a spark of awareness in my head. Some of my life you may already know. Here's the rest.

I've been asked to write a book for as long as I can remember. At first, I didn't think I'd lived enough, then I was so busy and distracted I couldn't be bothered. In more recent years, when the pressure to write my story got seriously intense, there was always a very painful consideration: I knew where it would, eventually, have to go, unless I wasn't truthful. I decided that I couldn't lie, so I never agreed to write it.

As you probably know, I have recently decided that the truth was the only thing that could save me. Let me stress, right from the start, that my 'truth' took a very long time to make itself clear to me. I have never deliberately hidden anything, but as my psychologist has pointed out on a number of occasions, we humans are complicated. We can evolve within ourselves. If we are lucky, we find clarity in our lives. As I got older, that is exactly what happened: I discovered something about myself that I had no idea was there. I found clarity, and that has taken a long time to process. So, it's as a by-product of a lot of pain – pain that continues – that this book can finally be written. That, coupled with the fact that, as I type, I'm sitting in lockdown as the Covid-19 pandemic has put the world on pause, so I have a shitload of time on my hands!

Writing this book has been a fascinating experience for me, a sort of controlled unravelling of my head, in some ways a reboot, remembering things I didn't realize I'd forgotten. I didn't think for a second, as I sat with my fingers poised over my laptop keyboard at the start of this adventure, that I'd learn anything new about myself. As it turns out, I have.

As I wrote about the big, conflicting decisions that I've made in my life, a pattern has emerged. I stress and I fret, I worry and tie myself up in ever-tighter knots. I keep myself awake at night in never-ending loops of turmoil, but the outcome always seems to be the same. As I enter into a huge life choice, it would appear that I already know what I'm going to do, it just takes me a while to get there – sometimes overnight, sometimes considerably longer. I seem to put myself through rounds of torture before I'm prepared to take a life-changing step. That's odd for me, because when it comes to major career choices I trust my judgement implicitly and I'll willingly jump into a new challenge without any great analysis – I go with my gut and act instinctively. Not so in my private life. I strap myself to the rack and let my mind stretch me out in unnecessary, elongated distress.

I've discovered that, in later life, I've become increasingly more adept at creating these 'thought loops' in my head. One big, mentally destructive loop encompassing everything, and then there are many smaller loops of unfixable issues around that, like planets orbiting the sun, going round and round in endless, exhausting cycles. I have recognized that they were always a part of my analysis process, but in recent times, these loops have been very much bigger and immensely challenging. Seemingly unfathomable, uncontrollable issues and impossible decisions. I've also learned that, in time, most things work out for the best, that each loop, taken in isolation, can be broken. With help, I have taken a careful note of this new knowledge and I will strive to be better at 'loop management'.

Perhaps most importantly of all, I've learned that we are indeed the masters of our own destiny, but life doesn't happen to us without the people we love and the people who love us. We can't do it on our own – we all need help, and we all need to trust that our families love us because we're worth loving, and that our friends are there because they care, no matter what. Take it from someone who has sat on the very edge and looked over: things do work out, things do get better.

It's so easy to go through our lives so quickly that we don't take the time to stop, look around, look up and appreciate the moments that should be celebrated. We're always looking to the 'next' rather than enjoying the 'now'. Those moments can be huge leaps forward or even the very tiny everyday steps, but just pause for that moment, give yourself permission to reflect on an achievement before you rush on. Now I've stopped, I've looked up, taken a deep breath and quietly celebrated in my head. I made it this far, I'm happy to have done the things that I've done, I'm grateful for everyone who has been with me on my life adventure. I most certainly could not have done it on my own. Everyone we meet is an influence on us in one way or another; they shape us, they guide us, they teach us to be wise or wary. So as I have taken a moment to pause and look around, I see you, we're still here, we're okay, and life is there waiting for us, if we are willing to allow ourselves to live it. Life, it seems, *is* what you make it.

Well, then, here we go, finally. I hope I'm what you expected me to be.

I

'Coke!' barked the large, bright-red man in front of me. At the age of fifteen, and safely separated from his painfully sunburnt fists and biceps by a wooden counter, I waited for a few seconds to see if he followed that with 'please'. He didn't. Game on.

I was born in Oldham, but I lived in Newquay, Cornwall, from the age of eighteen months. The beach was core to the life of the town, our family and my school friends, though I have a problem with sand (I'll come to that later). As the long summer holidays rolled out in front of me, the first thing I had to do was try and secure a summer job. As with most of the county, making enough money during the summer months means the difference between an easy winter and a difficult one. Obviously, for a business, hay in August has to be made to pay the employees' wages in February. For me personally, though, I needed enough money to buy my Christmas presents and some dodgy seventies Hai Karate talc, which I hoped might impress Louise Tucker. It never did. I did get to kiss her, however, when I was Prince Charming in our school panto and she was Cinderella. Louise lived on Pentire headland, like me, and was part of our school-bus gang. I never stood a chance, but she did appear on my *This is Your Life* twenty-five years later. Result.

The ice-cream kiosk was at the bottom of the steps at the Pentire end of Fistral beach. Landing a summer job in there was a triumph. Reasonable money, I could choose my hours, and occasionally a Pink Panther chocolate bar was thrown in, too. I have no idea why that was my sweet of choice, but it was bright pink and looked a bit avant garde. Because I was fickle, later I was to choose Walnut Whips, but I went off those because my nan kept asking for the walnut: 'Ooh, can I have the walnut off the top, Phillip?' Obviously, I said yes, but internally I was screaming, 'What's the point of having a Walnut Whip if I don't get to eat the bloody walnut?' Anyway, soon after, I moved on to Bounty, and stayed there for life. (The dark-chocolate ones are the best.)

My nan was a hard, uncompromising Northerner. Walking into her kitchen was a horror show – she would eat anything and everything. I'd sometimes pop in after school and there'd be a couple of hearts bubbling away in a pan on

A terrific nan, not such a great mother.

the stove. I deeply regret not getting her recipe for muffins but, other than that, I wasn't impressed with her cooking. The conversation would usually run something like this:

'Phillip, you've left your chicken.'

'It's fatty.'

'There is *no fat on a chicken*.'

Well, on hers, there was. She was a fun grandmother, but a terrible mother. She could regale me with the most wonderful stories, yet would show no approval or love to my mum. The way Nan treated her daughter did, however, benefit me and my brother, Tim. Every bit of affection my mum wished her mother had shown her, our mum compensated for by showering the two of us with love. She still does.

So here I am. It's a beautiful sunny day, I've run barefoot, at top speed, for no reason, from the guest house we ran ten minutes from the beach. I never wore shoes – the soles of my feet were like leather – and if I wasn't barefoot, I was wearing flip-flops. There's still a gap between my big toes and the ones next to them where the rubber gripper went through. My shift has started, I'm in a great mood, and up comes the rude, red fool for his Coke. If he had said thank you, or smiled, that would have been that; we would both have gone about our days, enjoying the beach. But he didn't, he just stared me down, with his bright-red face and his peeling back, standing menacingly at the front of the queue. Every morning, for just such an obnoxious customer, who treated summer workers like something on his shoe, I arrived early, took a can of Coke from the shelf and banged it swiftly ten times on the wooden floor of the kiosk. Not enough to dent it, just enough to make the contents angry and explosive. Then it was put back in its own special place, waiting for a moment like this.

'Sure,' I said. 'Anything else?'

'Crisps!'

'What flavour can I get you?'

'*Plain.*'

'Fine.' (You arsehole.)

He threw his money on the counter, turned and headed off down the beach, with his crisps and a specially prepped can of fizz. As I served the other customers, I watched, my eyes carefully following him down the steps and on to the sand as he picked his way through the jumble of towels, inflatables and windbreakers. I knew I'd lose sight of him, but it didn't matter, I'd soon see where he had set up camp for the day . . . three . . . two . . . one . . . *there* he is! From about a hundred feet away came the brown, sugary plume, bursting from the confines of the can, climbing up, up, into the air. That brief, delicious moment when it paused before gravity beckoned it back to the beach and the bright-red man with the peeling back below. He was soaked: bald head, beach towel, too-small shorts. An almost imperceptible smile washed across my face. As he bellowed, it was only moments before the second instalment began . . . the wasps!

I knew he'd be back, I knew he'd be furious, as the others had been before him. I knew I'd have to be careful, because I'm allergic to wasp stings (I'll come back to that). I would feign horror at his stickiness, apologize profusely, give him a replacement, 'Better open that one carefully. Did you shake the first one at all?'

If you're reading this, and you ever got sprayed by a can of Coke on the Pentire end of Fistral beach, pleased to meet you again and thank *you*.

I've always been thankful that my mum, Pat, and dad, Brian, fell in love with Cornwall on their honeymoon. Don't get me wrong, I'm proud of my Lancashire roots, but to grow up in the place where everybody else came on their holidays was lucky and then some. Mum and Dad had moved down from Oldham and my dad started work with Bilbo, a fledgling surfboard company. He was one of those guys who could turn his hand to pretty much anything, always busy, never still. In fact, the only time we ever rowed was when I said, 'I'm bored.' He couldn't understand what I meant by it.

'Get up, get off your arse and find something to do.'

He made the first surfboards in the UK. The factory on Pargolla Road was an adventure in itself, foam boards ready to be fibreglassed, each individually designed and coated in resin. I wish I had a picture of the resin room; there was every colour you can imagine, dripping waterfalls of colour that hardened into their own unique artwork. The fibreglass itched like hell, though, if you got it on your skin.

Downstairs was a vending machine that made the best chicken soup ever. It had never been within ten miles of a chicken, but its fakeness was delicious and is a lasting memory. I'm lucky to have eaten some of the best food in the best restaurants in the world, but give me a Pot Noodle or a Vesta Chow Mein and I'm yours. On the subject of food, if you ever ate a Matthews pasty in Newquay, you'll probably feel the same tantalizing thrill as I do when I mention them. Long since closed, their pasties were unbeatable. I think they used flaky pastry, but the meat juices would run out and caramelize on the underside. The pastry was just the right side of burned. (If you know how they did it, and you can re-create it, I'll come round.) No one could beat them but, even now, the family tradition when I go back to Cornwall is a pasty one day, and then the next day Flounders fish and chips, eaten out of the paper while overlooking Little Fistral, the wide Atlantic spread out in front of us. If you left the beach and travelled in a straight line, the next landfall would be Newfoundland.

Newquay has some of the best surfing beaches in the world. The swell can form perfect waves that peel over majestically before crashing on to the golden sand, but it can also be brutal and unruly. I can stand for hours on the headland and watch the sea with its wild, untamable power relentlessly crashing against the cliffs. The plaintive cry of the seagulls and the salty tang in the air always reboots my head. The reef off Little Fistral is quite close to the surface, so on a stormy day it can create an awesome sight with the 'Cribbar' wave. It's a monster, also known as 'the Widow Maker'. Climbing to over thirty feet, it was first surfed in 1966 and now, experienced big-wave surfers from all over the world put their trust in their skill and take their lives by the throat to ride it.

You'd think, with that surfboard heritage, I'd be able to surf. But I couldn't afford a wetsuit, I was painfully skinny and it was just too bloody cold, so I never really took to surfing. I can, however, body surf, which is cheaper, because you don't need any equipment. One of my proudest moments was when my mum and dad went to a surfing museum while on holiday in Hawaii and one of the boards my dad had made

Mum and Dad in Hawaii.

was hanging as an exhibit. He was thrilled. By the way, he couldn't surf either . . . same reason.

We took in visitors at our six-bedroom guest house on Lawton Close. Long hours and very hard work for my mum, but my grandma and grandad came down from Oldham every summer to help, which was great, apart from the fact that it wasn't, because my grandma drove my mum mad. However, Mum's hard work and our happy guests earned us a happy Christmas.

My dad was always at work in the garage, fixing things,

Stood at the front door of the house on Pentire with my grandma Hilda and grandad Harold, who were down for the summer.

making things. He was a French polisher by trade, so he was always polishing something for someone, so he had the best smell. He always smelled of wood. To me, my dad was made of mahogany.

In the summer we all slept in the garage, which Dad had converted into three bedrooms. During the winter, when the guests had left, I got the pick of the bedrooms. Which would I choose this year? Blue, yellow, pink, green? The yellow one upstairs was always my favourite, for two reasons. Firstly, I could climb out of the window, up the slate tiles and sit on the flat roof above my window. On a starry night, the view was beautiful, especially if I had a packet of Cadets! My best mate and I decided one summer holiday that we would smoke a packet of every brand of cigarettes from Mr Snell's tobacconist's down the road (there were lots more brands back then). Like a couple of elderly connoisseurs, we'd sit on the headland, open a new brand, and say, 'Hmm, I thought the Everest were much mintier than the Consulate,' or 'I thought the long, thin More would last longer,' or 'Christ! Capstan Full Strength?! Mate, I'm going to puke.' I know, I know, how utterly stupid we were, but those were heady days, when no one had told us what was going to kill us. For my night-time outing on the roof that particular summer, I'd chosen Cadets. I thought them 'very smooth'.

The second reason for loving the yellow bedroom was the secret camp I had in the wardrobe, where I could safely stash said contraband. Recently, I met a woman who lived in that house a few years after us. After telling her which bedroom I meant – 'As you look at the front of the house, it's upstairs on the left' – I went on to ask if there was still a removable panel on the inside of the built-in wardrobe. She was disappointed to relay that, unfortunately, she had never found it. Ah, what a pity. In my day, it was my hideaway. Through the wardrobe, fingernails at the top of the panel, and there was my own teenage Narnia in the eaves of the roof. Where it lacked Tumnus, it excelled in *Health & Efficiency*. Those thrilling naturist magazines full of naked people playing tennis, having a barbecue (a risky business; people were much hairier back then!) and sharing a sauna. Looking back, it was as tame as flicking through the underwear section in my mum's catalogues, but that's how we got our thrills. Add to that my Manchester United football cards, my collection of stones (to this day, I still take stones from memorable places I've been; sadly, I omitted to label them and I now have a reasonable collection of anonymous gravel), and my MI5 secret spy tape, and there you have it – a proper camp.

The secret spy MI5 tape? Well, when I found it by the side of the road I was terrified I'd get caught in possession of something so obviously highly classified. For weeks, I didn't tell anyone I had it, I just waited for a late-night banging at the door, the barking of the sniffer dogs and the splintering of wood as Her Majesty's Secret Service smashed their way into the hall. It was small, rectangular and plastic, with two spools of oxidized micro tape. I'd never seen anything like it before. It was only when the woman next door upgraded her sound system that I saw more of them. I was dumbstruck. She could definitely be a spy – after all, she and her boyfriend had matching E-Types; his was red, hers yellow . . . God, I loved that red E-type. The day he pranged it I felt almost as bad as he did. Anyway, so, obviously, they're spies! I've busted them wide open. It was only when she put her cassette into the new player and out came the music of Rick Wakeman that I realized what I had in my possession might not be quite so special. Turns out it was the Bee Gees' *Main Course* album. Wasn't a bad listen, actually, and when I got to 'Fanny, Be Tender with My Love', I laughed for days.

It's a wonder I survived, really. Only when you look back at the madness of youth do you realize how bloody close you got to calamity. We used to ride our bikes up to the headland to hang out. We'd sit, chatting (and smoking) with our feet dangling over the cliff edge, the sea crashing into the Tea Caverns about a hundred feet below. These huge caves were notorious in the town's history for stashing smuggled goods, usually China tea, which would provide rich rewards, if they got away with it. What never entered my head was the fact that the mighty Atlantic was boiling on the rocks below. If you look at that cliff edge now, the bit we sat on has long since fallen in . . . and that's my point! We were literally sitting on the thinnest outcrop of heather and air. We were a miracle away from a one-way Tea Cavern excursion. DO NOT DO THIS.

We each made a 'Dilly', essentially, a go-kart consisting of a plank of wood, a box at the back to sit in, big pram wheels at the rear and smaller wheels at the front mounted on a

My happy place on the rocks by the sea in Newquay.

cross plank with a rope attached to steer. We would push off, yelping with delight as we picked up ridiculous speed down Riverside Avenue. Now, I've always been shite at DIY – any family member will tell you – so it's inevitable that something I've made is going to come apart, and those Dillies did so with alarming regularity and in spectacular style. My mates would scream with laughter as I flew past. I'd feel the first vibrations of an impending systems failure, then something would come apart: a wheel, the box, the plank . . . me. As another creation tore itself to bits at breakneck speed, I would roll and bounce, along with the rest of the debris, down the road, but it was worth it. 'Mate, that was incredible, you're such an idiot,' was all I needed to hear.

One of the happiest days *ever* came when I walked out of the back door to see my new present. My birthday is in April, but I'd waited until July to take delivery of my yellow Chopper. Oh, I loved that bike, almost as much as I loved the red E-Type. Long seat, three-gear stick shift. It had to be yellow. I didn't like the orange, and I wanted either the red or the yellow to match one of the E-Types next door, and I preferred the yellow. There it was, brand new and gleaming. I saved my summer money and bought two battery horns, a switch on each handlebar, so if I pressed them alternately it sounded like a police car (what a nob). One thing was missing – it had to have a speedo; but this was stretching the finances, so I had to put in a few extra hours at the kiosk. Finally, it was fully kitted out – oh yeah! I put mirrors on it, too. I rode it for miles. It's funny how everyone needs to know where you are now, every second. Are you okay? You didn't call – when are you home? In those simpler times, it was 'I'm going out on my bike' at nine in the morning, and I'd come home at nine at night to a dried-out dinner and the threat of a grounding.

With my brother on the yellow Chopper; the Dutch VW van in the background.

The day I 'Choppered' Rejerrah hill is a day I shouldn't be proud of, but I am. A day I was lucky to survive and one of those days I'm glad my folks didn't know where I was. The hill is a few miles out of Newquay, on the way to Goonhavern on the A3705, steep down, then steep back up the other side. On a bike, my theory was, the more momentum you build up on the way down one side, the further up the other side you'd get and the less you'd knacker your legs trying to pedal up it. I'm not sure if it was a dare, but I'm pretty sure 'You've got a speedo, how fast can you go?' were among the words spoken.

We set out early because it's a fair old trek, and later that morning I sat astride the yellow lightning streak at the brow of the hill, looking at the drop and the climb on the other side. This is a main road: it was then; it is now. My dad's mate had a car accident on the hill in a Lotus Europa, bright orange, made out of fibreglass. Thankfully, no one was hurt, but he was flying down the hill and he only touched the other car, but the Europa literally disappeared in a puff of fibre around him. Apparently, by the time he got halfway up the other side, he was sitting on just the chassis! Still makes me laugh.

So it's a dangerous hill, especially if you're a teen fool on a Chopper, and as cycling helmets were a good few years away, a teen fool with a fully visible Noel Edmonds hairstyle, centre parting, wearing jeans, a T-shirt and . . . flip-flops. The agreement was that my mates would watch as I attempted the feat, then I'd rejoin them and we'd all ride home, and I'd be the hero.

As I set off, I'm pretty sure someone said something about dying, but it was too late. It became very obvious, very quickly, that my legs weren't going to be playing a major role in the descent. After about ten seconds they were flying round on the pedals so fast I was forced to retract the landing gear and put my feet up by the gear stick. Now I'm really shifting it (at this point spelt with an 'f'!), 20 . . . 30 . . . 40 . . . 50 mph. My seventies Noel Edmonds cut is streaming out behind me. I realize at that point, if there is the tiniest of quivers in my hands, the bike will begin a catastrophic 'Dilly-like' wobble. (Now change the 'f' to a 't'!) This is ridiculous, way too fast. The speedo only goes up to sixty and the needle is almost there.

Three quarters of the way down, it hits sixty, the needle stops on the limiter pin. I'm almost at the bottom, galvanized with fear, the noise of the wind is deafening. Please make it stop. I glance down to see the speedometer needle snap off. I don't have time to be angry that I broke it; it took a lot of red men and Coke cans to buy it, but I'll only consider anger and disappointment if I actually survive. I'm levelling off, at last. I start to fly up the other side.

One of the greatest surprises of the experience was that, on a bike, using only momentum, the speed bleeds off really quickly. In moments, I'm rapidly slowing. Did I really think I'd reach the top of the other side? A quarter of the way up, I can think about putting my feet on the pedals. Slower, slower, then stop. My heart is racing, my palms are wet through, I'm totally pumped with adrenaline. I turn back to my mates and wave, and they wave back to me. I'm alive, and surely that has to be some kind of yellow-Chopper record? I turn around, wheel the bike to the other side of the road and, using the brakes, coast back to the bottom and look up. Shit! There's no way I can pedal all the way up there, so I get off and push. It seems to take hours to get back to my starting place, and when I do, they're gone. Bored of waiting, they've set off home, and I ride back into town, tired but triumphant. I saw them the next day.

'How fast did you go?'

'The speedo needle snapped off at sixty.'

'Ah, right.'

'Yeah, broke the speedo.'

'Right.'

And that was it, but that was my mates. Next.

I can't say that my friends were always the best, if I'm honest, but that was partly my fault. There were principally three of us, never a great combination, and we were so good at making it difficult for ourselves. Only two of us were ever mates at any one time, so for the third there was an obligatory period in exile. It was so frustrating because I always seemed to be the one left out at the start of the summer

18

holidays. I say it was partly my fault, because when it was my turn to be 'in' the mix, I revelled in the attention and made whoever was the third wheel at that time pay. On the rare occasion the three of us would all get on and hang out together as a trio, that was when, for me, it was the best fun.

One of our summer holidays was spent working at the Tank Range. Obviously, you're now thinking Territorial Army and military hardware. Not quite. My dad's boss at the surf factory had diversified into boutiques and surf shops. The boutiques were a hippy cornucopia. I bought stupidly tight Karmann Ghia high-waisted jeans and cheesecloth shirts as the Beach Boys played. Every mystic fragrance of incense was there – sandalwood, patchouli, jasmine and pine (the back of that wardrobe smelled amazing). Quick note: you can't crush and smoke a patchouli incense stick, or indeed any incense stick; the taste is particularly awful.

So, with the shops came the brilliant idea of a tank range, built on the same principle as those remote-controlled boats on a lake. It was decided that twenty-five miniature Sherman tank kits should be bought. My dad designed the rolling hills, trees and pill boxes for the range and we were going to set it up in an empty shop next door to the boutique. The three amigos (currently all getting on) were to build the tanks over the winter. About a foot long each and incredibly intricate, they were pigs to build. The tracks alone consisted of hundreds of tiny parts. It wasn't long before one amigo got bored and didn't come back.

By the start of the summer, the range had been finished, thirty-two Sherman tanks built and individually sprayed. It was an impressive sight. My summer job that year was to supervise and fix. I worked in shifts, sometimes with Dad. The shifts with him were my least favourite, because he wouldn't let me sit down. It all seemed like a great idea, until we reached the fundamental flaw: the batteries were fantastically incendiary. I'd have my back to the range, standing in the fake supervisor's pill box, fixing another broken track, when I'd hear a child cry out in glee.

'Oh my God, Dad, that's so realistic! Did I shoot you?'

'I don't know, son, but this is the best 10p I've ever spent.'

A rapid turn to face the range and I could see that it was happening again: the batteries had overheated and the tank was comprehensively on fire. In the middle of the battlefield the horror of the combat theatre had visited us once more. As impressed customers watched the show, a skinny kid in high-waisted flares ran from the pill box with an extinguisher. Choking black smoke, molten plastic, red-hot batteries – all part of the job. I removed the smoking wreckage and decided that combat wasn't for me (a thought confirmed some years later, when I was involved in a very frightening Red Arrows crash, but that's for another chapter). There had to be an easier way to earn my summer money. I refunded the tourists their 10p and resigned.

Until I finally hit upon my greatest money-making idea, I was on the look-out for another job, so when the local wideboy offered me a gig selling candyfloss, I figured I was quids in. How hard could *that* be?! Turns out, on specific days of the year, it's tougher than it looks.

'So, you know what to do?'

'Yeah.'

'Just put the sugar and dye into the centre, turn the spinner on, turn the heater on, and then, when the floss sticks to the side, just hook it out and swirl it on to the stick.'

'Yeah, okay, cool.'

A word of advice: if your candyfloss audition should fall on a day that is both humid and windy, you're stuffed. As the queue lengthened, the farce unfolded. What the waiting tourists witnessed was really rather pathetic. As the floss spun out, the humidity prevented it from sticking to the sides, so it just hovered in there as a sugary-pink, gravity-defying hoop, waiting for a gust of wind to lift it, fully formed from the bowl, and throw it at me. In the hour that I was left alone, I didn't make one single candyfloss; however, I was wearing about 4 lbs of pink, sugary goo. When the wide-boy came back, it was to the forlorn sight of a lanky teen, virtually glued to the spot. It was in my hair, my nose; it had all but sealed my eyes shut. Flip-flops proved powerless to prevent it getting between my toes and the soles of my feet. He looked at me, I (coloured pink) looked back at him, the wasps lazily buzzed around me.

'I'm afraid I'm going to have to let you go.'

'Yeah, okay.'

Wasps and bees have always been an issue for me. I found out very early on in life that I'm allergic to both. If I get stung, it makes me, initially, very light-headed, and then as I start to black out I feel like I'm sliding down a well, wrapped in black velvet. It's scary, but not altogether unpleasant. It usually takes me about an hour to recover. The more severe the sting, the further down the well I slide. I'm aware of everything going on around me but I find it difficult to respond. Usually those around me keep asking if I'm okay, and as long as I can give them a thumbs-up, no one panics. I carry an EpiPen with me just in case – well, I say I carry it . . . If I get stung, it's in the kitchen cupboard.

I've only ever been fired twice in my life, from Arthur's candyfloss stand, and from Capital Radio. The second one wasn't really my fault either, as you will discover.

That walk home from the candyfloss episode was hideous. There are a few things that go right through me. The scraping of metal on metal, which is why I can't ever go on *I'm a*

Celeb – the eating utensils are all metal, so I'd just starve, covered in goosebumps. I told you earlier that I can't bear being wet and sandy. When I was tiny, apparently I'd just sit on the beach with my hands in the air! A habit all those around me are thrilled I have outgrown. I can't stand to be sticky, and 4 lbs of candyfloss more than qualifies. If I touch anything that is sticky and it gets on my hands, I have to wash them immediately or I feel really uncomfortable and anguished. Oh, and I don't like glitter, for the same reason. This is really annoying, because it is exploited by those who know me. Glitter on my hands is torture, so why not send me the glitteriest card you can find?! And then there's that one speck on your face that means someone suddenly has permission to grab your head, turn it back and forth, seeking the correct light, and then start picking at your face to get it off! Don't do it. I don't like it.

I never found out who sent a purple glitter bomb to my home recently. I'd just got in from work and I was alone in the kitchen, opening mail. I came to a small wrapped tube, the kind of thing that might have a scroll inside, and when I opened it, it exploded with a huge burst of purple glitter. I was covered, the kitchen was covered, and I just sat there, glittery mouth open, stunned. I had been got, comprehensively! If it was you, and you're reading this and you've decided to come clean, don't . . . it's still not funny.

So, what to do? Kiosk? Done that. Tank range? Resigned. Candyfloss? Fired. I was racking my brains, and then one night as I listened to Peter Powell on Radio Luxembourg, I knew what to do – I'd buy a disco. I would have the daytime to myself, as I'd work in the evenings, *and* I'd make more money than any of my mates. For a year, I saved all I could. I waited on tables at the guest house (that's where I got my love of cold toast, which I ate when the guests left it), I cleaned the rooms, did odd jobs, saved birthday and Christmas money, and by the following summer, I was there. We all drove to Bristol and I bought a pair of Citronic Hawaii decks, my dad built some lightboxes and, slowly but surely, I began buying the top forty.

Obviously, I had to think of a name. What should I call my new venture? This needed careful thought. And then . . .

'Your dad has got you a gig,' said Mum.

'No way.'

'They had to put it in the hotel events list,' said Dad.

'Oh, okay.'

'So, you needed a name.'

'Riiiight?'

'So, wait for it . . . you're the *Galaxy* Disco!' He beamed.

'That's a bloody chocolate bar!' I yelped, slapping my hand on my forehead.

'Oh, they'll never think of that,' said Mum. 'And don't swear.'

I was the Galaxy Disco by accident. We embraced it. Dad made me a lightbox with the name on it, which I still have, and I was in business. He was going to be my roadie. We'd always had VW caravanettes. He would fly to Amsterdam, buy an ex-company one cheap, then bring it home and kit it out as a camper van. As a family, Mum, Dad, my amazing brother Tim and me would celebrate the end of the summer by going camping, to France or Ireland. (In Ireland, I slid into an extremely precarious position and kissed the Blarney Stone, thinking maybe that might help me in the future and give me the promised 'gift of the gab' . . .) Though Mum could navigate beautifully, Dad would never listen, so we discovered all sorts of places we didn't mean to go and, as a consequence, never got to the places we intended to visit. Only trouble was, before it was pimped into a 'holiday home', it was still a former Dutch company van. So it was that I arrived at the Highbury Hotel for my first gig in a VW painted red and green with 'ACF Farmaceutische Groothandel' on the side.

I went inside and checked out the spacious dance floor as all the guests were having dinner. We loaded the kit through the window, set up the huge speakers and the light boxes (carefully placing the word 'Galaxy' in full view). I drew the curtains so it was nice and dark, then wandered off to get some chips. At 8 p.m. prompt, I arrived back alone and stood by the decks, staring in disbelief at the sight before me. The disco-goers had arrived, and they were all over eighty. What the hell! Four vital letters missed off my booking: SAGA. Well, I tried valiantly for ten minutes, but it was no use.

'The lights are making me dizzy.'

'It's too loud.'

'This *is not* music.'

Forced into a lighting and volume retreat, I walked up to the hotel owner and asked him for a week's sub. Les was a lovely guy and paid up. I ran through town to Newquay Electrical Services, which, as well as Hoovers and plugs, also had a reasonable record selection.

'I need old-people music.'

'What?'

'Stuff that isn't loud.'

In ten minutes I had what I needed: Victor Silvester, Sid Gateley, Max Bygraves. What a rave it was going to be.

That night, we had a ball. I turned the lights off, opened the curtains so the majesty of a sunset over Towan beach flooded in (it got a bit bright for a scary moment), and they danced and they danced. Everyone went to bed happy, I'd survived my first gig, and I was set for the summer. Those two weeks before and after the high season when the SAGA louts came to town were always fun, but, I'm not going to lie, I preferred the younger crowd in between.

During a few of the winters that followed, when the guests had all gone I would set up the decks in the now deserted dining room at home and present hours of radio shows . . . to myself. The disco was perfect for two reasons. Firstly, as all my mates worked in shops every day and missed the bulk of the summer, I had every day to myself and only worked for a few hours in the evenings. Secondly, I was performing! I had the bug, and the following week, the highlight of my year was coming to town. The Radio 1 Roadshow, live from Fistral beach.

There is no history of the 'broadcasting gene' in our family. I wanted to be something very different when I was at Trenance Infants' School. I was in the Blue Class and Barbie Reeve was my teacher. She had seen me through the highly traumatic first days of starting school. I had been perfectly happy to go once; in fact, I enjoyed it very much. However, when my mum got me up for the second day, I was traumatized. I'd been once; I very much did *not* intend to go again.

On the Fistral rocks with Tim in matching outfits.

As fast as Mum dressed me, I undressed myself. When I was finally crammed into my uniform, I was dragged sobbing down St Thomas's Road and up the hill to school. I was thrown in through the classroom door and Mrs Reeve had to put her back against it in an effort to stop me escaping. This went on for days. My dad would sneak up the hill in his lunch break to see if I was okay. He would report back to my mum and say that I was sitting on my own in the playground, back against a tree, sobbing. I had to have lunch in the classroom for a while, because I made the entire canteen cry.

After a time, as most kids do, I settled into school life. One afternoon, Mrs Reeve asked us what we wanted to do when we grew up. I announced that I wanted to be a gravedigger, but I'd leave holes in the coffin lid in case the bodies weren't

St Thomas's Road, Newquay.

dead. Mrs Reeve instantly created a new job in the classroom and I was the first to be given the role of 'Special Messenger'. I and those who followed me were given messages to take to the other teachers, a rudimentary internal-mail system. The job had been created for me solely so that I could be sent up the corridor to Mrs Chegwidden in the Yellow Class with a slip of paper. I handed it over, and she looked at me and thanked me. I found out years later that written on that slip of paper was: 'This is my little gravedigger.'

Barbie Reeve remained a friend long after I left school. She was round and bubbly and incredibly funny, with short dark hair and a slightly bohemian approach to life. Every summer, she and the local amateur dramatics society would put on a comedy show at the Cozy Nook Theatre on Towan beach called *Funzapoppin'*. I loved it. The Cozy Nook was also where our school put on its annual pantomime, in which I worked my way up from a mouse to Prince Charming. Miss Rowland, who always reminded me of the witch on the bike in *The Wizard of Oz*, was the teacher who organized it. She was so impressed by my princely performance that she gave me a grape. That was high praise indeed. The Cozy Nook Theatre on Towan beach is now an aquarium.

When I decided gravedigging wasn't for me and confided in Barbie that I wanted to work in radio, she was very encouraging. It has always been a source of sadness that she died before I 'made it'. I think she would have been very proud.

So, I have no idea where the 'broadcasting gene' came from. It started very early on in my life. I have always had a fascination with radio and television. I'd watch shows like *Top of the Pops* and *Tomorrow's World* not just for the content, but because I knew they were the shows where I was most likely to see cameras in their choreographed dance, capturing the action. It didn't really matter which cameras, but there was one particular kind that would deeply excite me. The EMI 2001 had a white top. It looked incredible – proper telly – and had 'BBCtv' written on the side. I can't describe the joy of catching a glimpse of one. James Burke used to do a science show, I think from the old Pebble Mill studios, and they didn't care about hiding the kit or the crew, so it was everything I wanted from a television show, behind-the-scenes shown in all its glory. I loved those cameras so much I finally managed to track one down, and I have it now, pointing at the pool table. Few people who come for dinner

My pride and joy, the EMI 2001.

can resist having a play. Sadly, it doesn't work. I have all the necessary equipment to fire it up, but I'm terrified it will burn the house down.

I would put a cardboard box on our wooden tea trolley (my camera), and fix an old microphone to my dad's fishing rod (my boom) and follow my poor brother around, asking for an interview. I'm pretty sure his first response was 'No comment,' but that soon turned to '*No, Phillip!!* Leave me alone,' and quickly progressed to 'Sod off.' He used to love his Lego, and I mastered the art of building a TV studio out of it. I tipped a cardboard box on its side and had a full Lego TV studio within, cardboard lights strung from the roof on cotton wires, mobile booms, six cameras, a set – the works. I broadcast many a virtual *Top of the Pops* from inside that box. Come to think of it, I was easily pleased as a kid: a cardboard box was all I needed. One was a camera, one was a studio and, when our new deep freeze was delivered, I lived in the box it came in for a fortnight.

My most treasured book was the *Ladybird Book of Television*. On the inside cover it had a full aerial map of BBC Television Centre. I studied every picture and knew every word; I knew that building better than our house. I was gutted many years later when I realized that I had lost the book, but how wonderful that my long-suffering brother was the one to find one online and buy it for me for Christmas. I'd watch the cameras dance on *Top of the Pops*, and years later I would be presenting *This Morning* from that very studio in the building that I had pored over in the pages of my favourite childhood book.

There are many people who didn't realize at the time that they were having a profound impact on my life. Bruce Connock was our careers adviser at Newquay Tretherras school. When he asked us all what we wanted to do for a career, I immediately said, 'Broadcasting.' Bless him, he never batted an eyelid; instead he spoke to a friend of his at the BBC in Plymouth and I was invited to go to watch the nightly local news, *Spotlight South West*, going out. It was so damned exciting, and I was so grateful that he didn't ridicule my ambition. I got the chance to properly thank him when he was a guest on my *This is Your Life*. We sometimes hear stories of teachers who were unsupportive of young dreams, only to be mentioned on the cover notes of a multimillion-selling album years later in a withering and public display of how unhelpful they were! Thankfully, Mr Connock wasn't one of those teachers, and the fact that he took me seriously has always

Bruce Connock at my *This Is Your Life*.

made me feel extremely grateful. Come to think of it, how lucky am I? When I told my mum and dad what my chosen career was, aside from my dad initially suggesting that might be more of a hobby than a job, they were never once anything other than totally supportive. Always watching, honest in their opinions, keeping my feet on the ground and, thank goodness . . . proud. I would eventually repay them by buying my dad a Hasselblad camera, which was his dream, and retiring him when he was fifty-seven after I got the role of Joseph.

You may be surprised that although I have been describing a fascination with telly, radio was my first love. I have a confused love affair with them both. A broadcasting threesome. I would listen to Radio Luxembourg in bed, in secret, and be captivated by the romance of a pirate-radio station forced to transmit from abroad. Whenever I could, I'd listen until it closed down at 3 a.m. The close-down sequence consisted of a song called 'Maybe the Morning', sung by Sunny, and the Luxembourg National Anthem. The signal was terrible and the station washed in and out like waves on a beach. The DJs – voices I knew so well – were Bob Stewart, Tony Prince, Stuart Henry, Emperor Rosko, Mark Wesley and Peter Powell. I always thought that Peter, who would go on to have a profound effect on my career and become one of my best friends, had the best taste in music, and I've had the chance to tell him many times.

Radio 1 was also an obsession. Every year, I'd buy the calendar; every day, I'd immerse myself in the station and its DJs. I wrote to all of them, asking how I could pursue a career in radio and, to their credit, in one way or another they all wrote back. Peter Powell had left Radio Luxembourg and was presenting a Saturday show from ten until one on Radio 1. I found out much later that the letter I had got back from him was actually written by his father, who was in charge of his personal mail. I eventually got that letter framed for him, and he now has it hanging on a wall in his house. One DJ wrote back with a piece of advice I use to this day: 'Never address the world at large. Radio and TV are personal. I am six inches from the mic, you are a foot from the radio or six feet from the TV. We're close, it's just you and me, so never say, "How are you *all* today?" It's just, "How are you?"'

If there's one thing I will change in any script, it's that. You won't ever hear me say, 'Lots of you have called,' or 'Hope you are all having a good morning.' It's old school, but it has stuck. Annie Nightingale (who shares 1 April as a birthday with me . . . hi, Annie) echoed much of the advice. It was a tough job to get into, very few succeeded, be prepared for setbacks, practise and be patient. I was prepped. I wanted it so badly.

Every year, the Radio 1 Roadshow came to Newquay, and it was a travelling circus coming to town, but with great music from huge orange speakers broadcast from a stage on a red, white and blue lorry. For two hours, that patch of Fistral beach was famous. The Roadshow was the brainchild of Johnny Beerling, a Radio 1 producer and later controller of the station, and it was in that capacity that I would work for him as a DJ in the then-distant future. The first Roadshow ever – and I was there – was held in 1973 on Fistral beach, with Alan Freeman, who also became a friend many years later. I would wake very early, run (barefoot) down the lane and across the mile of sand that was between the end of the beach where I lived and the other end, where the trucks would arrive. I was always there hours before a single other member of the crowd and I sat at the very front and watched. Watched the engineers set up, listened to the soundcheck, watched Smiley Miley set up his T-shirt and memorabilia shop (van). It was the highlight of my year. I hated the fact that in four hours I'd have to share the experience with 25,000 others. With about an hour to go, the DJ hosting the Devon and Cornwall leg of the tour would start their warm-up. Tony Blackburn, Noel Edmonds, Alan Freeman, Paul Burnett, and many more, I watched them all. By the time Paul Burnett hosted the show five years later I had managed to get a gig on Hospital Radio Plymouth, and he agreed to an interview. He was lucky to be alive that day – he'd drunk a wasp in his pint of beer and it had stung him in the throat! Being allergic, that would've done me in.

When I eventually got to work on Radio 1, in 1988, I found out that the Devon/Cornwall leg was the most sought after by the DJs. When I'd worked my way through other parts of the country the show visited, I was so thrilled to be offered Newquay. I made sure I looked very closely at the eager faces in the front row, knowing that, years before, it would have been my eager face looking back. Not one of the 25,000 ever knew, but, for a moment, I turned away from the crowd to wipe my eyes. The realization that a dream had come true washed over me and made me cry. Kismet.

If someone asks me how to get into broadcasting, I usually suggest hospital radio, if it exists in a hospital near them. That's the advice many of the DJs gave to me, and it proved to be fantastic experience. Finding the right hospital took a bit of trial and error. The first I approached was kind enough to ask me to go down and watch a broadcast, which I glee-fully did. My dad dropped me off at the hospital, because I was still learning to drive and had recently scared him sense-less when he was teaching me by threading his car through an impossibly small gap between two lorries in an unwise overtaking manoeuvre. I'll give him his credit, he never screamed, but he was silent for a mile or so, before saying, 'Don't *ever* do that again' . . . I haven't.

This was why I wasn't driving.

When I walked into the studio I was met by a very lovely gentleman who was about 150 years old, and he told me he was on air so could I sit quietly and watch. So I did.

I watched him open the mic, shakily introduce the next record, close the mic, then put his glasses on. He picked up the arm of the record player, bent down, squinted at the record on the turntable and then had three failed attempts at placing the needle at the start of the song. Whoever was listening in their hospital bed, and I suspected there were few, heard half a chorus of Boney M, then the end, then a couple of random bits in between before he managed to find the start. When the song was finally playing, he took his glasses off, beamed at me, and said, 'With experience, you'll get the hang of it. Don't forget, I've been at this game for twenty years.' I thanked him politely for his time, and left.

I found what I was looking for in Hospital Radio Plymouth, with a group of young, exciting broadcasters led by local telly celebrity David Rodgers. David became a mate and in time introduced me to Judi Spiers, Hugh Scully and Ruth Langsford. The radio station had great facilities and two well-equipped studios. The location, though, was terrifying. It was sat on the top floor of an old hospital on Lockyer Street. The hospital had been thriving until one day – I believe the lifts failed – it had been rapidly evacuated of all patients and staff. The only lighting that worked was at the top for the studios, so the walk from the front door to the top floor had to be done by touch in pitch darkness, and by trial and error I had to learn the route. That walk scared the crap out of me every time. I went wrong and ended up in the morgue; I went wrong and ended up in the operating theatre; I went wrong and fell into a room that was full, floor to ceiling, of old X-ray pictures, dimly lit by a skylight. I have to admit I might have spent a few minutes looking through the X-rays. Man, some people were in a bad way.

I had so much fun at Hospital Radio Plymouth and learned much of what I carry with me today. However, there is one evening I'd love to forget. Most of the programmes were live but, occasionally, if a DJ couldn't be there, they would record a programme instead. I was given the job of being the technical operator for a show David Rodgers was recording. I was the engineer for a TV star! I perfectly rolled in his interviews, seamlessly played in the music and made sure the levels were good. Sadly, I failed to press record and two hours of work were never to be heard. He didn't let me forget that for a long time. Another particularly memorable time was one evening when we came off air and I was sitting with everyone in the staff room. In a moment of silence one word came from an unoccupied corner of the room. Whispered, but perfectly clear in a woman's soft voice came the word 'money'. We all stopped and stared at each other. It couldn't possibly have been one of us. That woman's voice, whispering, 'Money,' has stuck with me. I can hear it still. The story was, in the distant past, one of the nurses had taken her own life because she was in debt. It was scary, but also very sad.

About ten years ago I was asked if I would be regressed to my past lives for *This Morning*, which was running a series of 'past life' films. I was interested so I agreed.

I lay on a couch in a quiet, modern sitting room, and the camera rolled. The lady guiding me into my past lives had a curiously distracting high voice, so, rather than finding myself regressing anywhere, all I could hear were squirrels in the roof and the whir of the camera. She asked me to picture doors to walk through, but all I could picture was the editor's face as we went back with hours of useless tape. Then, suddenly, and I have no idea how or why, I walked through a door. I was on a muddy street in a town; it seemed like the seventeenth century. There was a man two doors up selling end-of-season apples from a wooden crate. As people scuttled by on this cold, bleak day, I knew I was on the threshold of my home. I walked two steps down to the front door, and there my heart was gripped by a fearful sense of impending doom. I opened the door to silence and felt horror wash over me. Three steps in, and I saw them: two murdered bodies on the floor. I knew they were my wife and small child. Horror turned to fury. I knew why they were dead. I owed money to two brothers who worked at the end of the street in a sawmill. I ran, crying, from the scene of this cruel act of retribution, straight to the sawmill. One of the brothers was there, but I couldn't see the other. I ran straight to him, picked up a large piece of cut four-by-two and clubbed him repeatedly. The noise brought out the other brother and I ran from the mill, through the streets, and hid in a church. Running to the back of the church to hide, I looked out of a window. If I'm ever in a church that is high up, I look out of a window if I can – not easy, as most are stained glass. If I ever see a long, sloping field rolling down to a grey, lazy river, I'll know I've lived before. Until then, I'm putting these events down to a vivid imagination. Because what happened next was a horrific continuation of what had already been a particularly unpleasant experience. The brother found me, dragged me outside, punched me to the ground and, as my head hit the mud, he repeatedly stamped on it until I was dead!

I asked the lady afterwards what the use of these new pictures in my head actually was, and she said it was the comfort of knowing that we live again. I'm not so sure I agree. That terrible set of events are as fresh in my head now as they were when I walked through that door, and I don't know that they bring me any comfort at all. However, interestingly, if we do take characteristics from life to life, I can't owe anyone money.

We had a typewriter in our house on Pentire, and I was pretty much the only person to use it. From the age of ten, I had been applying for jobs at the BBC. I've often thought what would have happened if I'd been successful at that early age and actually got a job interview! I regularly typed my application letters so they couldn't see from my handwriting how old I was. I'm pretty sure that the BBC finally caved after seven years because it was cheaper to hire me than to pay the postage on the rejection letters. One day, I got the shock of my life. At the age of seventeen, I was asked to travel to London to have an interview for the job of a clerk in the Radio Sports and Outside Broadcast department. It had taken seven years of typing, but I was a step closer.

I travelled to the interview on the train with my dad. It was a memorable day for two reasons. Firstly, and obviously, I was about to go through the doors of Broadcasting House. Secondly, our train was the first-ever Penzance to Paddington Intercity 125. It felt almost as fast as my Chopper ride down Rejerrah hill.

My dad sat on the steps of All Souls Church in Langham Place as I walked to my interview, sadly not in Broadcasting House but in a dull building across the road. There I met a lady called Margaret Skidmore. She had quite a sizeable file on me, unsurprisingly, and was impressed by my 'continued interest in the BBC'. We chatted, I performed reasonably well in my typing test, she thanked me and sent me on my way back to Cornwall, promising to 'let me know'.

The days were endless, the waiting painful. Then it arrived, the franked envelope with the red BBC letters in the corner.

My trembling hands opened the letter. *I was in!* That night, the reality struck me like a freight train: I was about to leave home. Everything I had always known, everyone I knew and loved, was here. At seventeen, I was launching myself into the unknown, moving away from an idyllic seaside life to a city I knew literally nothing about. What the hell was I doing? Night after night, I lay in the dark of my room, worrying myself senseless: family versus a job, seaside over an office job. What if that was as far as I progressed? Would I end up sheepishly returning home, carrying the smouldering embers of a failed dream? Obviously, I knew the answer. Of course I would go – damn the consequences! I talked myself into refusing to acknowledge potential failure, but it took a few sleepless nights . . . the first thought loop of my life.

One of my friends said to me as I packed my bags to go, 'Why would you want to leave Cornwall? Everything you could ever want is here.' A small part of me agreed. I was lucky to live in a place where people had to save up to come on holiday. I got to stay there when they had to go home. My dad had built a beautiful Cornish cottage on Beach Road in Crantock. I had the most loving, caring, fun family. I get my sense of humour from my dad, and I get my grey hair from my mum; like me, she got her first grey hairs at sixteen – though I like to call it 'Arctic blond'. There are seven years between me and my brother, Tim. I would miss him so much. It was tough to leave. But I knew I had to take that huge step into the unknown.

2

When I got to London, I stayed with a family friend in Chiswick until I found a place of my own. That first night was horrific. Waves of desperate homesickness washed over me. I had travelled on the train from Cornwall, and when, on my arrival in Chiswick, I unpacked my suitcase, there, sitting on the top of my clothes, was a letter from my mum. 'We're so proud of you. This will be the start of a great adventure. Watch the pennies and don't get anyone pregnant' was the general gist. I already missed them so much.

After a couple of weeks, I applied for a bedsit in St John's Wood in North London, a very nice part of London and walkable to the BBC. I had difficulty finding it, so I knocked on the nearest door. Peter Gilmore from the seventies television series *The Onedin Line* opened it and pointed me kindly in the right direction! London, eh?

I met Mr Horn, the landlord, and from the off, I knew I had to impress him. He made it plain that he hand-picked the people in the house and that his concern was that everyone got on, which, looking back, was quite caring of him. He liked me, and offered me a deal: someone in the house had to take responsibility for cleaning. The person who had been doing it had just left and so, for a reduced rent, would I like to take on the job? The terraced house comprised seven bedsits: a couple of doubles and the rest singles. I would be responsible for cleaning the three communal loos, vacuuming all communal carpets and – he stressed this most emphatically – cleaning the brass on the front door. He said, 'If I drive

St John's Wood Terrace.

past – and I *regularly* drive past – and that brass isn't shining, the deal is off and you go back to full rent.' Needless to say, the loos were constantly sparkling, the carpets were spotless and the brass knocker and the number 93 on the door in St John's Wood Terrace would burn your retina if the sun caught them. From the day I moved in, to the day I left to emigrate to New Zealand, Mr Horn was happy. I'm the sort of person that seizes a task and won't let it go. It has to be right before I'm happy, so there was no way that brass was going to be anything other than perfect. Having said that, leaving Cornwall had stressed me out and, even now, if I'm stressed, I clean. If my head is struggling, I'll usually be found wiping kitchen surfaces, tidying up, loading or unloading the dishwasher, or cleaning out entire neglected cupboards. As I type, the cupboards at home are spotless. When I drove past

Stair party with my friend Ruth (left).

that door on St John's Wood Terrace a year or so ago and the brass was dull and abandoned, I felt a pang of sadness.

My bedsit contained a tiny single bed, a small cooker, a table, two chairs and a wardrobe. On the landing there was a shared fridge and a payphone beside it – thieving piece of shit that it was. My electricity meter swallowed fifty-pence pieces faster than a blue whale sucking plankton. I was still desperately homesick, but Mr Horn was good at his tenant selection and everyone in that house was lovely. In one of the other bedsits there was a young couple (my *God*, did she scream when they were having sex!), and in another, Eddie, who was a middle-aged, recently divorced guy (he worked for BT and will crop up again in a bit). Ruth, who was a friend of mine from school, lived downstairs, and there were a couple of nurses, who were so busy we didn't see them that much. None of our bedsits was big enough to house everyone, so each Friday we'd put in what money we could afford, pop down to the offie and buy as much cheap wine as we could, then we'd sit on the stairs and have a party. I still remember those stair parties with great affection *and*, of course, the carpet was immaculate! If it was sunny, we'd open the front door and listen to the lions roaring in nearby Regent's Park Zoo.

I may have been homesick, but I don't think I was ever lonely. I have, until recently, always been happy with my own company. I love being with friends and family, too, but I never struggled if I was on my own. Perhaps, in my head, stability always overpowered loneliness. In recent times, when stability has faltered, I've found that no amount of loving company can stop me feeling lonely in my own head.

After months of missing home, I can clearly remember waking up one morning and feeling . . . what? Joy? Yes, that

With Ruth.

was it. I wasn't homesick any more. I finally felt at home in the big city. I loved my friends and my tiny home, but I *never* had any money. I think I earned £4,000 pounds a year. The meter would run out, I wouldn't have 50p for it, so I'd sit in the dark with one candle and a book. I phoned my folks every evening from the thieving payphone. I'd make the call, pump in the ten-pence pieces, say a brief 'Hi, it's me,' and it would cut me off and eat my money. On my very tight budget, this was provocative in the extreme and, on one particular day, when I knew I only had thirty pence and would be sitting in the dark all night, it ate my money again. I'd reported it so many times, but nobody ever came. I will admit to having a temper. It takes a lot of provocation for me to see red, but when it happens . . . losing my last 30p *again* was the final straw, and I can't tell you how good it felt to kick the bastard off the wall. I'm not proud of it, I instantly regretted it, but for one brief moment I felt I'd taken control. Obviously, it was stupid and Eddie (the BT guy) was singularly unimpressed. However, he did organize another one for us, which was much better behaved.

Constantly being penniless was certainly an issue. I'd walk past restaurants and look at the people sitting inside and wonder how the hell they could afford it. On one grocery-shopping trip I only had enough money for a handful of green beans and a potato. I decided to make a soup, only to discover that the beans were in fact chillis, and though I tried my sweating best, the soup was inedible and I had to go hungry. My folks would, thankfully, send me bail-out money when things got really bad. I looked forward so much to the times my family would visit – my parents would cram into the single bed, and my brother and I would sleep on the floor. I think it was those times that proved what hopeless gigglers we all were. In the night, my dad would say something funny, or someone would accidentally fart, and we'd be screaming with laughter in the dark for an hour. When they left, there'd be a note on the bed when I got back from work: 'Milk, cheese, veg, butter in the fridge, bread by the cooker, and we've bought you a couple of cushions.' If I could, I'd put a heart emoji here.

My job was as a clerk in the Sport and Outside Broadcast department of BBC radio. The office was in Room 130 of Broadcasting House, overlooking Portland Place. I can't pass that building now without looking up at those windows. My first day didn't start well. I had finally got to walk through those huge brass doors (though they weren't as shiny as the knocker and plate on No. 93). The feeling of supreme elation as I walked through on my first day was extreme. I'm sure I was glowing. I'd bought myself a briefcase, but only had a newspaper, a banana, house keys and my (empty) wallet in it. I had been given my instructions to find the office: 'Into reception, sweeping staircase on the left, up to the first floor, 130 is a few doors down on your left.' I strolled through reception, set off up the grand spiral staircase and disappeared out of view of reception. At that moment, I slipped on the stairs and fell. My briefcase opened, I clattered back down the stairs and into full view of a now-silent reception. I slid into a heap at the bottom and my briefcase followed a split second later, followed by my keys, the paper and the banana! A very smart middle-aged man ran to pick me up and asked if I was okay. I squeaked, 'Yes,' and so it was that Sir Ian Trethowan, then Director General of the BBC, helped me to put an empty wallet and a banana back into my briefcase.

At the time, at seventeen, I was the youngest employee of the BBC in London. This was something they took very seriously. I was constantly asked if I was okay and, looking back, in a remarkable show of care, they paid for my second-class

Room 130 in Broadcasting House. My desk is in the corner,
the Uher booking sheet on the right.

return rail ticket to Cornwall every fortnight, an agreement
they committed to 'until I had reached the age of nineteen or
had been there for two years'. I got to know the journey from
Paddington to Penzance very well. For a time, I took the
sleeper down, but I did learn one lesson very quickly: always
take the top bunk. If you take the bottom bunk, at some
stage in the night some hairy-bollocked bloke is going to
descend the ladder to go for a pee! Far better to be up top
with a bladder of steel than be subjected to that.

My dad loved fishing of all kinds, but he was happiest fly
fishing. Just before he died, we all had a wonderful sunny
afternoon in the garden watching him cast a fly on to a side
plate on the grass from further and further away, with
remarkable accuracy. On my fortnightly trip home, I would

get off the train at Bodmin Parkway (then Bodmin Road) station at about 11 p.m. His car would be the only one in the dark car park. In the wheel arch of the front-right tyre, hidden, he'd leave a torch. I would take it and cross the car park, go through a gate and walk down the most scary-assed lane in the darkness to where he was fishing about a mile away. It always played out the same way. I'd start off nervously, swinging the torch from side to side, then slowly start to freak myself out and walk a little faster. As I walked past the huge, brooding rhododendron bushes, my pace would quicken. The more I scared myself, the faster I went: walk, fast walk, trot, run, Olympic panic sprint. Dad always laughed and said he could hear me coming, crazy running down the lane until I burst, breathless, through the bushes to where he was silently casting his fly.

'Hi [pant, wheeze, cough]. It's me.'

'I heard you.'

'Caught anything?'

'Nope.'

Much later on in life, the actor (and fellow Oldhamer) Bernard Cribbins would become a friend, and because of his love of fly fishing, he was the only 'famous' friend my dad was ever in awe of!

My job at the BBC was to manage the diaries of the thirty-two radio engineers, putting in the jobs they were to do and their location. I was only responsible for the recorded events; anything live was handled by John Goodman, who sat opposite me. I wasn't yet qualified for live, and I left before I ever reached that level of competence. I was still a radio geek and I recognized some of the engineers' names from the Roadshow days; to me, they were famous. Another part of my job was to book out Uhers, portable recorders that could be taken out for non-studio work. I booked out the Uher

Clay shooting with my brother-in-law Tim, Mike Smith and Bernard Cribbins.

that Andy Peebles took to New York to record the last-ever interview with John Lennon. I made a copy of the booking form and kept the original, because it had Andy's signature (which to me was an autograph) on it, but no one had any idea of how important that interview would be until a few days later. I was also responsible for the Uhers' timely return and it was my job to chase up any that were overdue. I'd been chasing one for days and, finally, I got hold of the very kind but obviously busy journalist. I politely told her that her recorder was overdue, she apologized profusely and said she'd got caught up in a war zone. I replied to Kate Adie that it was fine, but could I have it back asap.

I was introduced to the profound joy of real ale in that office. Thirty-two engineers travelled the entire country and almost every one collected beer mats from wherever they'd been. On a map on the wall, each and every one was displayed – it was an exceptional collection. Even now, I can drink spirits and wine to a reasonable level, but beer always writes me off. I can't count the amount of times I fell forward in the urinal of the Crown and Sceptre pub and banged my head on the ceramic tiles. That pub, and the Yorkshire Grey, were where we would gather after work to have a drink, and I'd watch in awe as the guys from Technical Stores sank fifteen pints and were still able to walk to the Tube. When I did the one thing I *never* thought I'd do – resign from the BBC to emigrate to New Zealand – as a real-ale aficionado, John Goodman was furious I'd chosen a country that only drank lager.

It was a very male-orientated department at the time, with only one female engineer (Liz Rorison), and sport was always a topic of conversation, mainly cricket. John had a cricket bat in the office and there was a wicket drawn on the wall. We'd roll up Sellotape tightly into a cricket ball and play in the office. If you ever walked past Broadcasting House in 1980

John Goodman (with his real-ale bible) and Rachel Pryor
from the religious department.

and a Sellotape ball flew out of a window and into Portland Place, that was us.

As I've said, our office was on the first floor, which was incredibly lucky for me. The end of our corridor opened up into a kind of foyer and at the end were four steps leading down to a set of double doors. At the top of those steps was a camera and a button, and if you pressed that button you were scrutinized from within. If you were deemed safe, a green sign would illuminate above the double doors, simply saying: 'Enter.'

As the junior, it was obviously my job to get the teas in. Joyce, the tea lady, stood proudly by her trolley and urn, ready to provide it. She was a middle-aged cockney who looked uncannily like my Auntie Jean. Joyce was a delightful dream of a woman. She knew everything and everyone and we quickly became friends. On day two of my new job I asked her what was behind the MI5-style security. When she told me, I was awestruck. Behind those doors was the main control room for all BBC Radio, linked to the Post Office Tower and the entire world. However, that was just half the story. If you walked through the control room you would find the studios, or 'cons', two studios each for Radios 1, 2, 3 and 4. It was, for me, the holy grail. It was all in there – *they* were all in there, at the end of my corridor.

In the weeks and months that followed, Joyce, who seemed to know more than she should, would say to me in hushed tones, 'Princess Grace of Monaco, this afternoon at four.' I'd make sure that was the time for the day's tea run and stand waiting with Joyce, and there she was, spot on four, Grace Kelly being escorted to a studio. 'Enter,' read the green sign, and in she went, graceful and beautiful, to be swallowed up by the black double doors.

''Ello, lovey. Margaret Thatcher, in at ten.'

'The Police . . . here at five.'

Indira Gandhi, Muhammed Ali, David Bowie . . . and so it went. Joyce and I stood and watched as the VIPs of the world walked by and the office teas went cold.

It was fun to watch the massive stars drift by, but much more appealing to me was the daily arrival of the DJs, off to do their shows, from Jimmy Young to Peter Powell. I was on nodding terms with them all. Me, the radio anorak from Sport and OBs.

But it wasn't enough! I needed to get through those doors. Access came in the form of a memo that I had to type and put in the internal post every Friday to the 'TOM'. It was the weekly schedule of OB activities. For weeks, I typed it up and posted it without question until, one day, I asked John who TOM was. He didn't look up from his work.

'Technical Operations Manager.'

'Ah, right, where is he?'

'In the control room.'

Holy shit!! Access! The address on the envelope was just an office number, with no indication that this piece of paper was a passport to 'enter'.

'I may as well deliver it, rather than post it.'

'Why?'

'Seems silly to post it if I can drop it off when I get the tea.'

'Please yourself.'

Friday took *ages* to come round. I typed the memo with trembling hands, I was so excited at what was to come. My legs were shaky as I walked to the top of the stairs, my heart pounded as I pressed the button . . . I waited . . . *enter.*

Literally, excitement off the scale. I walked down the steps and in through the doors. I'm not sure if anyone has ever delivered a sheet of paper as slowly as I did. On that day, and every Friday afterwards, I walked like a tortoise. It was the bridge of the *Enterprise* on speed. There were screens, monitors, buttons and dials by the thousand, links to every corner of the globe. My eager eyes drank it all in. I could see the corridor to the studios, but that was for another day, as my brief access didn't allow that. I put the schedule on the desk of the TOM, and he said thanks but didn't look up. I walked very slowly back through the nerve centre, heard the doors click behind me, and that was it for another week. Except one week, it wasn't. A bout of flu (for someone else) was the fledgling beginning of a life-altering friendship.

Our office was next door to the motoring unit, a supervisor and two secretaries responsible for typing up the travel news for all four networks. 'Beep beep, beep beep, yeah, traffic news on Radio Oooone' was the jingle. One morning the motoring unit supervisor walked into my supervisor's office, Alastair McLachlan or 'Mac'. Small, Scottish and very kind, always keen on enhancing our love lives, usually by saying of one or other of the girls in the building: 'Aye, she's a cutie, better give her a wee tickle.'

Only a couple of months into my booking-clerk job, both secretaries in the motoring unit had gone down with the flu, and the supervisor was, as Mac pointed out in his lilting Scottish accent, 'in a pickle'. One of us had to go in and type up the travel newsflashes.

John didn't want to. I did. It was something different. I was sent next door to help out.

The job was simple. The supervisor, with the information coming in before him, dictated it to me, and I typed it. I had no idea what happened to it after that. First flash of the morning came in, he spoke, I typed on to four sheets of carbon paper. 'Crash on the motorway, M1 closed . . .' I concentrated as I typed, but on completion I had to correct the four copies because the crash hadn't been on the K1. Well, 'K' and 'M' *are* very close on the keyboard . . .

'What next?'

'Right, now you have to go to the control room at the end of the corridor. Know where that is?'

'Err. Yes.'

'Walk through the control room, there's a corridor at the back, go down that corridor to the studios.'

'Okay!!'

'You deliver one sheet to each of the four studios that are on air. Walk into each of the control rooms and they'll either take it from you or send you into the studio to give it to the person on air.'

Imagine a very loud, choral burst of 'Hallelujah!' exploding in your head.

'Enter' had never looked so good. I almost ran through the control room this time. There was the corridor, there were the doors to each of the studios, four red on-air lights shone like beacons and called out to me in their siren voices. Radio 4 first: heavy news debate going on; the producer took the sheet from me. Radio 3 next: orchestral tones echoed out; I woke the engineer and gave him the sheet. Now it got interesting: Radio 2. The producer said hi, a record was playing, he pointed to the door of the studio and said, 'Go straight in.' I walked into the studio, and there was Terry Wogan. The mighty, affable and brilliant Tel. I told him this story of our first encounter years later, and he was as charming and gracious then as he was that morning. Paper was strewn everywhere in the studio and there was a bright, cheery atmosphere. Terry looked up, said hello and I gave him the traffic flash. He asked if I was new, I said I was filling in, he smiled and said thank you and I distinctly remember backing out as if I was leaving the presence of a king – which, in a way, I was. How could this day get any better? Well, Radio 1 was next. I'm sure I must have been bright red as I stood at the door of the control room. Here I was, eighteen, standing at the heart of British radio broadcasting. My memory flashed back to that conversation with my mate.

'Why would you want to leave Cornwall? Everything you could ever want is here.' In my head, I was screaming, 'Because of this, mate, because of *this*!'

In through the door, a nod from the engineer to go into the studio of the radio station I'd been listening to for years from a bedroom with a secret door in the wardrobe. Only a few months before, I had listened to the last Noel Edmonds breakfast show as he handed over to Dave Lee Travis. The final thing Noel played was 'It's Over' by Roy Orbison and the sound effect of a door slamming. Now I was in that studio and big, hairy DLT was in the seat. He was known as 'The Hairy Cornflake' on the show. The music was loud. As a matter of fact, he was out of his seat and dancing around. 'Morning!' he shouted, over the

Reunited with DLT, 'The Hairy Cornflake', when I finally got my Radio 1 show.

noise. I gave the traffic report to the producer and left. As I walked back down that corridor I was grinning from ear to ear. What a geek, but a happy geek. When I eventually got my Sunday show on Radio 1, I used the studio after Dave. He laughed when I told him the story and said, 'I remember you!!'

'No way! Do you?'

'Do I bollocks.'

Being in his studio with him for an hour or so on a Sunday was a joy. DLT was utterly bonkers, very loud and very funny.

As I delivered my traffic report I admit I was a bit disappointed I'd missed Noel Edmonds on the breakfast show by a few months. Noel was who I wanted to be, great fun on the radio, a sort of more restrained Kenny Everett.

I had watched the first show of *Multi-coloured Swap Shop* on BBC1 in 1976, open-mouthed at how live and exciting Saturday-morning TV had just become, and how clever the

The gang surprise me on my birthday. From left to right: production secretary Cathy Mellor, DLT, me and producer Louise Musgrave.

producer, Chris Bellinger, must be. Two hours totally live, famous guests, phone-ins, sketches, music, cooking – it was all there and would cast the mould of all the following Saturday-morning juggernauts to follow. Noel was in his broadcasting prime and would remain there for some considerable time. How could I know that in only seven years I would be presenting *Going Live* with Sarah Greene in that same Saturday slot and that the brilliant Chris Bellinger would be my producer and friend. I certainly couldn't have guessed that one day I would watch him slide down the wall in my house in Chiswick, full of over-proof rum. Noel and I would eventually become friends, too. I always cited him as my TV inspiration. Sadly, many years later, he and I would strongly disagree over an interview on *This Morning* when he suggested that 'negative energy' could cause cancer. I still take a different point of view to Noel, but I think it's a terrible shame we fell out over it.

That day helping out with the traffic news was amazing. I ran back and forth and met pretty much every DJ as I delivered the bulletins, but it was at about four o'clock that afternoon that, unbeknown to either of us, a friendship would be forged that lasts until this very day. I took a traffic flash down to Radio 1, and Peter Powell was presenting the afternoon show. This was the guy I'd been illicitly listening to late at night on Radio Luxembourg. One of the best voices on the radio, the same taste in music as me, a flag-bearer for new bands. I walked into the studio and he said, 'Hello, mate,' in a way that only Pete can. I gave him the travel flash and said I'd loved his show on Luxembourg. I think I blurted out that I wanted to work in radio, too. The song finished, he said, 'Hang on,' opened the mic, did a link and then he was back. It was just a brief chat, but he was very charming, said something like 'Good luck, it's tough to get into.' I said thank you and left. What a day.

In the months that followed I bumped into him in the corridor a few times and he always said hi. Eventually, he was given the tea-time show and one day, as we passed each other, he asked if I was still interested in getting into radio. I said yes and told him that I'd recently used a lot of BBC resources and favours to make a Christmas show to send back to Hospital Radio Plymouth. He said, 'Well done,' or something equally generic, and said I was welcome to pop down to watch the show for a bit after I'd finished work. I didn't want to be a nuisance, so I only took up the invitation two or three times, but to sit in a studio and watch a show go out was priceless in helping me get to where I wanted to be. The life-changing moment came a couple of years later when I told Peter in the corridor outside Room 130 one day that I had just handed in my notice and was emigrating to New Zealand. He said three words that would shape my career. He swears he can remember, but I'm pretty sure he can't. Peter Powell said to me, 'Keep in touch.'

The Hospital Radio Christmas show happened simply because Hospital Radio Plymouth asked whether, now I was in the BBC, I could record anything for them. I dropped a cheeky note to a few presenters and all of them replied that yes, of course they'd be happy to help, as it was for Hospital Radio. Brian Matthew, John Dunn, Ray Moore, Libby Purves, Pete Murray and others all recorded a passage from *A Christmas Carol* for me. Arthur, my friend down in Technical Stores, blagged one of the basement war-time studios for me. It even came with an engineer! I recorded my show for a few hours in the middle of the night when everything was quiet. Those studios are the historic soul of the BBC, deep below the building. I spent a lot of time wondering what landmark broadcasts had been made from there as I felt the Tube trains on the Bakerloo Line rumble beneath my feet.

One of my proudest moments on getting my job was being given my BBC pass. I still have that first one. When it arrived in the internal mail I tore up my temporary pass and studied my new official one. I was reasonably happy with the picture and I remember asking John a burning question.

'Where can I go with this?'

'Anywhere.'

'Which buildings?'

'All of them. Why?'

'Well, I was wondering if it would get me into TV Centre?'

'Yeah, of course. Why would you want to go there?'

'Dunno. Just wondered.'

The 'Hallelujah!' chorus burst forth in my head once more. As most companies do, the BBC shortened many locations into acronyms. Broadcasting House was BH; the Royal Albert Hall was RAH; RFH was the Royal Festival Hall; and so on. Television Centre was just TC, and I had just been given a pass into TC, the building I knew so well from my *Ladybird Book of Television*. I made a decision: that weekend I would go, to test access, to snoop, to finally be there.

Saturday morning arrived and my head was buzzing all the way on the Tube. St John's Wood to White City seemed to take an age. I walked out of the Tube station and on to Wood Lane. A look to the left, and there it was, this imposing, minimalist seat of British television, which opened in June 1960 and was respected around the world. The architect, Graham Dawbarn, allegedly drew a question mark on a sheet of paper when he was given the job of designing the BBC's new home of television and, viewed from the air at the time, that's exactly what was built. Even now, though so much has been made residential, that original shape remains. I knew what to expect. The mighty brick wall that was the side of Studio 1 (TC1) with its iconic BBC Television Centre logo, and twenty-six white square lights below, in three rows. The centre of the main block was circular, and affectionately known as the 'Doughnut'. In the middle of that was the golden statue of Helios, the Greek god of the sun, to represent television radiating around the world. I knew that there were eight studios of varying size built around that circle. I knew because I'd studied it. I knew because I was obsessed.

As I walked down Wood Lane, it revealed itself to me brick by brick. If I'd walked past Mick Jagger at that moment, I wouldn't have cared, because this building was the star I'd dreamt of meeting from the moment I put that cardboard box on top of a tea trolley. My God, it was majestic. I thought then, and have felt ever since, that this building was designed perfectly for its purpose. It was, as Sarah Greene and I would say to each other in a few years' time, the Fun Factory.

I stood at the barrier and walked up to the commissionaire's window. This was *never* going to work. He looked at me, I shakily showed him my pass, he nodded and looked back at his paper: entry had been granted. I spent the entire day exploring. Any door that would let me through, I walked through. I looked into all the studios I could that weren't flashing their red transmission light. In TC1 a huge drama set was nearing completion; in TC6 a set for what looked like a sitcom. There was a studio for sport, for current affairs, too, and in all of them the white-topped EMI 2001 cameras. My breath caught as I saw them for real for the first time. In one silent studio, I went up close to look. In my eyes, it was a work of art. It's a source of regret to me that by the time I got in front of a UK camera, the 2001 had been mostly phased out. I would have loved to have looked 'down the barrel' of one of those as a presenter. I've often wondered which shows and which stars had been in front of the camera I now have pointing at the pool table.

I've tried all my life to be as encouraging as I can to those who want to get into broadcasting. I've always remembered those kind replies I got and the help I've received along the way. Some of the presenters and performers who are working now wrote to me, and I gave them advice. Although she wasn't asking for advice, Sarah Millican sent me a birthday card at my Radio 1 show. She had made a gag about the fact there was a hamster on the card and called herself 'Hilary Hamster' as an encouragement to get others hamsters to write in. I apparently said, 'And remember, if you're going to send stuff in, you don't have to *try* to be funny.' Apparently, she was crushed. I've insisted on a number of occasions since that I wasn't being dismissive and that she *was* funny. Having said that, she has told me that it was the first step on her path to becoming a comedian, so the misunderstanding didn't do any lasting damage. I'm in her book, now she's in mine, and we have a secret love for each other. (Hi, Sarah.)

In all of the letters I've sent and all the interviews with students I've had, I have always stressed one thing: I'm not interested in helping you if you just want to be famous; you have to want it, in your bones. I didn't want to be a presenter, I wanted to be a broadcaster, and that's the profession I write down in official paperwork, though, obviously, some may disagree.

There's a reason I mention this right now, and it comes down to smell. As I walked into those television studios that very first time I realized that they had their own unique smell. It's hard to describe. One of my favourite smells is petrichor: the smell that comes off baking tarmac when a brief shower hits a hot road on a summer's day. A television studio is similar, but it has an unidentifiable smell. I've joked with other presenters that it's the smell of adrenaline and fear, but that's not it. It's vaguely electrical, I suppose, maybe with hints of floor paint and the wood of the sets. Every studio has its own distinct smell. Studio one at the old ITV studios smelled differently to Studio 8, the home of *This Morning*. They must retain their own personal aroma, because the smell of TC3 on that day as they were striking a music show was imprinted on my mind. Many years later, when *This Morning* moved from the Southbank to Television Centre and we moved into our new home, I walked back into TC3 and my memory exploded with wonder: the smell was exactly the same. So, if you write to me about wanting to pursue a career in broadcasting, I'm not interested if you just want to be famous, but if the smell of a studio gets you, you have my attention.

On that first day at Television Centre I walked through the scene docks, saw the Tardis and the set for *The Generation Game*. I smiled at sports presenter Des Lynam. Diana Dors, the actor, apologized as she trod on my toe in the lift as I made my way to the canteen. That was my final stop of the day, because the food at the BBC was subsidized then, so you could eat great food at ridiculously affordable prices (a cup of tea was three pence). I had steak and chips with big field mushrooms for my dinner, my only proper meal of the week, and then left to go back to St John's Wood with a feeling of utter satisfaction. I had just enjoyed the *best* day out. I wish I'd known then how well I'd get to know TC in the future, how much telly I'd make there, the friendships that would be forged and the fun I'd have. It would have made what was about to happen a lot easier.

I can't say that my job as a clerk was fulfilling me, but I was with fun people and felt like I was on the beginning of some sort of ladder. I was at the BBC! Behind the scenes, I was sent to the Guildhall for the Lord Mayor's Banquet. (I got horribly drunk and threw up behind John's desk when I got back to work. I cleaned that mark for hours and he never knew what had caused it.) I was sent to Centre Court at Wimbledon, and to Wembley in May 1981 for England v Brazil (Brazil won 1–0). At the bedsit, life was also good. I was seeing an older lady in Swiss Cottage called Madeline who was . . . fascinating. I felt like I was in *The Graduate*, an older lady and an eighteen-year-old, and she taught me things that were never in those copies of *Health & Efficiency* in the den under the roof of my bedroom in Newquay. Our stair parties continued apace, I went to Regent's Park open-air theatre with my friend from school, Ruth, and to make her laugh I learned the 'Now is the winter of our discontent' passage from *Richard III* and quoted it back to her in full-on thespian tones. I still have it in my head now, along with the Pepsi ad of the time: Lipsmackinthirstquenchinacetastinmotivatingood buzzincooltalkinhiwalkinfastlivinevergivincoolfizzin Pepsi. That was a bitch to type, but it's amazing how these things lodge for ever, like the colours of Joseph's coat!

So, life was good, until one day the payphone in the hallway rang, someone picked it up and shouted, 'Phillip, it's your mum.' My heart sank. When she had called in the past, that phone had delivered two horrid pieces of news, the death of my Uncle Alan and the passing of my grandad. My Grandad Harold was truly one of the world's kindest men. He died at seventy-eight while sorting his record collection on the floor of the sitting room in Oldham. He told great stories, taught me brilliant rhymes and never, ever lost his temper. He left me his ring and, from that day, I've worn it on my right hand in his glorious memory. So, had someone died? I picked up the phone.

'Hi, darling, it's me.'

'Hi, Mum.'

'We've got something to tell you.'

'Okay.'

'You know your dad has always wanted to go to New Zealand?'

'Er, yeah.'

'Well, we're going to go, but we're not coming back. We've decided to emigrate and wondered if you'd like to come.'

My world disappeared from under my feet. I had to hold on to the payphone to steady myself. I had no idea what to say. I probably said, 'Let me think about it,' but I'm not sure. The loops began to spin in my head. I felt despair and confusion. I loved my family completely, unconditionally. How could I be separated from them by 12,000 miles? On the other hand, I had been writing to the BBC since I was ten, I'd got my job at seventeen, I was now nearly nineteen and I felt happy with where I was. What was I expected to do? After almost two years in London, did I have to resign? WTF hadn't been invented then; if it had been, that would have been at the forefront of my mind. I lay in bed and listened to the chaos. 'You can't go, you don't have a job to go to.' 'You have to go, you can't be separated from your family.' 'You love London, you don't know anything about Auckland, all your friends are here.' 'When will you be able to afford to visit? You have to go.' All night long, and for night after night, I went round and round. Pointless, really. I knew I would go, I just had to torture myself a bit first, which was the start of that annoying habit. I wrote my letter of resignation to the BBC.

At the time, I felt that I could be making inroads in my attempt to get on air. I was in the right building, I was meeting the right people – who knows? It *might* happen.

I've thought long and hard about including this next bit. But what is known now wasn't known then and at the time it was a great day for the Schofield family. It's also a momentous occasion in my journey to making it from working behind the scenes to talking into a microphone or standing in front of a camera.

Jimmy Savile was a broadcasting god at the BBC and in the country at large. With *Jim'll Fix It* on the telly and his various radio shows, he was a big name – one of the biggest. He couldn't use one of the usual Radio 1 studios at the end of the corridor to record his shows, because they weren't big enough to hold all his guests, so he recorded in one of the big drama studios in the basement. *Jimmy Savile's Old Record Club* was a weekly event in the building. It was recorded during the week and broadcast on Radio 1 on a Sunday afternoon, and I listened every week. It was clear he had a sort of informal audience in the studio with him, and sometimes he put them on air. I wondered, if I dropped an internal memo to his producer, Ted Beston, perhaps I could attend one of the recordings? Ted wrote back: of course! He said to come down and see us, they'd be expecting me. I asked John and Mac if I could be excused. They were always a little bemused by my radio obsession, but they agreed so I set off for the basement.

When I walked into the studio, it was as if I'd walked into a religious gathering. There were about fifty people there – old, young, disabled, some with special needs, some wearing Scout leader uniforms. It was quite the most eclectic audience I'd ever seen. Ted Beston met me and showed me to a seat. Savile was standing behind a lectern with a script and a large microphone. We were all in awe; we felt truly blessed to be there. He'd play a record, then walk to the various attendees, chat to them, make them feel welcome, ask them why they were there, how he could help them. I'm pretty sure that if he had touched the head of the woman in the wheelchair, she would have considered trying to walk. He came over to me.

'Now then, now then, young man. Ted told me you worked upstairs in OBs?'

'Yes,' I gasped.

'He said you were interested in getting a job on the radio.'

'Er, yes. Yes, it's my dream.'

'Well, we like to make dreams come true down here. Come with me.'

I got up and he led me to the lectern.

'This is the next record. Why don't you introduce it?'

'Okay, thank you.'

The previous record finished, and Jimmy Savile spoke.

'This is my friend Phillip from the Outside Broadcast department, but he has always wanted to be on the radio, so today we're going to make that happen.'

We briefly chatted, and I made the introduction. I was going to be on Radio 1. I thanked him and Ted, and calmly left, then I ran. I ran all the way from the basement to Room 130, where I phoned my mum and dad.

'I'm going to be on the radio on Sunday.'

'What? How?'

'I've just been downstairs to a recording of Jimmy Savile's show and he let me introduce a record!'

'Oh my goodness, darling, that's so wonderful, we're so happy for you. We'll tell everyone to listen.'

Sunday came, and every Schofield was glued to their radio. So were all the people in Newquay and Oldham that had been told. The moment arrived. Here it was, my first-ever broadcast. It was brief, yes, but it had happened – I'd been on Radio 1. My family were so proud.

I went a couple more times to the adoration club, and Savile remembered me and was free with his advice. It was the first time someone had told me: 'Be nice to everyone on the way up, you'll need them all on the way down.' He reiterated the 'addressing the world at large' advice and gave me tips on broadcasting techniques. I was incredibly grateful. In fact, I was so grateful that I asked him if I could buy him a drink. He replied with 'That's kind, thank you, but no, I don't think it would be appropriate.' You couldn't make it up.

I met Jimmy Savile a number of times over my career. He always remembered me. The last time I saw him was at the launch of a new cruise liner. I was on board with my wife, Steph. He was standing alone, looking old, at the top of the grand staircase, and I introduced him to Steph. He bowed low and kissed her hand, said he was proud that I'd done so well, that he'd followed my career with great interest.

A short time later he was dead. I tweeted my sadness at his passing. It is the only tweet I have ever retrospectively searched for. When it became clear how he had behaved all of those years, I scrolled back for hours to find it so that I could delete it.

In any of the brief times I had contact with him, there wasn't one hint of who he really was, from either him or anyone I met. I just wish that, back then, victims had been believed or had felt they had enough support to speak up against this monster, who was hiding in plain sight, and that 'possibly Britain's most predatory sex offender' had not died before he was brought to justice.

I'd come close to realizing my broadcasting dream, but it still felt so far away. Writing my resignation letter was deeply painful. I hesitated before I put it in the brown internal-mail envelope, but I knew I had to send it. It was 'regretfully' accepted. 'The BBC and all my colleagues would miss me.' They all wished me well in my new life in New Zealand.

I worked out my notice. I would finish in OBs, pack up the bedsit, travel down to Cornwall to help with the packing there, then Mum, Dad, me and Tim would all travel back to London to fly.

Reluctantly, I said goodbye to my BBC colleagues. At the bedsit, Eddie told me to send him my phone number as soon as I had one; he could be 'helpful' to us. I had no idea what that meant, but I promised I would. I kissed my friends at 93 St John's Wood Terrace farewell and left the shining door knocker behind.

Dad had been accepted into New Zealand because of their points system. Nobody got in unless the country needed you. As I mentioned, he was a gifted French polisher, and that was an occupation that happened to be on the 'needed' list. We had to have an interview at New Zealand House on Haymarket, which turned out to be quite controversial. All three male members of the family were asked numerous questions about why we wanted to go, what we would contribute to the country and whether we had ever been to prison. Throughout the entire process, they didn't speak to my mother once, and it didn't go unnoticed. She was furious.

'If that's the kind of chauvinistic environment I'm going to, I'm not interested,' she said. Thankfully, it wasn't.

Those weeks packing up in Cornwall were painful. I didn't want to leave. Everyone tried so hard to cheer me up, but I was moody and morose. We drove to the river at Bodmin so Dad could have a final fish. The weather was glorious, brilliant sunshine, the happy babbling of the river; a chorus of birds sang, dragonflies drifted over the long green grass and there was the sapphire flash of a kingfisher. It was literally the perfect day, except it wasn't, because I *didn't want to go*! I think if I had changed my mind at the last minute, they would have accepted it, but they would have been heartbroken. As the loops continued to spin in my head in Cornwall, I knew that, having resigned, there was no way back. I had made my

The last thing loaded on to the van for New Zealand . . . the vacuum cleaner.

choice. I tried to smother any anxiety by thinking, 'This will be an adventure and we'll all be together.' I was talking myself into a decision that, really, I had already made.

Our furniture was en route to NZ in a container, and we said a tearful goodbye to the rest of the family, locked up the cottage and set off for London.

Perhaps if I'd known that emigrating would allow me to save my dad's life, I wouldn't have been so bloody miserable.

3

I always wanted to be a pilot. I think if the broadcasting gene hadn't been so strong, that's where my path might have led. Up until recently, I had a very sophisticated flight simulator game on my desktop and I'd sit for hours and fly all over the world. I got pretty good, too. I took it very seriously, so much so that I paid a fortune for AERAD charts. They are an impressive set of loose-bound books that have plates of every airport in the world, how to approach them and the frequencies needed to land. They're used by real pilots, so my year's subscription included any critical updates. If a runway was closed or a new part of the world had been deemed too dangerous to fly into, an update arrived in the post. Obviously, the updates were useless for my flight sim because it wasn't updated, but it was worth it to see the postman's face when he delivered another envelope marked: 'Urgent: Contents Critical to Flight Safety'.

If I had been the pilot on that plane flying us to Auckland, I would have pointed out the view from the window. For some reason, we couldn't all sit together, so I was at the back of the 747, in a window seat. A few hours into the flight, when it was fully dark outside, I slid up the window blind and gasped. We were flying under the Northern Lights, a stunning spectacle of flashing purple and green that whipped and swirled in the night sky above us. Nothing was said from the flight deck. I took it upon myself to start to inform my fellow passengers, walking the length of the plane, saying, 'Excuse me. If you look out of the window, you can see the Northern Lights.'

The plane was filled with the sound of sliding window blinds. Most were thrilled; some were not. Not surprisingly, perhaps, a few people were unimpressed by being woken up in the dead of night by a total stranger advising them to look out of the window.

Steph and I went on holiday to see them a couple of years ago in Norway. It was the second time I'd seen them in my life and, both times, it was truly majestic.

As the Schofield family sped through the sky at the start of our 12,000-mile journey, I hoped that the beautiful sight outside in the night sky was a good sign of a happy arrival. It wasn't.

At Heathrow, my mum had had her manicure set confiscated because it contained sharp objects, and she was furious. My dad, on the other hand, had been doing some last-minute jobs on the cottage before we left and had accidentally wandered through security with a massive screwdriver in his hand luggage, totally unchallenged.

As we left the plane at our halfway stop-off in Los Angeles, my thumb moved to my ring finger on my right hand. I always twiddle my grandad's signet ring if I'm nervous or concentrating, but it wasn't there. I'd taken it off in the loo on the plane when I washed my hands, and left it there.

I was utterly bereft. Could this shit adventure get any worse? I tried to go back, but they wouldn't let me. I asked the ground crew, but they weren't interested. This was the second time I'd done this. The first was when I took it off, for the same reason, on one of my weekend train journeys home, courtesy of the BBC. I only realized it wasn't on my finger and was still in the loo when my dad met me as I got off at Bodmin Parkway. I yelped, 'I've left my ring on the train!', but the doors were closing and the train was moving defiantly out of the station. We jumped in the car . . . and chased the train. We missed it at Par and St Austell, but finally caught up with it in Truro, where I burst on to the train, ran into the loo, and there it was, waiting for me by the sink.

So, I'd done it again. This time there was no chasing. I walked, sullen and moody, my head down, to collect our bags. We stood and waited by the carousel. The first thing to come through the flaps at the end of the luggage conveyer belt was a little plastic tub. Curious as it passed me, I looked inside, and there, on its own and unannounced, was my grandad's ring. I was stunned. It was only beaten by a second plastic container following behind containing . . . a confiscated manicure set.

Our arrival in New Zealand didn't go particularly well. We were knackered after the flight and we all felt deeply unsettled. Here we were, in a different hemisphere, about as far as you can go without coming back, and 11,386 miles from everyone and everything we knew. The only people we knew in the country were Jim and Irene, who were friends of a friend, so it was a tenuous connection. Jim was kind enough to meet us at the airport to take us to our motel. Unfortunately, he didn't know the way. International airports are seldom built in the prettiest parts of a city, and the suburbs surrounding Auckland airport are not the city at its shimmering best. We had no way of knowing that the drive should have taken us about forty-five minutes. An hour and a half in, and not realizing we were going in large circles, we were still driving through one of Auckland's more run-down neighbourhoods. After mile after mile of rusty cars in unkempt gardens, my mood wasn't good. It was only months later, when I made the drive myself, that I realized what he'd done. The poor man had got himself hopelessly lost and was bluffing furiously as he tried to find his way out. Jim dropped us at the Best Western Motel in Cockle Bay. His profession was driving instructor, and he would come in very useful a few months later when he 'manipulated' me through my driving test.

New Zealand is an incredibly beautiful country, with a, rightly, very proud population. I say to any Kiwi reading this: any criticism you may read is fleeting. This was the eighties, we were on a journey of slow discovery and it was a while before we found our feet. I'm also very proud of my dual citizenship, which I was lucky to be given during my time there. I haven't visited for many years and I know that Auckland has changed enormously and is a spectacular city. We went at a time when the now world-renowned wine industry was still in its infancy and long before Peter Jackson showed the world with his *Lord of the Rings* films what a stunning filming location New Zealand is and released the potential for a massive international film industry. It was also before the internet and, for all my dad's passion to go, he hadn't done much research.

Cockle Bay wasn't the romantic perfection that we had expected and the motel was as basic as motels are built to be. We were in sprawling suburbia. It wasn't what I wanted and it wasn't the Cornwall that my parents loved. I know that's unreasonable and unfair, but we were very tired, very alone, and I could see in my mum's eyes that she was thinking that this was the biggest mistake she had ever made. Over the years, my folks had moved a number of times, buying or building houses and then moving on. A guest house and a cottage built from scratch were just a couple of their impressive achievements. I could tell that, for Mum, this time my dad may have asked too much. The family mood in the motel that night was extremely low.

I needed a cigarette. I'm not proud of the fact that at the time I was smoking again, not many a day, but certainly more than none. I tried to be respectful and never smoked in front of my parents, not that they would let me. In my childhood, my dad smoked half a cigarette a day. He would light a new one, smoke half of it then put it out and leave it in the ashtray for the next evening. He called the unfinished portion his 'dimp'. Other than the occasional relaxing spark-up when he was fishing, he hardly touched them, and they both deeply disapproved of me smoking. Back in the bedsit, in London, when my parents had come to stay for the weekend, I would excuse myself from my room and go to the loo for a crafty smoke. There were two toilets separated by a wall and their windows were very close to each other. After each puff, I would put the hand holding my fag out of the window. Dad knew what I was up to, so he would go into the loo next door, put his arm out of that window and pluck the cigarette from between my fingers. I would feel it go but had no idea what had happened. One minute it was there, the next it was gone. Had I dropped it? Was it stolen by a bird? Only when I rejoined them and they were all laughing did the penny – or cigarette – drop.

Back in Cockle Bay, Dad read the mood and said he was just popping up to the petrol station. When he returned, he tossed a packet of Peter Stuyvesant into my lap. Without a word, we both went outside and smoked together in silence.

A couple of days later we took the bus into Auckland city centre. I think they thought that a sniff round the city might perk me up. We got off the bus on Queen Street and it looked promising. At the end where we stood, the sea was at our backs; out in the bay was Rangitoto, a volcano cone, where, sometime in the future, I would get marooned with a member of Hot Gossip, an all-girl, raunchy British dance group started by Arlene Phillips and made famous by Kenny Everett.

The waterfront was interesting, the ferry buildings full of boats and cafés. Queen Street stretched out in front of us and we started to walk. It mostly housed banks, but there were shops and bars, too. My folks said that there was no need for me to stick with them – why didn't I set off on my own and explore? They would meet me back at a coffee shop in an hour and I should try not to get lost. I set off up the central street. It was quiet, but felt like a city, so I was happier. I looked up Shortland Street (which would soon become a very important street to me): not much up there, so I carried on walking up the main street then branched off up Victoria Street, a large side-street. There was nothing much up there, either; then, the city ran out. I walked back and tried Hobson Street. The same. I tried every side-street and, again, there was nothing more. Twenty minutes later I was back at the coffee shop.

'You're back early.'

'This is it! This is all there is, it's just one street!'

Eventually, we moved into 15 Alexander Street, in Howick, one of Auckland's eastern suburbs, close to Cockle Bay. It was a *Neighbours*-style house, with a garage underneath and

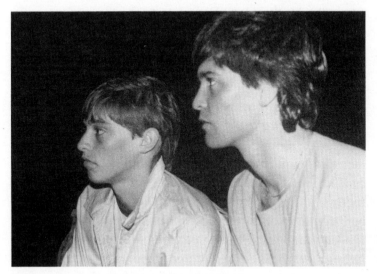

Tim and I far from home.

steps up to the front door and a sloping driveway to the road with a postbox at the end. Many houses in the suburbs had a 'quarter-acre plot' – in other words, a pretty big garden – and ours was one of them. I found our garden fascinating. Orange and lemon trees drooping with heavy, ripe fruit; there was a vegetable patch and, at the back of the garden, a huge kiwi-fruit bush that was so big you could crawl right into the middle of it. Tim and I would walk to the end of the garden with a knife and two teaspoons, sit inside the bush, reach up and pluck the fruit from the branches, cut them in half and scoop out the flesh, the green juice dripping down our chins. There were also Feijoa trees. I'd never seen them before, but their fruit is a bit like a bald kiwi and eaten the same way, but they have pale, fragrant pulp. I loved them. So much so I've tried to grow them over the years. I get the red flowers, but not one has ever borne fruit. For my Christmas present this year my brother found an importer and bought twenty of the fruit for me. I would imagine that those days back in that garden were probably the times when I was most full of vitamins.

One morning, Tim and I decided that a rotten branch of one of the orange trees needed to be sawn off. We positioned ourselves on either end of the saw, and it came off easily, revealing a hole in the centre of the stub left on the tree. We both looked in growing terror as two large flicking antennae appeared out of the hole. They grew longer and longer and we started to back away. After a few moments of ever-increasing antennae length, the biggest, ugliest insect we'd ever set eyes on slowly emerged from the tree. Our screams brought out the neighbours, who watched as our legs ran, but, like in cartoon characters, wouldn't gain the traction needed to move us. We fought each other to get away, both yelling, *'Monster in the garden!'*

We sprinted away and almost knocked the fly-screen door

off its hinges as we skidded into the kitchen, both gabbling about what we'd seen to Mum. There was a knock, and in came Harold, our neighbour, to explain what we'd seen. It turned out to be a weta. Google it!! You'll discover that it's native to New Zealand, a sort of flightless cricket and one of the heaviest insects in the world, and it's a big, scary-assed four-inch monster of a thing when it climbs out of a hole in a fecking tree.

I was later told by a friend that one morning she took her snorkelling gear out of the garage to go crabbing. When she got in the water, she put on her goggles and snorkel and launched herself into the sea. She'd gone about ten feet when she felt a tickling sensation on her tongue. Confused, she started to tread water as she removed the mouthpiece. Out of the pipe which moments before had been in her mouth crawled a weta. It will come as no surprise that, from that day, she always checked her kit.

With the next-door Schofields.

Our neighbours were, coincidentally, also called Schofield. A couple from Yorkshire, Harold and Doreen, they had two daughters: Sally, at twelve, the same age as Tim, and Catherine, nineteen, the same age as me. They were an absolutely delightful and fun family who couldn't have been more welcoming when we arrived. I used to ride into Auckland with Catherine, and we'd share a Milky Bar. She was bright, funny and very sporty. One day she found a lump on her leg, and when she told her mum they decided to get it checked out. Only months later, the cancer that it turned out to be took her young life. I have never seen anyone go through such a terrible ordeal with such calm dignity as her and her family. We all said at her funeral that, if you have to go, go with the resolution and style that Catherine did. Catherine was the second friend I lost.

The first was in Newquay. I won't name my two schoolfriends, but they married and had two lovely children. She became dangerously depressed. At that time in the eighties, there was very little care available and depression was deeply misunderstood and poorly treated. One day she went missing, leaving her two very young daughters at home with her husband. Shortly afterwards, my friend got 'the knock'. Two policemen came into his sitting room, and one of them threw a bag on to the coffee table. My friend looked inside. It was full of her rings. 'They your wife's?' said the copper, 'Yes,' said my friend. And that was how he was told that his wife had thrown herself from a very high rockface and was dead. I couldn't understand then how a loving parent could ever be in such a dark place that the only way out was the one she took. I came to develop a far clearer understanding much later in my life.

Dad had settled into his job at Goode Industries in high spirits, even though the skilled craftsman was now making television cabinets. My brother started school. In a wily move and to avoid any 'new Pom in town' teasing, he made friends with the biggest Maori schoolkid we'd ever seen. It was hilarious to see them side by side, little Tim and a combine-harvester-sized guy. He was a gentle giant, but not to be messed with, so Tim was protected.

Mum and I were struggling, though. We were both still hopelessly homesick and just couldn't settle. Mum was heard to complain that even the stars were different.

On the day I left the bedsit, Eddie had asked me to send him my number when we finally got a phone connected. When the phone was installed, I wrote to him and told him what the number was. A few weeks later, on a Saturday night as we all watched TV, the phone rang. It was Eddie. I was thrilled to hear his voice, and we chatted for a while, telling each other our news, and then:

'How are you all?' asked Eddie.

'Struggling a bit, if I'm honest,' I replied.

'Well, I told you I'd look after you.'

'Er . . . okay.'

'Who would you like to talk to? I can put you through to whoever you like, and you can talk for as long as you like, no charge.'

'What?!!'

And so it was. I'm not sure what Eddie actually did, but he had 'access' to something. In those days, with no internet, mobiles or FaceTime, the only way to contact family, other than extreme snail-mail, was to phone internationally, and it was fiendishly expensive; for us, prohibitively so. Wonderful Eddie saved us all. Each week he would call on a Saturday evening and connect us to people back home. Mum could talk to her sister Diane, who she missed painfully; we could all talk to family or friends for as long as we liked, for free. We never took the piss – none of the calls were longer than thirty minutes – but it was the most incredible lifeline and I think it saved Mum's sanity. Eddie is no longer with us. If he had been, I wouldn't have told the story, because I wouldn't want to get him into trouble at work. (Sorry, BT.)

I'd been applying for jobs on the radio. Auckland was rich in stations, and 1ZB, 1ZM and Radio Hauraki were the ones I liked and wrote to first. I didn't exactly lie; I was just a little light on the truth. Yes, I had worked at the BBC, I just didn't say I was a bookings clerk. They all invited me in and asked me to audition. I was pleased that they all seemed to like what I did, but they all had the same issue.

'I'm afraid you sound a bit English, mate.'

Of course! It had never crossed my mind that my accent would be an issue. I wrote to other stations – even to the ones I didn't like! The response was comprehensively the same. I was screwed. I had no idea what to do or where to go next. My mood plummeted and I moped about the house and garden, deep in thought. It was painfully obvious that I'd have to go back to London. I felt completely torn and lay in bed agonizing over the decision night after night, staring at the ceiling. Could I leave my family in New Zealand? How long could I hold out before I had to admit that my dream job had eluded me? Could I honestly travel back on my own with no money, no prospect of a job? Where would I live? Round and round the loop went in my head.

My folks knew that I was struggling. How could they get me to stay? Apparently, as they lay in bed one evening worrying about me, they hit upon an idea that just might at least stall my departure. The next morning, they pitched the idea:

'We're thinking of putting a swimming pool in the back garden.'

Clever move – almost sneaky, you could say. It was an idea that was met with a very positive response. The days were long and sunny, I was learning how to barbecue, taught by Harold next door, and a pool would be amazing. And so, we got one. Don't jump to the conclusion that it was a sunken pool with a shallow and a deep end, or that it might be tiled in blue and have a diving board. Nope, this was a much simpler affair, comprising a circular metal frame about five feet deep with a plastic liner. Dad built some steps so we could get in, and a small wooden platform. It was perfect. We were never out of it and it did the trick. It delayed my departure, which was very lucky, because I was soon to be shown a life-changing newspaper advertisement. I've thought a lot about those anguished nights. Could I have left my family? No chance.

We were approaching our first Christmas, the sun was blazing, the giant pohutukawa tree on the front lawn had exploded with red flowers, the pool was cool and welcoming, and yes, still the shops were full of Christmas cards with pictures of robins and snow. We never did understand that one.

Mum was about to make a critical error. Still hankering after the festive seasons of old in Cornwall, she had decided that we were *not* going to change our traditions, we *would* have a full Christmas lunch with all the trimmings.

Christmas Day dawned bright and clear and preparations began in the kitchen. As the jobs were handed out, the thermometer began to rise. As the temperature climbed outside, so did the temperature in our small kitchen. Four people all bumping into each other, the oven roaring, gas rings blazing, pots bubbling. I'm not exactly sure when it began to go wrong. It was becoming clear that Mum was getting fraught. My mother doesn't have a quick temper, it takes a while for her to blow, but when she does it's usually pretty nuclear. Any time in my childhood that she decided to take out the sewing machine, the three male members of the family would literally run and hide. Without doubt, every single time she turned it on it was inevitable that it wouldn't do what she wanted and that the air would turn a deep shade of purple.

'Mum's just taken out the sewing machine, boys,' Dad would say. 'Go now!'

The sight of him scurrying to the garage just made me smile. I will also admit to provoking Mum occasionally, which was deeply unwise. We both have the same temperament, and neither of us will back down. Where my dad and Tim were endlessly calm and placid, Mum and I were both very much fire signs. One day, after school and in the kitchen in Newquay, I wound her up so much she threw a mug at me. It missed by inches and took a huge chunk out of the wall. Fiery temper; thankfully, a rubbish shot. I hasten to add that all this was a long time ago. Life is much calmer these days, and my eighty-four-year-old mum is my wise rock.

The air in that sweltering, cramped kitchen in Auckland was beginning to change. It was ninety degrees outside and the beads of perspiration were showing on Mum's brow. We could sense the change. As the chirping of the cicadas scraped lazily across the lawn, the sound of pans being slammed got louder. The pressure was building. Steadily, she moved from red to purple, like the pressure gauge on a malfunctioning reactor. One wrong move and we knew it would be carnage. Things were beginning to boil over, to burn. Her limit was about to be exceeded. Just . . . one . . . wrong . . . word.

I don't know who accidentally pressed the detonate button (I suspect it was probably me), but *bang!* She went off with spectacular fury. This woman, who desperately wanted only to maintain a thread of connection to the tradition of our old lives back home, had had enough. We heard the yell of her reaching breaking point before we felt the wave of heat that announced she was in meltdown. In slow motion we all turned, saw what was happening and ran for cover. She picked up every single boiling pot and pan, burst out of the fly-screen door and threw them up the garden. Every potato, Brussels sprout and parsnip flew out of the door. The turkey in its roasting tray followed and the pigs flew from their blankets, joined moments later by the arching flight of the stuffing. If it had been remotely funny at the time, we might have smiled that the final addition to Christmas lunch on the grass was the gravy, but this was no time for a grin or a smart-arsed comment. We all stood silently, watching her and looking at the grass. There was a profound silence, broken only by the continuing chirp of the cicadas, although even they had briefly paused.

'Right then, that's that,' she said to no one in particular. Then we went next door to join the other Schofields for a barbecue.

I had decided I should learn to drive. I'd had a few lessons with Dad when I was younger (and scared him witless) and I'd also had two lessons in North London, but our departure had put a stop to those. It was time to pick up where I had left off, and it would be a further distraction. I mentioned earlier that Jim, who had so kindly picked us up when we arrived in New Zealand, ran a driving school, so I called him. Of course, he'd be more than happy to take me on, so my lessons started. Thankfully, Kiwis drive on the same side of the road as the UK, so that was a blessing. I did well, but was prone to distraction. Ten lessons in, Jim concluded that I was ready for my test.

'You have to take your test at five o'clock on 30 December,' he said.

'Okay, but why then?'

'Because you won't fail,' was his reply.

New Zealand was policed by two separate teams. The

police handled crime and drove calm-looking blue-and-white cars with blue lights and wore 'policey'-type uniforms. The traffic cops were in charge of the roads, speeding, accidents and the like, and they drove black-and-white cars with red lights and wore *Chips*-style uniforms made up of sunglasses and leather jackboots. They were scary. The driving test was conducted by the traffic cops, so Jim parked up outside their headquarters at 4.50 p.m. on 30 December. It soon became clear why he had been so specific about this particular time. He walked to the back of his car, opened the boot and lifted out a huge hamper. My allocated cop sauntered menacingly through the front doors of the HQ and walked in his creaking leather jackboots towards us.

'G'day, Jim,' said the cop.

'How ya goin', mate?' said Jim.

Jim then proceeded to hand him the hamper, which the cop carefully carried inside. When he emerged, he creaked back to the car. Jim went for a coffee in HQ and I slid into the driver's seat.

I went a little too fast on occasion, I forgot to indicate, I should definitely have checked my mirrors more and my three-point turn was a clumsy eight-point turn. Dammit, I knew I'd messed it up.

Deflated, I drove us back to HQ, whereupon my jack-booted passenger smiled and told me I'd passed . . . I'd what? Yep, I had passed. He wrote me a licence application slip and gave me the 'pass' form, smiled convivially, got out and strode back to the building, nodding to Jim as they passed.

'Well done,' said Jim.

'How did you know I would pass?'

'I gave you the hamper slot. It's when, every year, I thank the cops for all their help and wish them a happy New Year.'

'Oh.'

'Yeah, mate. No one has ever failed in that slot. You'd have had to have broadsided a bus or run over a vicar to screw it up.'

As I said earlier: 'manipulated'.

I bought a green Hillman Hunter, reg. FR 1865, and it was the key to a new freedom. I didn't drive as much as I would have liked, because I couldn't afford the petrol, but I could run errands to the mall down the road in Pakuranga and pick up my brother from his mate's house.

I'm sure things have changed, and I don't want to offend drivers in New Zealand in 2020, but they were terrifying times on the road back then, and that taught me to have sharp wits and rapid responses. At the time, you could drive when you reached the age of sixteen and, though the most popular cars were Japanese, many were huge American-style gas-guzzlers. One night I drove down the off ramp of a motorway with high concrete sides, and in front of me was a big Commodore with, seemingly, no one at the wheel. It

My first car, the Hillman Hunter.

drifted from side to side, scraping the wall on one side, then wandered slowly across the road to the other. Each time it touched, a huge plume of sparks left the bodywork. Was it rolling on its own? How had it got on to the motorway? I hung back at a safe distance – there was no one at the wheel for sure – so I was surprised when, a mile or so later, the brake lights came on and it slowed for the traffic lights and stopped and I pulled alongside. There were two small hands on the wheel. He may have been a very small sixteen or he may have been a child, I have no clue, but he could barely see above the dashboard. The lights turned green, I hung back again, and he meandered off into the night.

Hanging back at traffic lights was an essential trick to learn. Thankfully, I'd been prepped by a friend. On a Friday night in the city, when stopped at traffic lights, 'leave two car-lengths between you and the car in front', a popular game was for the car in front to suddenly be thrown into reverse and lurch back into you. Everyone was ready for this, we all left a gap, and when the white reversing lights of the car in front came on and it jumped back, we all did the same, a whole row of traffic reversing back into the spaces that had been left by the car behind.

Each week the death toll on the roads was released, and each week I was stunned by the magnitude of the numbers in comparison to the country's population of only 3 million. I saw more dead bodies by the side of the road and in car crashes than at any other time of my life. As I've pointed out, I'm sure that's not the case now.

I'd given up on ever getting a shot on the radio; it obviously wasn't going to happen and I had no idea what to do next. Yes, I was still homesick, but I had the car, we could swim in the sunshine and my dad had bought a pool table and put it in the garage. Every evening he and I would go down to play and I was allowed one cigarette per evening. Life was good, but I was uneasy and impatient: would I have to give up on my dream career? Or, to pursue it, would I need to leave the family and travel back to England on my own? I had no idea where I wanted to be.

Doreen from next door regularly popped in. She was hilariously funny in her haphazard approach to life. In either house, we never knocked during the day, just shouted, 'Only me!' as we walked through the fly-screen doors. And that's what happened on the day that changed my life.

'Only me!' chirped Doreen.

She walked into the kitchen carrying the *Auckland Star* newspaper. Mum put the kettle on and they chatted a bit. I was just pottering around the kitchen.

'There's an advertisement in here you might be interested in,' Doreen said.

'Oh, okay,' I said.

'It's been put in by Television New Zealand. They're looking for a young TV host.'

'Oh, right, thank you, I'll have a look.'

The Schofield family next door knew us very well by now, so they all knew what I wanted to do. They knew how disappointed I was by the constantly slamming Kiwi doors. Doreen finished her tea and left.

I didn't pick up the paper. In fact, it was only later, when everyone was home, that the subject was revisited. I remember it so clearly. We were watching *Prisoner: Cell Block H* in the sitting room.

'Have you looked at that advertisement?' Mum asked.

'Nah, not yet.'

'What advertisement?' said Dad.

He was informed of Doreen's visit earlier that afternoon.

'Go and get it, let's have a look,' he said.

'I'm not really interested,' I replied.

I fetched the newspaper and we all had a look. It was an ad for a young person to host a new teenage-magazine-style pop show. My family were all very enthusiastic; I was less so.

'Apply,' said Tim.

'Call them,' said Dad.

'But I don't want to work in telly, I want to be on the radio' was my forceful response; strangely ironic, if you consider how many years I've now been in front of a television camera!

'For God's sake,' said Dad, 'it's something to do. It'll get you out of the bloody house for a bit, and at least it'll be interesting and different. Phone them for an audition.'

I sighed. They had a point. I called the next morning. A couple of hours later a lady called Evelyn phoned me back. There was an audition slot available the following evening; could I be at the studios at 7 p.m.? I said I could. My folks were right: it would be interesting, if nothing else.

I drove into Auckland city centre, down Queen Street, and turned right into Shortland Street. At the top on the left was a windowless, fort-like red-bricked building, the home of Television New Zealand in Auckland. I walked into reception and stood next to their star newsreader, Philip Sherry. Okay, it was turning out to be interesting to have come after all. I waited until I was called. Evelyn, who I'd spoken to on the phone, came to meet me. She was obviously very efficient. I was to follow her to the studio, where I would meet Peter Grattan, the producer. It was the second time I'd walked into a TV studio since my visit to the BBC in Plymouth to watch Joe Pengelly read the evening news on *Spotlight South West* and my snoop around Television Centre. I liked the smell. Peter met me. A tall, smiley, curly-haired Brit, he seemed fun. They were taking it seriously: there were three cameras, a makeshift set and a member of the crew sitting on a stool who I was to interview, pretending they were in a band.

Maybe it was because I was just doing this for a night out and out of nothing more than curiosity, but I wasn't nervous. I sat on my stool and, for the first time in my life, looked into the black, glassy eye of a television camera. I was asked to talk about myself, introduce a couple of pop videos and then conduct a mock interview with the crew member, who I think I turned into Smokey Robinson. I was enjoying myself; it was fascinating. I was remembering the key advice I'd been given: 'Don't address the world at large' and 'Be yourself.'

The audition was done. I said thank you to the studio crew, which I've done in every studio I've been in since, even today, to our Covid-19 skeleton crew on *This Morning* thirty-nine years later.

Peter and Evelyn came on to the studio floor and said they'd give me a call in a day or so. I thanked them and drove home to tell my family that I'd stood next to Philip Sherry.

Next morning the phone rang. Could I pop into the TVNZ offices on Queen Street to have a chat?

About an hour later, I was met by Evelyn, who told me about her Maori heritage. She chatted convivially to me, asked if I'd like a cuppa, and we talked a bit more. She was lovely. She apologized that Peter Grattan was running late but said he'd be back in a minute. I wondered if they were going to question me more on my very sparse CV. I had listed 'presenter of a regular radio show in Plymouth', omitting the fact that it was hospital radio; 'extensive work at the BBC' – for that, read booking clerk; 'worked on Radio 1' – that was the twenty-second link with Jimmy Savile; 'produced and presented a star-studded Christmas special for radio at the BBC' – well, yes, it was *at* the BBC, just not *for* the BBC. Oh, and I was twenty-two, when I was actually nineteen.

If I was quizzed on the details, I was going to come seriously unstuck.

Affable Peter bounded into the room. He was sorry he was late, hoped 'Ev' had looked after me, did I need another tea? He chatted about his ideas for the show: it was going to be called *Shazam!* and would be a half-hour pop-video show with interviews of any guests that were in town and, if he could get the budget, some interviews could be done in Australia. It all sounded great. Obviously, whoever got the gig was going to have a ball. I was beginning to get confused. Why was he telling me all this? The conversation went like this:

'It sounds like it's going to be great,' I enthused through my confusion.

'It's going to be so much fun. I can't wait,' smiled Peter.

'I bet,' I said.

'Are you excited?' Peter asked.

'It's a great idea,' I generically answered.

'Er, you're being very calm, mate. Oh, hang on, did Ev tell you that you'd got the job?'

'Er . . . no.'

'Oh shit, well, yes, you have, *Evelyn*?'

'I thought you wanted to tell him, *Peeteeer*!'

'Oh, right. Well, welcome on board.'

And that was it!! Without the slightest fanfare, I had just become a TV host. No, wait: I had just become a broadcaster.

The conversation continued, though. I had to come clean.

'I might have exaggerated a bit on my CV.'

'Oh, I don't care! You got it because you were great in the audition.'

'And . . . I lied about my age, I'm not twenty-two, I'm nineteen.'

'Oh! That's good, you nearly didn't get it because you were too old!'

It seems to be a pattern when I'm hired for a big gig – it seems to just . . . happen. When I got the job on *Going Live* six years later, Chris Bellinger said to me, 'Would you like to come and play on Saturday mornings?'

I couldn't believe it. I had my own show. I was going to be on the telly. My family exploded with excitement, partly because they had pushed me to go to the audition, partly because I had a foot on the ladder, but mostly because we could all stay together. Doreen was thrilled to have played a part, too, and for ever more said, 'I took the paper over, you know.'

Work on the show started in earnest. We sorted out my fee. I didn't haggle, I'd have done it for free. It wasn't a big salary, but it would keep me in petrol and meant I could afford to take the family out for dinner occasionally. There were just the three of us in the office: me, Peter and Ev. I wasn't hired

Publicity stunt for *Shazam*.

just to be a presenter, I was expected to be part of the production team, too. In the UK, much like in America now, the unions were all-powerful. If it wasn't your designated job to move a chair, you didn't touch the chair. New Zealand was nothing like that. Jobs were wonderfully fluid, and part of my job was to drive to the record companies around the city and watch the music videos they would pitch to me. I would then take a long list back to Peter, who would build the show. I made some great friends at those record companies and there was a real buzz about music in the city, not just international music, but also a very healthy and exciting 'home-grown' music industry: Split Enz, DD Smash, The Chills, Auckland Walk – just some of the many great Kiwi bands of the time. One afternoon in 1983 I drove to CBS because they said there was a new video we had to see; it was unlike anything that had been seen before and was utterly ground-breaking, it was over thirteen minutes long! What? The show was only thirty minutes, with commercials, so that was a full part! They said I shouldn't be put off by that, that we'd want to show it, to drive over and watch. I walked into the viewing room and spent thirteen minutes and forty-two seconds with my mouth agape as I watched Michael Jackson's *Thriller* for the first time.

The day of recording the first show was getting very close. Peter and I had one slightly awkward conversation about my hair.

'Er, mate, can we just talk about your hair?'

'What's wrong with my hair?'

'Well, you've got a few, well, you see, you can see them on camera, and, well . . .'

'Pete, what are you talking about?'

'Mate, you've got grey hairs.'

'I know, the first ones appeared when I was sixteen. It happened at the same age to my mum.'

'Well, you're going to be the young host of a new pop show.'

'And?'

'They have to go.'

A couple of days later, and for the first time, I had my hair dyed the same brown that most of it was. My real colour wouldn't see the light of day until I moved from the BBC to ITV years later. I decided to take the opportunity to let it grow out, and was quickly told, 'ITV say they didn't hire a grey guy.'

So, I dyed it back. I've always been a bit sheepish and embarrassed that I did this. A local TV newsreader in London saw that I had come out of the 'grey closet' and, inspired by me, followed suit. He proudly showed his new hair colour on the news, citing me as his inspiration. Two days later, I was brown and had left him out there alone. It was only when Fern Britton finally persuaded me to embrace it that I allowed myself to be a 'silver fox'.

I seem to have a habit of changing my appearance just as I become known for it: just as I won 'Spectacle Wearer of the Year' in 2015, I had my eyes lasered.

Recording day for *Shazam!* had arrived. I was ready, my hair was fully brown, I'd done all the publicity, I'd bought new clothes and we were walking from the office, up Shortland Street to the studios.

It was the first time I had ever sat in a make-up chair, and the ladies were so reassuring. I've come to learn that make-up is the last calm place you'll be before you walk into a studio. After make-up, it's back to the dressing room for production briefings and final checks. It's a bit like an airport: make-up is an emotional 'land-side' for me; anything after is 'air-side'. All good make-up artists are very clever at reading the mood of whoever is sitting in their chair. Would that person like to chat, did they need quiet, did they need reassurance, did they need counselling? A make-up artist

can be a therapist at the same time as making you look considerably better than you actually do. Massaging your ego, telling you how great you're going to be and that there is 'absolutely nothing to worry about'.

Fern Britton once told me of a presenter who was sitting in a make-up chair with a gown covering his body. As his face was being attended to, the make-up lady noticed that he was vigorously 'fiddling' under the gown. Quite rightly, she was deeply offended, smacked his hand and told him, 'Stop it!' The presenter was equally offended and lifted the gown to show her that he was, in fact, filling his pipe with tobacco.

That first day in the make-up chair in Shortland Street, I needed reassurance. I surprised myself by how nervous I was. I really didn't want to arse it up. The lady powdering my face was utterly charming. I would very rapidly come to love that building and everyone in it.

After make-up, I walked down to the studio. The news studio was by reception; the bigger entertainment studio – where I was to go – was downstairs. I walked on to the studio floor to be met by Jimmy Biggum, the hilarious Scottish floor manager. There in front of me was the brand-new *Shazam!* set. Not elaborate, but perfect for the show. It was going to be recorded, so I knew if I messed it up I could have another go. We were ready, and I took my place on the sofa and the opening titles rolled, electronic graphics of a TV and the stylized image of a guitarist, which I'm pretty sure was Peter Grattan (he had a band called PG and the Hot Tips). An electric guitar provided the music. The red light on camera one lit up, Jimmy waved his cue, and I began. Looking back at the footage, I'm more alarmed by my flat hair than anything else, but I'm pretty sure that style was acceptable at the time. In future shows, I occasionally wore glasses that were so large they looked like two perfectly aligned satellite dishes. Watching it back afterwards, I could see that I looked nervous, but not too much. I picked nervously at the cushion as I introduced Quarterflash's 'Harden My Heart', but other than that, I was happy with how it went. It's both deeply nostalgic and a little unnerving how many of the moments I'm recounting can be found on YouTube. It has been invaluable for research as I write this, but it results in more than an occasional wince of embarrassment.

When I finished recording, Peter and Evelyn were thrilled. It had gone well; it was what they had envisaged, thankfully. Now all we had to do was to transmit it a couple of days later and hope that the viewers felt the same.

I felt a sense of calm once I got into my stride in that studio. It was easy for me to see the camera as the person I was talking to. It would take a few programmes before I'd feel totally at ease, but I knew even on that first day that it wasn't

My first studio set.

going to be intimidating, that a studio, to me, was a friendly, happy place, not a hostile, scary one.

I watched the show go out with my family at home in Howick. They all watched in silence and I held my breath for thirty minutes. As the closing credits rolled the room was full of 'That was great' and 'You did so well, we're so proud.' From that day on, my family have been my most honest critics. What they think is immensely important to me. They have all become very good judges of what I got right and when I've got it wrong. Telling me they're proud has a huge currency, and telling me I messed up keeps my feet firmly on the ground. The Schofields next door were also thrilled, and Doreen was happy to reiterate that she was so relieved it had been her that had brought over the newspaper that set everything in motion.

A couple of days later I drove into Auckland to start planning the second show in the office. Peter was a happy man. The network executives were happy with both my and the show's performance and, consequently, they were also very happy with Peter. We worked away on the planning of the next recording. At lunchtime Evelyn apologized for not pointing me in the direction of the large grey sack in the corner.

'What is it?' I asked.

'It's your fan mail.'

'It's *what*?!'

It had never crossed my mind. Throughout all of my love of TV and radio from the age of ten, and in my pursuit of a job in the industry I loved so much, my concentration had only been on getting into a studio. At no point had I considered that people might actually watch, let alone that I might have fans and that they might bother to write to me. I took the first couple of letters from the top of the sack. I had absolutely no idea what to expect, but mercifully the response was positive. I was going to have to practise a suitable signature for my replies.

Shazam! was a success. It didn't seem to matter that I was British and had an accent. In fact, all eyes were on Britain at the time. It was 1982 and we were all watching the horrors of the Falklands War each night on the news. The phone rang in the *Shazam!* office. A man called Ross Goodwin was asking to talk to me. I recognized the name. He had been the guy who was with me during my audition at Radio Hauraki. He was also the programme controller and a DJ on the station and it was he who, very gently, had told me I was too English.

'G'day, Phil, well done on the show. Do you want to complement that TV shit with some proper broadcasting?'

'I would like that a lot.'

'Great, fancy a tinny?'

Working in television was an unexpected surprise, and I was loving it, but the pull of radio was still very powerful.

Radio Hauraki was the Auckland station I loved the most. It had begun life as a pirate station broadcasting offshore from a ship called *Tiri* in the sixties. Ross was one of the original DJs. In my eyes, Hauraki was the coolest station, played the best music and had the best studio location. I was eager to have that beer with Ross as soon as possible. I asked Peter if he was okay with that. But what if he said no? I was hugely relieved when he said it was a great idea and that it would be a benefit for *Shazam!* if I was on the radio as well. I went for a beer and was given Sunday mornings on the station. I was ecstatic.

There have been many memorable, proud and exciting moments in my career, and just a few utterly sublime moments. Radio Hauraki provided a moment that was both sublime and, briefly, terrifying. The studios were about five floors up, in a glass building that stood on its own on the waterfront. My first Sunday show started just before dawn. There was only one studio, so you had to hot-seat. I waited for the night-time DJ to finish, then, during the news, he packed his stuff away and I slid into the chair. I'd been shown how to use the desk, the music was ready and I'd had a play to see which jingles I liked.

The news finished, I hit the button to play my first ever jingle – 'Radio Hauraki Auckland's *best* music' – and segued into the first track. I was on my own and beaming from ear to ear. I was on the radio, with my own show, on the best station in Auckland, with the *best* music. The studio sat in the corner of the building with glass windows on two sides that looked out over the harbour, one behind, one to my right. The view to my right was the Auckland Harbour Bridge. The view from the window behind was even more spectacular – the waterfront of the city with ships and wharves. Beyond that, the perfect sloping volcanic cone of Rangitoto. Beyond that, the shimmering Hauraki Gulf. It was a view that was happening behind me. I had my back to it and was deeply embedded in being on the radio, oblivious to anything else and having the time of my life.

About ten minutes into the show and, thankfully, during a record, the studio was suddenly flooded with red and golden light. What the hell? I turned and was utterly horri-fied at the scene. Rangitoto was erupting – but it hadn't been part of an eruption for six hundred years! I wondered if the next thoughts racing rapidly through my mind might be my last. If they had been, my final petrified, angry thoughts would have been: 'Are you fucking *kidding* me?! I finally make it, I get a show on TV, I'm ten minutes into my first-ever radio show and I get killed by an erupting volcano? This is *so unfair.*'

Yes, those would have been my final thoughts on the planet, if indeed Rangitoto had been erupting. But it was happening too slowly. There was no explosion, no flying boulders, no lava rushing into the sea and no pyroclastic flow smashing through the windows to preserve me as a stone DJ statue for all eternity. What I was witnessing was . . . a sunrise, one of the most beautiful and sublime I have ever seen. That particular day, my first-ever day on the radio, was one of only a handful of days in the year when the sun rose directly out of the cone on the volcanic island. I didn't speak when the track finished. I went straight into the next song and stood watching. From thinking I was witnessing my final moments on Earth, to witnessing one of the most beautiful natural events I've ever seen, all in about thirty seconds. The next day I told Ross Goodwin what had happened, and he roared with laughter and said, 'Oh, yeah, I forgot to tell you about that. Proper shits you up the first time, doesn't it?'

I was outrageously happy: all the pieces of the jigsaw were falling into place. *Shazam!* was a success. We were showcasing home-grown talent in a nationwide Battle of the Bands and I was hosting live events in front of thousands of people. And, at the weekends, I loved my two hours on the radio and I was making some great friends.

I think perhaps the reason life in New Zealand was so chilled back then was because of the dope. It was taken very seriously. Kevin Black was the breakfast DJ on Hauraki and he was the biggest name on the radio and a very talented broadcaster. He was also a top bloke. As I've mentioned, we all used the same studio. There were two pot plants in the studio, and I'm assuming, at some stage, someone was having a midnight toke and stubbed it out in the pot plant that was directly in the eyeline of all the DJs. There must've been a seed in the stub, because slowly but surely green shoots started to show themselves and it really did become a pot plant. Kevin was the first to identify what was going on and, as the senior DJ, in an unspoken agreement, all the other DJs silently agreed that the spoils were his. He watered the plant lovingly during his show every morning. Conditions were obviously perfect because it was thriving and beautifully healthy. Kevin was so excited by his studio horticulture.

The station cleaners came during the breakfast show. When they were in the studio, they would go about their work as the music played, dusting, emptying the bins, cleaning the windows and vacuuming. Kevin would tell them he was about to open the mic and they would turn off the vacuum cleaner and stand quietly until the red light went off.

Some of us were listening to his show one morning when Kevin was reading the weather. Suddenly, during the report . . .

'It's going to be a fine day over the city, temperatures sitting somewhere in the region of . . . *Oh God, no!* . . . I'm so sorry, in the region of twenty-three degrees.'

A jingle played, then music. In fact, three records in a row. What the hell had happened?

They were still laughing about it later that day when I popped into the station. It turned out that the cleaner had been vacuuming and Kevin had asked them to hang on as he opened the mic. He said later that as he was reading the weather, the cleaner was looking around for something to do quietly, spotted the weed (meaning one thing to the diligent cleaner, another thing to us) and deftly plucked it out and threw it in the bin. The outburst on the radio was an involuntary yelp from a DJ who had just seen weeks of work ripped out in front of him.

That wasn't the only time the DJs at the station dabbled with drugs. My mate was a DJ. He pulled into the station one Sunday after I'd finished on air to show me a car he'd just bought. I looked it over.

'Yeah, very nice. How much?' I said.

He told me. I was a bit surprised at how much he'd paid. It was a reasonably throaty Mitsubishi, but not worth that much. I said I thought he'd been ripped off.

'Nah, mate, look. It came with extras.'

He opened the glove box: it was full of dope. He walked round to the boot and popped it open: another stash in there!

'See, mate, great deal.'

I had to agree: he had got a bargain. He was, to be fair, pretty sly with money. He still owes me quite a bit.

When Kevin left the breakfast show he was replaced by Pat Courtenay, a very high-flying, high-octane Irish DJ who had just arrived from Australia. At the time, I believe, he was the highest-paid DJ in the country. He was amazing on the radio and was a massive asset to the station. His show was fast, original, occasionally controversial and very funny. I absolutely loved it. We were all a bit in awe of Pat. Our paths didn't cross at the station, but he took offices above the production office of *Shazam!* and I was hoping to bump into him to say hi. It took about a week. He was fast-talking, took no prisoners, brash and sharp as a knife. We hit it off instantly and became great friends. We both joined the press club, an industry-only speakeasy kind of place. When you were accepted, you were sent a key. It opened a nondescript door in a bland building, on Wellesley Street, I think. Through the door, up a flight of stairs, and there was the private bar, a sort of Kiwi Soho House, full of industry professionals who were all very discreet, especially if you fell over full of whisky, which Pat and I regularly did. We played pool into the early hours and he educated me on Irish politics, a subject he was extremely passionate about. One evening we were playing pool and talking about the sectarian divide. Pat was in full, passionate flight. He stopped playing and looked me dead in the eyes. I met his gaze as he told me, that under different circumstances and in a different place, he wouldn't hesitate to shoot me. I believed him.

It was after one of those very long nights of pool-playing and challenging conversations that Pat caused me to frighten the life out of my parents.

Dad had decided we were too cramped in our house. Unable to suppress his creative urges, he designed and built an extension to the Howick house. A new, large bedroom for him and Mum with an impressive en suite. He was extremely proud of his creation. They had been waiting to move into their new bedroom with increasing anticipation. Eventually, it was completed and they decided it was the night to move in. I may have been on the TV and radio, but I still lived at home and slept in the same bed in the same small room as I had when we moved in. Their departure from their old room would free up a bit of space for me and Tim.

On the night in question, they were proudly and comfortably tucked up in their new 'suite' for the first time. I was out with Pat. It was a very long night and it had been a tiring week. As I was driving home my eyes were beginning to droop. I was in reckless danger of falling asleep at the wheel. I swung the car off Alexander Street and up the drive, not concentrating and too fast. I got to the end of the drive, misjudged the stopping distance and ran into the metal garage doors. The noise was spectacular, a huge reverberating boom!

In the new bedroom, the eyes of my parents flew open at the deafening roar and, for the first time, my dad doubted his building skills.

'Christ, Pat, it's coming down!'

'What?'

'The bloody extension is coming down. Get into the garden, quickly!'

I surveyed the damage: nothing to the car, dents in the

garage door. I shrugged and walked up the steps into the house. Walking into the kitchen and looking out of the window, I saw both of my parents, in their night clothes, holding on to each other and looking at the extension. It still makes me laugh. It took a long time before they did.

Although it was fun being around my occasionally stoned friends, I'm not suited to marijuana and I don't like it. On the rare occasions I've tried it, it has either made me sick, or made me feel like I have been darted with a tranquillizer. The first time I ever tried it was with Pat. He invited me over to his house for dinner; his lovely girlfriend, Trish, was going to cook. His hefty salary at Hauraki had enabled him to rent a house that, to this day, I'd like to revisit. It was on stilts, built of beautiful local wood and set in a silver-fern grove in the swanky Takapuna suburb. Big double doors opened on to a large veranda that was built out into the ferns. It was stunning.

Trish cooked a lovely dinner, we drank wine and whisky, chatted and listened to music. I think Pat played the guitar. Then he rolled a joint. I was hesitant but decided to give it a try. It seemed like only moments before the waves of nausea hit me, followed by the tranquillizer effect. Obviously, I was now rubbish company. Pat told me the next day that I just crumpled on the sofa, but I had a smile on my face. He carried me into the spare bedroom and he and Trish tidied up the dinner things. As they did, they put on some music. They wouldn't know, but in my stoned state, I was about to have an intimate relationship with an album.

The album they were playing as they did the washing-up was Dire Straits' *Love over Gold*.

They assumed I was asleep on the bed in the spare room. That wasn't the case. I was *in* the album, living every note and loving every word. It was an intense musical experience, and I feel I know that album more than any other, not just to listen to, but to be an integral part of ... like ... to really know, maaan ... you know? When I've subsequently told that story, some have said, 'That's a shite album.' I won't hear a word said against it, because ... I know. Haha.

A while later, Pat was too controversial for the radio to take any more, and he resigned. That was it. I was distraught. I drove to the Takapuna house, but he and Trish were gone and I never saw them again. He's on the radio in Dublin now, I think. I should call.

I don't think there are many areas in which both Tim and I disappointed Dad, but sport was definitely one. In his youth, he'd played for the feeder team for Oldham Athletic. We have newspaper cuttings from those days. 'Schofield scores 6' – that type of thing. He could have been a pro, but he hated the politics. He was always watching the footie; it was his passion. Tim and I couldn't have cared less. He tried to get us involved, but it was never going to happen. So, when I was asked by TVNZ if I would play for the station in a charity match, I couldn't have said no fast enough. But they were having none of it and Peter was exerting enormous pressure.

'It would be great for the show, mate.'

'No.'

'Great publicity.'

'No.'

'The channel would be really appreciative.'

'*No*, Peter.'

So I played, obviously.

I didn't breathe a word of it to anyone. My folks didn't know, and I was not going to tell them.

On the day of the match, it was pissing down. I was given shorts and a shirt (branded) by the station. I borrowed the boots from the wardrobe department and I was in a very bad mood.

I don't like being pressured into things, and this had been extreme pressure.

The rain was relentless, and it was cold, too. Wet and cold and football. Seriously?

I think the team realized very quickly that I wasn't interested, and they made sure the ball didn't come anywhere near me. I made a few obligatory runs, but nothing that merited anyone risking a pass in my direction. I was wet through to the skin, shivering with cold and pissed off in the extreme. The match ended and I got changed and went to the pub with everyone, where I was heartily ribbed for my performance.

There was no mention of where I'd been when I got home, and I was not going to tell for sure.

Three days later I walked into the kitchen and on the table were about twenty pictures of me, lanky, bedraggled, cold and sullen. My dad had found out about the game somehow and hidden in the trees with his camera.

'I thought you did okay.' He laughed.

'Sod off.'

Becoming a recognized face of TVNZ came with responsibilities besides charity football matches. Before I ever considered answering that fateful newspaper advert, I'd spent hours watching TVNZ as I tried to figure out what I was going to do with my life. Sometimes I watched until the channel closed down at around one in the morning. The close-down sequence was a cute animation featuring a Kiwi who was switching everything off, accompanied by his friend the cat, who followed him up to bed. The Kiwi put in a cassette to start the 'goodnight' music, walked through a deserted studio, put the milk bottle out and then went up in a lift, to where they both slept, in a satellite dish. You can find that 1982 sequence on YouTube – it is called 'The Goodnight Kiwi'. Now I was one of TVNZ's presenters, I was occasionally asked if I would help with a bit of brand promotion. I got a call from publicity. Would I be prepared to do a handful of public appearances with the iconic Kiwi & Cat from the close-down cartoon. Of course. I'd be honoured.

The appearances were in large shopping malls in the Auckland area. I would go onstage and give away a few TVNZ T-shirts and introduce the Kiwi and the Cat, both of whom were girls of about fifteen dressed in costumes that were a very good representation of the animated characters. The children in the audience were to line up to have their pictures taken with the three of us. It went down a storm. The audience loved it. We had successfully completed the first two shows of the day that morning. After a quick break, we set out to do the final two in other malls in the afternoon. It was getting hot, the day was sweltering and, combined with the lights on the stage, it was pretty uncomfortable. I was in a shirt and shorts, the Kiwi and the Cat were in full, heavy character costumes. The crowd was clapping and cheering, and children's faces beamed up at me. It was time to introduce the characters.

'You all know who I'm about to introduce, the stars of TVNZ and icons to all of us. Please welcome the Goodnight Kiwi and the Cat!'

The crowd went wild.

I knew something was wrong right from the off. The Cat bounded out, as it had done on the previous two occasions, but something was wrong with the Kiwi. It walked slowly forward and seemed a bit confused. I was immediately on high alert, but the crowd was oblivious. The show continued, and I did my best to keep it going while keeping an eye on the motionless Kiwi. When I could, I sidled over and whispered, 'Are you okay?' Nothing from the Kiwi. 'I think I should help you off the stage . . .' Still nothing.

As the children smiled and clapped, the Kiwi puked. From inside the costume, I heard the loud and expansive sound of a teenager comprehensively losing her lunch. I grabbed the feathers of the bird in the knowledge that it was about to keel over.

'Thank you to the Cat and the Kiwi . . . yaaaay . . . I think it's time they both went back to their satellite dish to go to sleep. Come on, you two.'

The crowd was still totally oblivious, until, as I led the stricken animal from the stage, a large splosh of vomit gushed forth from its feet.

The costume was beyond the hope of any dry-cleaner. The Kiwi was incinerated, and the remaining shows cancelled.

As we felt more settled in our new country, we began to explore. The scenery in New Zealand is breathtaking, as you will know if you've visited or watched the *Lord of the Rings* films. We drove through the stunning hills of the Coromandel Peninsula, covered in temperate rainforest, and then down to the black volcanic sands of Piha beach. A note of caution: the black sand gets substantially hotter in the sun than the golden sand of Fistral beach. I attempted to run across it barefoot to the sea. After six paces, I ran back, yelping.

My folks had made friends with a British couple called Alec and Vera. Along with their two grown-up children, they lived in Taupo, in the centre of the North Island. Taupo is a pretty town beside the lake from which it takes its name. Again, the scenery is spectacular. The entire area is volcanic and much of it is still active. In the distance are three rumbling volcanos, Ruapehu, Tongariro and Ngauruhoe. In fact, Lake Taupo is in the caldera of an ancient volcano. Given that the freshwater lake has a surface area of 616 square kilometres, it must've been a bloody big bang when it went off.

Alec and Vera invited us all down to stay and asked if I would like to learn to water-ski from their boat, out in the lake. I don't know how much of what they then told me was true, but it all seemed highly plausible, given the geographic location. They said that the ground beneath the town was entirely pumice and that if there was ever a water shortage in New Zealand, the residents of Taupo would always be able to water their gardens because the water soaked through the grass, into the pumice and straight back into the lake. The other fact was thrown casually into the conversation as we sat in the boat on a cloudless day, the lake beneath us as flat as glass and the mountains mirrored on its surface. I was getting kitted up for my first attempt at water-skiing when Alec told me that at the bottom of the 110-metre-deep lake were pumice caves. If anyone drowned in the lake, the bodies were hardly ever found because, as they sank, they were pulled into the pumice caves and were impossible to recover. Well, that put the shits up me, for starters.

I jumped into the water and bobbed as the boat circled to leave me the rope. The clarity of the lake was astonishing. As I looked down to my feet, it was as if there wasn't any water there at all. I looked past the water-skis and into the crystal-clear depths beyond; no chance of seeing the bottom. As I thought about those pumice caves below, waiting to steal my drowned body, I felt something happen in my head and I shivered. It was the beginning of a phobia, a fear of deep water that would stick with me for years. A fear that was compounded years later when I was scuba-diving in Antigua and swam over the edge of the continental shelf. The water went from warm aquamarine to cold black as I looked down the sheer, rocky wall into the abyss. My instructor laughed for hours. He said he'd never seen a human bend so much in a turn. 'It's a miracle you didn't snap,' he said.

Anyway, turns out I'm not a bad water-skier. Maybe it was the fear of falling in that kept me upright on the skis.

We only had two experiences of earthquakes in the four years we were in New Zealand. Mine was about five floors up in a hotel room in Christchurch on the South Island, where I was about to host a concert. It felt at first as if a large truck was driving past. I only looked up from learning my lines when I realized that not only was it taking a very long time for the truck to pass, but now everything was falling off the shelves. I was new to this, so I ran down the corridor to tell the crew there had been an earthquake. They looked at me bewildered. To them, what I'd felt was just an everyday occurrence to be ignored.

My folks had a far more interesting experience. They were on a weekend break with friends in Napier, on the east coast of the North Island. The women decided they needed to use the public loo and the blokes were standing on the pavement, waiting. As the fairly large quake hit, both my mum and her friend Ann were sitting down having a wee, and a chat through the cubicle wall. They were rocked, screaming, from side to side as they sat. Mum told me later that she felt like she was trying to stay on one of those bucking-bronco machines, all the time trying to pull her pants up!

My most frightening moment came not from shifting tectonic plates but in front of a camera on a talent show. Anyone who knows me will tell you how terrible I am at maths. Right from school, I knew it wasn't for me. English, biology, history, politics – yes. In physics and chemistry, I showed a passing interest. Maths – literally, no chance. My folks even paid for private lessons, but Mr Holmes gave up. It's funny how these weaknesses have a habit of manifesting themselves when you least expect it.

One of New Zealand's most highly regarded entertainers at the time was Ray Woolf, a genuinely lovely ex-pat who had become a very well-respected singer and TV host. Ray was launching a new talent show called *Star Quest* and I was invited to be on the panel. This was a big honour for me and was an establishment seal of approval. Ray was a talented, affable host. As with pretty much every talent show in the world that would follow, a performer performed and a panel of four judges gave their critique.

There had been no rehearsal for the judges because the acts were to be a surprise.

The studio audience clapped the end of the first act, a singer. Ray asked us all to vote out of twenty for presentation, content and star quality. We all complied. I gave the performer marks of sixteen, fourteen and seventeen, respectively. I completed my scoring, sat back and waited for my turn. Ray went to the first judge, who I think was a charming kids-TV host called Olly Ohlson. Olly chatted through how he thought the performer had done, and then:

'So, Olly,' said Ray. 'Could I have your scores, please?'

'Well, Ray, I gave Alison fifteen for presentation, fourteen for content and sixteen for star quality.'

'Thank you, Olly, so that makes your grand total?' asked smiling Ray.

'My grand total for Alison, Ray, is forty-five,' beamed Olly.

Oh dear God! We had to do our own adding up!

I told my family what had happened and my dad was helpless with laughter. We all sat down to watch when the show went out.

'Thank you, Olly. So that makes your grand total?'

You could see my head snap round to look at Olly and

Ray, my eyes wide with panic, then both my hands shot under the desk so that I could frantically try to add up my total score on my fingers. It was hopeless, I hadn't left enough time, the cameras would very soon be pointing at me and Alison would be waiting for her score. The family screamed with laughter every time there was a shot of me. Head down, looking at my fingers, deep in panicked concentration.

I couldn't do it: I'd have to change her score. Poor Alison got straight fifteens from me because it was easier to add up. She didn't win, by two points.

One afternoon in the *Shazam!* office, Peter and I were discussing music and musicians and he told me a story that he assured me was true. I'm not going to name the person, in case it isn't.

At the time, Auckland bar-opening hours and their accompanying rules were confusing. There was a hangover from the 1920s, when they were only open for an hour between 5 and 6 p.m. This was called 'the six o'clock swill'. You got as much down you in that hour as you could then staggered off into the dry suburbs. Sixty years later, even though the law had been very much relaxed, that first hour of opening time was often carnage. If the bars in the city were raucous, the bars out in the deep country were like the Wild West, with larger versions of Kiosk Kev's shack in *I'm a Celebrity Get Me Out of Here!* There was a long wooden building with a single shutter which, when open, revealed the bar, but it could be slammed shut if things got out of hand or if it was closing time. It was seldom ever closing time, so things often got out of hand!

In the story I was told, this particular artist had a false lower leg, but no one knew. He was at the bar, in the bush, and was being seriously ribbed by the locals about how soft he was because he was from the city, how he had no idea how rough life was out here, how they could 'out-tough' him at every turn. As it was in the middle of nowhere and as rough as hell, naturally, there was a bloke standing nearby with a beer and a shotgun. The artist in question said, 'You wanna know how fuckin' tough I am?'

He picked up the shotgun, pointed it at his (false) foot, pulled the trigger and blew it off. A dozen hard-nosed drinkers were apparently sick on the spot and ran off. Our artist calmly finished his beer. How he got from the bar to his car with only one foot, I wasn't told, nor indeed, come to think of it, how he drove home.

I was desperate to learn as much as I could now I was finally on the inside of the business. Peter was happy to facilitate my education. He sent me on a public-speaking course and I travelled to Wellington and Christchurch to complete courses in TV production, directing and film-making. I like to think that, these days, it helps me see the work that goes on in a studio from other people's perspective. At the time, I was just happy to learn anything I could. It's strange, though. It's not what you learn from working *in* television that can make the greatest difference, it's what you learn from *watching* television that can profoundly change the course of your life and the lives of those around you. Our family was about to discover that fact on the most traumatic night of our lives.

I was never home in those days. I was always out with mates, out with girlfriends, working. I loved the city, the country and my jobs on radio and TV. Life had got very exciting and varied; it was full and fun. I'd ditched the Hillman Hunter and was the proud owner of a Honda Civic, which, admittedly, wasn't very showbiz for someone who had by now interviewed some of the world's biggest stars of the time.

My first-ever 'star' interview was Cliff Richard. He is a great friend of Gloria Hunniford, mother to Caron Keating, who I would later go out with. We've laughed about the fact that I interviewed him in New Zealand – Cliff remembered his trip to NZ, but not our interview. He said he didn't remember any terrible interviews, so I must've done a reasonable job.

I wish I could remember who taught me the most valuable piece of interviewing technique I possess; it would have been in one of those letters I got when I was about ten. The most important thing in an interview is to *listen*! Don't have a list of questions that you relentlessly stick to. I learned in the early days to have a structure but to be prepared to throw it out of the window, to engage in whatever is said, to be interested and to listen.

I've mischievously used this technique in interviews I have given, when I know the person asking the questions isn't really listening to a word I'm saying. Halfway through the interview, at the end of an answer, I'll say:

'So, you see, that's how I got my first job in TV . . . and then I ran over the nun.'

'Right,' says the interviewer. 'And were you excited to be in television?'

Only when they got the recording back and listened to it would they realize what I'd said and think, *He did what?!*

I had interviewed Elton John, who had just got married and surprised the world. I'd recorded a TV special with Boy George and Culture Club. I'd driven in the back of a limo with Billy Idol as his screaming female fans bounced off it. At one party in Auckland, Laura Brannigan, who was riding high on the success of 'Gloria', had decided I needed to learn how to put a lighted match in my mouth without burning myself. She must have been a pretty good teacher, because I didn't singe the roof of my mouth. One of the most surreal moments was interviewing Sting and The Police, because the last time I'd seen the band was when I was standing beside Joyce at the tea urn, watching them press the 'Enter' button in Broadcasting House.

I'd also flown to Australia to record a special with Duran Duran. It was while Peter, Ev and I were in Australia that we were introduced to an Australian performer who was, as yet, unknown outside the country. He was charming, enigmatic, sexually charismatic and fascinating. We all had a beer, and he asked if we would like to go to the studio to listen to the album he had just recorded. We all eagerly agreed. The album was incredible. He was incredible. And so it was, that night in Sydney, that we spent a wonderful evening listening to *Shabooh Shoobah* with Michael Hutchence of INXS.

I had celebrated my twenty-first birthday with all my family and friends and my dad had made me a wooden key with '21' on it that everyone had signed. We had applied for and

Happy 21st birthday.

been granted New Zealand citizenship, so I now had dual nationality.

My girlfriend at the time was part Russian, and I was asked over to her house for dinner to celebrate my birthday a couple of days later. It was a messy affair, as her Russian father toasted everything with a shot of vodka. My arrival: toasted. Sitting at the table: toasted. The wonderful company: toasted. The wonderful vodka: toasted! Being totally smashed certainly helped with the main course. There is nothing I *can't* eat. In company, I'll always be polite, even if it's something I don't like. I love the yolk of an egg, but I never fancy the gloopy white, and I don't like polenta, because it should be packaging and not food, but I'll eat it if I have to. That night, in the midst of incredible Russian hospitality, I was served something that I, literally, couldn't eat.

Imagine a fish that dies from unnatural causes, then washes up in a harbour in August and lies on the tideline for a week before being picked up by a seagull and dropped on to the deck of a cargo ship, which then takes it around the world. After arriving in the tropics, it is kicked off the ship by a passing sailor, falls over the side of the ship and on to the dock, where it is scraped up, put on a plate and posted to a Russian who lives in Auckland because he's having a dinner party. The amazing fish, toasted . . . and hidden in a napkin.

So, my social life was full and fun, but on one rare occasion – that traumatic night – I happened to be at home. Mum, Tim and I were sitting watching TV. Dad had enrolled in an art night-class and was out painting and we were waiting for the sound of his car in the drive. It was a surprise when we heard his key in the door, but no car. He walked in.

'I've locked my bloody keys in the car at night school,' he said.

'Oh, okay,' I said. 'Get your spare ones and I'll take you back down the hill.'

Dad was skinny and fit. He'd jogged up the hill from the class to home – he usually jogged everywhere when he was out on his own. None of us noticed him do something he very rarely did: he walked into the kitchen and poured himself a glass of water. Then he walked back into the sitting room and sat down with us to watch TV. My mum was beside him on her chair, my brother and I were in our usual places, Tim lying on the floor, face down, head in hands, propping him up as he watched, me sitting on the floor with my back to Dad's chair.

'Brian!' cried my mum suddenly. *'Brian!!'*

I turned and looked up. He was having a heart attack in his chair. It's a sight I will carry with me for ever. He was gasping and clutching and it was utterly horrific. It's strange how, in times of deep trauma, your mind and vision focus to a laser-sharp pinprick. There was a whooshing in my ears. All I could see was him. Mum and Tim were blurs in my peripheral vision. I was aware that Tim was phoning for an ambulance and that Mum had run next door.

I pulled him from the chair on to the floor. He was dead.

I have no idea where I had seen CPR or mouth to mouth, but it had to have been on television because, back then, there were no lessons or any real awareness and I'd never been in a situation like that. I started compressing his chest and breathing into his mouth, again and again and again and again. Nothing was happening. I kept trying. I looked at the lamp and wondered, if I pulled the cord out, could I hit him with 240 volts? No, the fuse board would trip and I'd be in the dark. Again and again I compressed and breathed into him. His lips were blue and he was totally lifeless. It wasn't working. I put my left hand flat on his chest over his heart, lifted my right hand over my head in an arc and crashed the side of my right fist on to my left hand, over and over, then breathed again into his blue lips. I thumped more, I breathed more, he made a small gasp, but nothing else. *Again and again and again and again.* Small signs of something. Was it life?

I was oblivious to everything but him, but then I heard a siren. As I kept up the thumping and the breathing, two paramedics arrived. They were pulling kit out of a bag, and one of them said:

'Well, mate, that's an unorthodox method, but it seems to be working. Keep going until we're set up – only thirty more seconds.'

I kept going.

'Clear.'

I stopped, sat back on my feet and watched. They had cut his favourite T-shirt. He wouldn't be happy with that. A high-pitched whine, two paddles on his chest and a *thunk*.

His eyes shot open.

'I'm all right,' he said.

'What's his name?' asked the paramedic.

'Brian,' I told them.

'Okay, Brian, nothing to worry about. You've had a bit of a heart attack, mate.'

They gently strapped him on to a stretcher and I became aware that Mum, Tim, Doreen and Harold were all in the room. Mum was distraught. Tim was as transparent as a ghost.

One of the paramedics was writing in a pad. He didn't ask my name. He gave me a small certificate, and it read, 'Tonight, Phillip Schofield saved a life.'

As he handed it over, he said, 'Nice work, mate.'

Out of every small scrap of paper I have saved in my life – and I save everything – that certificate is the only thing I have lost.

The stretcher was lifted past the pohutakawa tree and loaded into the ambulance. Mum got inside. The doors slammed shut, the red-and-white flashing lights burst into life and it tore off into the night.

'Get in the car!' I shouted to Tim.

And we chased the ambulance.

If they had stayed in rural Cornwall, there is no chance that an ambulance could have reached them in the ten minutes it had taken in Auckland, and I would have been in London and wouldn't have been able to administer incorrect but effective CPR. The move to New Zealand had saved his life.

Dad was rushed into intensive care and the three of us sat on a bench in a nondescript corridor to wait for news. After an hour, a nurse came to tell us that he was critical but stable, and was in the best hands. She then exclaimed, 'Oh, my dear God, your hands!' We looked at each other. Who was she talking about? She was looking at me. 'You have to go to X-ray straight away.'

The back of my left hand was black from the tips of my fingers to beyond my wrist. My right hand was the same: purple-black bruising from my little finger, up the side of my hand and halfway up my arm. I had obviously been hitting Dad very hard. My hand was checked – nothing broken – and we were then allowed in to see Dad. Surrounded by the usual ICU paraphernalia, he looked so fragile and vulnerable. I had never seen him like that. He wasn't a big man, but to me he was invincible and immortal. Clearly not.

He opened his eyes and smiled and we asked if he was okay.

'I feel fine, apart from my chest.'

'Your chest? What's wrong with your chest?'

'I feel like I've been kicked by a bloody horse, repeatedly!'

'Ah, yes, sorry about that.'

He was fine that I had battered him, but really pissed off

they had cut up his favourite T-shirt. Like I said, I knew he would be.

Two days later, I had to fly to Christchurch to host an awards ceremony live on TVNZ. The show must go on.

In the days that followed, Dad had a quadruple heart bypass. It was months before he was back to normal – well, normal apart from having what looked like a huge zip from his neck to his navel.

We suddenly all felt a very long way from family and friends. It was time to make another seemingly impossible decision and, collectively, we made it. We were going home. The loops fired up in my head with a vengeance. What the hell was I doing? I had everything. I had been looking at apartments and had found a beautiful wooden cabin deep in a fern grove. I had great friends, I was on television and radio, I loved Auckland and my way of life. One loop said, 'You have to stay, you've finally got where you want to be. You can't leave this; if you go back, you start from scratch.' The other loop screamed, 'You can't stay behind, you have to go with them. You have felt for a few moments what it's like to lose your dad. You brought him back. How could you contemplate being 12,000 miles away from him, Mum and Tim?' Night after tormented night; again, utterly pointless. Obviously, I would be with them on the flight home.

Let me take you back to that conversation with Peter Powell in the corridor of Broadcasting House, outside the door of Room 130: 'Keep in touch.' That was exactly what I had done. I had sent numerous VHS tapes of my best TV moments and cassettes of my radio highlights. In fact, I had sent a lot.

I had been writing to Peter on and off to update him of my progress. By a magnificent stroke of luck, he had set up his own management company in London. He had called it James Grant Management. James was his middle name and Grant was the middle name of his new business partner, Russ Lindsay. I had been really concerned that my parcels would get 'wiped' by some unknown magnetic force as they travelled across the globe, so I had wrapped them all tightly in tinfoil. Back in London, this had caused great amusement in the JG offices.

'Pete, you've got more sandwiches from New Zealand.'

Though obviously an unnecessary touch of over-caution, the contents of the foil packages had been well received. Pete had said that if I ever found myself in London, I should pop over to the office in Chiswick for a chat. Well, turns out, that was only a few short months away.

It was happening all over again. I was saying goodbye to all my friends. I was resigning from jobs that I adored. I was totally uprooting myself. Radio Hauraki had a small gift that they gave to friends on special occasions, a small gold pendant fashioned in the image of the ship, *Tiri*, that had been the original home to the pirate station in the sixties. I was presented with one by the team, and as I accepted it I seemed to have something in my eyes that made them water. I have my *Tiri* to this day, and Peter Grattan, Evelyn and Jo from the *Shazam!* office remain my friends.

As the 747 rumbled down the runway of Auckland International Airport, I was sitting by the window, looking out. We lifted laboriously into the air, and my eyes were transfixed on the golden lights of the city – my city. I wanted it to be a long goodbye, to watch them twinkle ever smaller as we climbed, but the clouds that night were low and, in a flash, the city was gone.

I will forever be grateful to beautiful New Zealand. For trusting in a kid with no experience, for teaching me so much and for allowing me to have my dad for another twenty-five years.

4

It was very strange to be back. My family returned to Cornwall. I moved back to London and was very kindly put up by family friends called Joan and Les in Finchley, North London, until I found my feet and somewhere to live. They pointed out the Kiwi twang I had picked up over the four years in Auckland and which would take months to disappear.

London was just as exciting as it had always been: busy, vibrant and full of opportunity.

I can clearly remember walking through Piccadilly Circus on a hot, sunny day, feeling happy and excited to be back. My bright mood wasn't dampened in the slightest by a sudden sharp shower. I took cover in a restaurant doorway and watched the hustle of the street. After a minute or so the rain stopped and I re-emerged. There was my favourite smell, petrichor: rain on hot tarmac. If I smell it now, it will always take me back to that day.

As I reacquainted myself with friends and family, I knew my money would run out. Not only did I need work, I was also itching to get back on to either TV or radio, but it was to prove much harder than I thought. One of my first priorities was to travel to see Peter Powell and Russ Lindsay. The offices of the fledgling James Grant Management were upstairs in Pete's lovely house by the river in Chiswick. Russ was interested to meet the guy who had been sending the tinfoil packages from New Zealand. He was and is a wonderful guy, and remains among my very closest and trusted friends. We chatted, drank tea and they agreed to take me on. I have stayed ever since. Recently, after Pete and Russ sold the company, it became YMU. (I still think the change of name was a bad idea.) I was the second artist on the roster. The first had been signed a few months before – a singer called Owen Paul. He got to number three, I think, with 'My Favourite Waste of Time'.

James Grant was a management company, not an agency, which meant they looked after every aspect of your life, if you needed it. They helped me to find a flat and a car. My flat was on Madeley Road in Ealing and my car a black Ford XR3i that had a very appealing throaty growl.

Everything was new to me – I hadn't even seen a mobile phone. Pete showed me how his worked, saying that I'd look like a dick if I didn't know how to use one. However, it would be a while before I could afford one, because work was proving to be elusive. I was being pitched everywhere, but no one was particularly interested.

Thankfully, I had continuing associations with TVNZ to keep my dwindling finances afloat. Everyone was buzzing about the upcoming Live Aid concert at Wembley and I was desperate to go. I got a call from Peter Grattan. He was travelling to London to produce coverage of the event and asked if I would like to be the UK host. I didn't just bite his hand off, I took his arm off to the elbow! Jo Hulton, who had replaced Ev at TVNZ and become a friend before I left Auckland, came on board as PA, and the three of us were reunited. The biggest concert the world had ever seen, the world's greatest musicians, and I was backstage, recording interviews with them all. Later in the evening, we moved into the arena to watch. That was a hell of a day.

I recorded a few interviews with the pop stars of the time to send back to *Shazam!*, which was now being hosted by Pip Dann. The music was as positive as my mood – shit, it was

Jo Hulton and Peter Grattan.

good to be back. Nik Kershaw, Howard Jones, Simply Red and Go West – I chatted to them all and the tapes were dispatched to New Zealand.

TVNZ had started to run an annual Telethon and I was asked if I'd consider flying back to host some of it. I had a job interview a few days after, so I said I would go but would have to come back immediately. I wondered if sleeping pills might be a good idea for the return journey and figured that I might be able to get a few from the oldest member of my family, my nan. She popped a couple in an envelope for me and I packed them in my case. I flew to Auckland, where I was picked up and driven directly to the studio to present for twenty-four hours, live on TV. My co-host was Erik Estrada from *Chips*, who reminded me of the New Zealand traffic cops. After that, I did a further twelve hours on Radio Hauraki, during which I abseiled down a hotel and scared the bejesus out of a bloke sitting on the toilet. After that, I went

Interviewing Howard Jones.

straight to the airport and boarded my flight home. I was on the ragged edge of exhaustion, so I took the pills. I have no idea how the hell my nan could even walk after taking them – they acted like cattle tranquillizers. I fell asleep about an hour out of Auckland and woke up in my bed at the flat. I have absolutely no recollection of changing planes in Singapore or how I got from Heathrow to Ealing. That was the last time I visited New Zealand. Life, work and timing have all prevented a return trip, but I've often thought how lovely it would be to reacquaint myself with Auckland. My Kiwi passport has long since run out, but I sometimes wonder if I still have my dual citizenship.

Pete still remembers a conversation I had with him about money when I told him I was getting worried because I had £1.47 in my bank account. My new friends were making sure I wouldn't starve, and I spent most evenings with Russ and his girlfriend, Lesley, and their circle of mates.

Sometimes Pete would join the group. But I was beginning to get worried about my lack of employment.

Satellite TV had only just begun and Pete was hosting a weekly music show on Sky Trax. In an incredibly selfless move, he asked for a fortnight off and said that he wanted me to fill in. Remarkably, they agreed and I hosted two shows. Sadly, they weren't all that impressed.

Things took a small step forward when I was asked if I would present the weekend graveyard shift on Capital Radio, I think from 2 a.m. to 6 a.m. It would be a toe in the door, and I was happy to be back on the radio. Unfortunately for me, Capital being a commercial network, timings were critical. The news had to happen exactly at the top of the hour, to the second. I had to back-time the record into the news and add up the commercials I would play, then add in the news jingle. For me, it was impossible maths. I was bad enough adding up at the best of times, but doing it in minutes and seconds was something I couldn't get my head round. On the first night, as I sat in the chair, I spotted what was going to happen at about 2.45 a.m. I tried the maths but I just couldn't do it. I phoned my mum.

'Sorry to wake you up, but I have a problem.'

'What's the matter? What have you done?!'

'I'm on the radio, and I need you to add these up, quickly.'

'Bloody hell. Okay.'

'Three minutes forty-nine seconds, then twenty-eight seconds, then thirty-one seconds, then fourteen seconds, then twenty-six seconds, then eight seconds.'

I hit the news bang on time! Each week after that I phoned mum before I went on air and she did that night's maths for me. She couldn't help me when I locked myself out of the studio, though.

The loo was down a corridor, on the other side of a door

that was opened by a key card. At about 3.30 a.m., I decided I needed a wee. I put on a record of a suitable length and set off. The station output played throughout the building so I could hear the music even in the loo. When I got back to the studio door, I put my hand in my pocket: nothing – the access card was still in the studio. The record continued to play. I phoned security to tell them I was locked out. It was an age before they picked up. The music played on. The guard was on his way. As I stood, panic-stricken, outside the door, I heard the music start to fade, followed by the *tick*, *tick*, *tick* as the stylus nudged the centre of the record. About five minutes later, the security guard sauntered down the corridor, smiling at the silence I was broadcasting across London.

'You're going to be in trouble.'

'Hopefully, nobody is up.'

He let me in, I ran to the studio and pressed 'play' on the next record, but already the phone was ringing. The programme controller was up. I lifted the phone to my ear and listened in silence to my bollocking.

He was *always* up! I got a second dressing-down when I broke the rules. To save money through the night, I could only play music that didn't cost the station any performing-rights fees. So that ruled out all chart music, past or present. In fact, it ruled out anything that I had ever heard of. Essentially, I spent the night playing shite. All the forbidden chart records were in a huge box beside me. One night, I couldn't stand the temptation any longer. It was 4 a.m. – surely I was safe. I reached into the box. I'm pretty sure my hand settled on 'Easy Lover' by Phil Collins. I put it on the turntable. I waited for the record by someone no one knew and would probably never know to finish. A jingle first, then I pressed 'play'. I settled back in my chair. It sounded good. Fifteen seconds later the phone rang and I got my second bollocking. The man was *never* asleep!

Regardless of all the restrictions and the fact it was the middle of the night, I loved being on Capital. It was an exciting station, and made better by the fact that Kenny Everett was presenting the weekend breakfast show and I handed over to him. Kenny would arrive into the studio next door to set up and give me a cheery wave. Sometimes he would pop in for a chat and bring me a cuppa. He was brilliantly eccentric and outrageously funny. Kenny told the best stories, and those handovers were the highlight of my week.

JG Management were still tirelessly trying to get me a job on TV, but no one was interested. Russ heard that the BBC in Manchester were looking for presenters for a show called *No Limits*. It had been running for a series, and they were recasting. They sent my CV and show reel to Manchester. It took a few days for the rejection to arrive on Russ's desk. Apparently, I didn't get it because I wasn't blond. It had gone to Tony Baker, who was.

I was getting used to the disappointment. It's a tough business – you have to be patient and have a thick skin – however, I was both impatient, and upset that my hair was the wrong colour! The surprise came a few weeks later when my show-reel VHS was returned. It was in a BBC envelope but had been sent from London. I had posted it to Manchester, so why had it travelled internally? It was probably nothing to get excited about, but I was intrigued.

In fact, it *was* something to get excited about – wildly excited. A couple of days later Russ got a call from Pat Hubbard, who was the BBC's Presentation Head of Promotions. The BBC were looking for a presenter to link the afternoon children's programmes. ITV had had the idea first, and it was beginning to hurt the BBC's viewing figures. The ITV content was recorded, but the BBC wanted to do it live. They were working very quickly and hadn't had time to hold their own auditions, so they had gone to the last show that had: *No Limits*. They had, essentially, asked to see their rejects – and I was one of them. If I was interested, they would like to see me.

As I write this, it's got me thinking about my fickle relationship with television and radio, how I waver between the two, and, from the outside, how confused it seems. In the earlier years it was a bit like the tides of Fistral beach, washing in and out. I wrote to all the radio DJs when I was younger, but I also had a TV studio made out of Lego in a cardboard box. I was entranced by the cameras sliding into view on television, but I waited for hours to watch a Radio 1 Roadshow.

In New Zealand, I had landed a job on TV accidentally, but had only felt completed by working on Hauraki. Back in London, I was applying for jobs in television but also wanted to be on Radio 1. I think perhaps that, in New Zealand, television had taken the lead. It had become the career, with radio the sexy accompaniment. On contemplation, currently, television is my life and my love. I'll have to see if, in the future, the tide changes and I look towards radio again. The thread that ties them together is the fact that I have loved learning the art of communication on both platforms, and the lessons continue.

Anyway, this day in London in 1985 was *all* about TV, because there was that feeling again as I walked down Wood Lane to the TV building I loved so much. I hadn't seen it since the day I had explored before we left for New Zealand. It was no less spectacular. The 'Atomic Dots' on the side of TC1 were still there. Apparently, Arthur Hayes, who worked on the building, was rushed at the time he was designing parts of it, stuck drawing pins into a polystyrene model, and thus, the dots were created. This time, though, I wasn't going for an uninvited snoop. This time was different. I had been asked to go.

As I walked confidently up to the commissionaire, I was able to say, 'I have an appointment.'

I was waved through and pointed in the direction of the main reception. I knew my way. There was the iconic John Piper mosaic on the wall. I waited for a few minutes, watching the hustle and bustle, until I was collected and taken up to meet Pat Hubbard in his office on the fifth floor. He told me what they were planning and that it had never been done before. He also told me that the idea was being met with resistance from a number of different areas, but 'Fuck 'em!' He was very blunt. After an initial chat, he introduced me to his deputy, Stuart Dewey, and I was led to Presentation, where I would audition in front of a camera.

If the way to Hogwarts is the magical platform 9¾, then the way to Presentation was a magical 4½. We walked to the stairs in the South Hall. I've always thought that the cantilevered staircase in the South Hall is a work of art, with its apparently suspended dogleg stairs. Thankfully, after most of the building was made residential and reopened in 2017, the staircase was left intact.

On all the floors in the South Hall there was nothing behind the lifts, except on the fourth floor, where, to the left of the lifts, was another, smaller set of steps that took us behind the lifts, and at the top was a door. I had not discovered this secret part of the building during my previous adventure. Pat explained that this was the home of Presentation, the unsung department of the BBC that was responsible for playing out all the shows on both BBC1 and BBC2 and all the bits between them. It was Presentation who ensured that the *Six o'Clock News* started at exactly that time. As we walked down the corridor, he pointed out a door to a gallery on the right with an announcer's 'continuity booth' at the far end, which was the brain of BBC1 Presentation. A door on the left of the corridor led to a similar set-up for BBC2. At the end of the corridor were two small studios. The one on the left was 'Pres A', where the weather forecast was transmitted from. It was from there that Michael Fish would say in 1987 that a woman had phoned the BBC, concerned that there was a hurricane coming. He assured her and everyone watching that there wasn't. That night, the great storm ravaged Britain, and Sevenoaks became Oneoak. Next to 'Pres A' was, unsurprisingly, 'Pres B'. This was used mostly for recording graphics to go into trailers and promos, but it was also the home of *The Old Grey Whistle Test*, where 'Whispering Bob' Harris played host to some of the greatest musical names in the world. We turned right and I found myself in an emergency gallery which was usually 'dark' and stood waiting in case either of the other two broke down. On a tripod in the corner was a small TV camera with a chair in front of it.

Pat asked me to imagine that I was introducing the various children's programmes that day and gave me a copy of the *Radio Times* so I could see what they were. He said each link should be thirty seconds to a minute, and that was it. Pat and Stuart left me to prep for five minutes or so, then Pat popped his head back in to tell me I could begin when I was ready. He then disappeared back to wherever they were watching me from and I set about introducing the shows for the day.

Nothing was said after I'd completed my audition, they just chatted politely as I was led to the lifts.

'Thanks for coming,' said Pat.

'Thank you for seeing me,' I replied.

Down to the ground floor, out of the South Hall lifts, past the golden statue of Helios and through the 'Doughnut' I walked, out into the August sunshine. The next day, Pat Hubbard changed my life.

It was morning when the phone in my flat rang. It was Russ. Could I pop over to the office? Many agents/managers would impart important information over the phone, but we were a team, we were all friends, they wanted to see my face.

I drove to Ibis Lane, knocked and waited. Pete opened the door.

'Come in, matey.'

Pete and I both walked up to the office. Russ was behind his desk and I stood there, looking at them both.

'You've got it, mate! You've bloody got it!' Pete shouted.

The three of us cheered, we hugged, we had a celebratory drink and I phoned my folks. It had happened: my dreams had finally come true. Thirteen years after my ten-year-old self had typed the first of many letters to the BBC, I was now a presenter for them.

My first job was to talk to the programme controller at Capital Radio. I told him that I had just been offered a job on BBC1, but I hoped that wouldn't be a problem. He informed me that it was indeed a problem. I couldn't work for both Capital and the BBC; it would be a hideous conflict of interests.

'But,' I explained, 'you're asking me to choose between presenting every afternoon on the telly and presenting a couple of weekend graveyard shifts for you.'

'Yes, that is a tricky dilemma,' he agreed.

I told him that I was going to take the TV job and he apologized for having to let me go. Candyfloss and a radio show – not a bad collection of sackings to have on my CV. I should perhaps have been more upset to lose my radio job, but although I would miss the handovers with Kenny, on the whole, it was pretty unfulfilling. I was playing terrible music in the middle of the night to practically no one other than an insomniac controller, and I couldn't be remotely creative. Also the studio didn't have a window that looked out on to an extinct volcano.

In the balance of things, to be the first live in-vision presenter on the BBC in a generation certainly had the edge!

'How did the Capital meeting go?' asked Russ on the phone later that day.

'They fired me.'

'Oh.'

The next couple of weeks were blissfully frantic. I had publicity shots taken, I did interviews for the press and we set up the new 'Children's BBC' office. My producer was Ian Stubbs. We were in the circular section of the 'Doughnut' on the fifth floor. Pat Hubbard's office was along the corridor. Our full team was only me and Ian, and we were a few doors down, in a little spur corridor opposite the office of the weather presenters. Bill Giles, Michael Fish, Ian McCaskill and John Kettley were always fun and friendly neighbours. Ian Stubbs was a great character and full of stories. He had

My first publicity shot for the Broom Cupboard.

previously worked as a cameraman, and though I think, looking back, those were the 'golden' years of TV for me, Ian had witnessed a far wilder BBC.

The BBC club was a major hang-out for everyone. Far from the gaze of the public, everyone could let their hair down. I had been a member in my Broadcasting House days. There was a club in most buildings and, if you joined, you were a member of them all. No matter where a BBC employee or correspondent might be in the world, there was probably a BBC club nearby. They were relatively straightforward bars with a bit of food where everyone knew they were safe from the outside world and they were always buzzing with countless interesting people. A major presenter could get smashed and fall over and no one would ever tell. Mind you, that was before camera phones and online news. The one in Television Centre had a very appealing outside area overlooking the studio roofs. Ian told me that when he was a cameraman for *Top of the Pops*, one particular director would get crashingly drunk. As the countdown to the live show began, his friends would persuade him that he really should leave the bar and go to the gallery to direct his live show.

As the studio waited to go live, the camera team, Ian among them, would be listening to their headphones to find out what state the director would be in. On more than one occasion, as the opening titles rolled, the gallery door would burst open and the director would fall through it and shout, 'Okay, lads, away you go!' That was the only direction they got. He fell asleep in his chair and they and the rest of the team made it up on the hoof.

On 9 September 1985 at around three forty in the afternoon, I walked with Ian Stubbs from our office on the fifth floor to the Presentation gallery of BBC1 for my first broadcast. Everyone had wished me well, and the producers of the various shows I would introduce had sent good-luck messages. Everyone in both the Children's Department and the Presentation Department was extremely nervous. This could be a terrible idea; it was extremely un-BBC. Live and unscripted, it had embarrassment written all over it. Nothing like this had been done before and my face was going to be all over it. I should probably have been more nervous, but it was so huge, I was swept up in the excitement of not only creating something new but creating something new on BBC1.

I was given two very strict instructions. Under no circumstances was I to press the button that would put the iconic spinning globe on air, and I was not to touch the button that would do the same to the BBC clock. The set-up was simple. In the booth, a small Ikegami camera had been bolted to the stack of monitors in front of the announcer's control desk. Other than the two and a half hours we were on air, it would have a lens cap covering it. When I came in, the afternoon announcer would vacate the chair and I would take their place until five thirty. When I finished, after introducing *Neighbours*, I would place the lens cap back on the camera and the announcer would return to the chair to introduce the *Six o'Clock News*.

At ten to four, the announcer, lovely Peter Bolgar, vacated the booth, the camera lens cap was removed and I selected the correct button on the desk to enable the camera to go live. A simple, tiny gesture – removing a piece of black plastic from a camera lens – but it was so much more, it opened up the black, glassy eye of the camera, a camera that could put me into every living room in the country. I sat in the chair and waited. At five to four, the cutting-edge computer-generated ident that had been specially created played. It looks shockingly dated now, but back then it was a revelation. For the first time, my face appeared on British television and the 'Broom Cupboard' entered television legend. Children's BBC was born. Just the week before, it had been the stern, totally 'correct' invisible BBC announcer who had introduced the programmes; now it was an unrehearsed guy in questionable jumpers who took the nation's children through their afternoon. Over the years, I watched 'Children's BBC' be shortened to 'CBBC' (I wish I'd thought of that!). It grew, from my links, to Andy Crane and beyond, eventually having its own channel and non-stop broadcasts.

I can't remember a single moment of that very first day. It went by in a blur. But at 5.30 p.m. I vacated the chair, the announcer returned, the lens cap was replaced and normal service was resumed. I was euphoric: it had worked. All departments were thrilled. It had gone well. I hadn't disgraced either myself or the BBC. In the coming two years, I would come close to doing both.

Pat Hubbard was extremely happy. If it had gone wrong, he would have carried the can, and I wouldn't have wanted

The Broom Cupboard . . . my view.

to make him angry! I had witnessed his explosive temper on a number of occasions. Mercifully, I was never directly in the firing line. I have, over time, described Pat as rude, bombastic, blustering, incredibly loud and outspoken. His fury would ignite over the smallest of things and his rage could be a terrifying tempest. If you didn't know him, he could scare you rigid. I did know him, and so when he 'went off' I'd make myself scarce or sit quietly and wait for the storm to pass. And it did, as quickly as it had erupted. As a counterbalance to that side of him, this 'father of the Broom Cupboard' was incredibly kind to me. He was very protective and always open to new ideas and silliness. This was in contrast to the BBC as a whole, which, at the time, had one stock word: 'No.' For a centre of television, sometimes those further up the ladder made it very hard to actually make television. Could we do this? 'No.' Could we go here with a camera? 'No.' It always really annoyed Pat, though I have to admit some of our ideas weren't necessarily fully thought through. One afternoon it snowed. Could I go out on to the roof of TC1 with a camera to ice-skate? 'No.' Pat was furious, until it was pointed out that there was no safety barrier or any kind of wall up there. If I skated too far, I would fly off the edge and on to the inner ring road far below. They had a point.

So, my time in the Broom Cupboard got off to a great start, but I eventually found out that my new position had not been without controversy. Firstly, the Children's Department didn't like the fact that someone employed by Presentation would be introducing their programmes and that they had little or no control over what I said. Secondly, some people in the Presentation Department were unhappy that I would be presenting from the BBC1 continuity booth. It was, for some announcers, but by no means all, very much beyond the pale. An upstart twenty-three-year-old, in their booth – what *had* the BBC come to?

There were mutterings that I had been a little disrespectful by calling the booth the 'Broom Cupboard' because it was so small. For me, it was a term of deep affection. Even now, I'm often stopped in the street by parents who remember watching me in the Broom Cupboard when they came home from school. Some of them are captains of industry now, and some of them have entered the worlds of television or advertising and employed me! As I was quickly discovered by the nation's viewing children, they would send pictures and toys to our office, and I stuck them to a board that sat behind me. It forever amused me that, as I sat at home watching BBC1 and the solemn unseen announcer said, 'There now follows a Party Political Broadcast on behalf of the whatever Party,' behind them would be a colourful array of pictures of *Jimbo and the Jet Set* and *SuperTed*, along with a stuffed orang-utan called Hogan.

The mail was flooding in, so we hired a secretary because neither Ian nor I could keep up with it. Doreen Harden joined our team. She was and is one of the funniest, kindest and most delightful women I have ever had the pleasure of working with. She very quickly became a friend and has remained so ever since. She used to have 'ladies' evenings', when all her friends from the Women's Institute would gather at her house. Fellow presenter and my successor, Andy Crane, and I loved dropping by to surprise them. The grub was great, too.

Doreen was also incredibly protective and I was shielded from any mail that was negative. Thankfully, as I understood it, little was – until the day I said on air that I didn't like the dentist and hundreds of mothers wrote in to angrily berate me for giving their kids an excuse not to go. Sometimes I learned the hard way. It was a very fair reaction. Obviously,

Doreen Harden.

Reunited years later with Doreen and her 'supper club' ladies,
recreating the picture she is holding.

I didn't have children at the time so occasionally I needed reminding of the influence I had and the trouble I could cause if I was careless with my words. I was also scolded for using the word 'berk' on children's television. I had absolutely no idea of the origins of the word, but was horrified when I found out. (I bet you're googling it right now.)

One afternoon as Doreen was opening the mail she let out a chilling scream, which was unlike her. She had opened a letter and an entire bush of pubic hair fell into her lap. The fan in question had shaved herself for me and sent the proof. Ian and I were helpless with laughter, but Doreen said that she looked like she had a Bearskin cap in her lap.

Even with Doreen on board, I still liked to open my mail myself if I could. Doing that led to a very unfortunate misunderstanding on one particular occasion. We had decided to have a badge of the day each afternoon, and the theme had to be a show on CBBC. The badges arrived in their hundreds. One day, I opened a letter from a gentleman who sweetly professed his undying love for me. He said that he was going to be out of the country for a fortnight, but when he returned, could I please give him a sign if I was interested. On a specific date, he asked if I could present CBBC wearing yellow for yes or red for no. It was a very kind letter, but it went in the bin and I forgot all about it. Over the course of that fortnight, the kids got wise to the fact that, as our camera was on a 'locked-off' shot and couldn't zoom in, the bigger the badge, the more you could see it.

Paul Daniels was presenting a show called *Wizbit* at the time about an alien magician. Wizbit was a yellow cone-shaped character. Totally by accident and in a twist of cruel coincidence, on the day the gentleman had specified, I wore an absolutely enormous yellow *Wizbit* badge that had been sent in. Two days later the letter arrived. He was overjoyed:

Heron Street in Oldham, my first home. Looks like Dad has ingeniously secured my bath on an upturned table.

On the rocks at Little Fistral. Incidentally, Mum said I hated that outfit with a vengeance.

One of my first school photos from Trenance Infant School in Newquay. Why didn't the photographer tell me to stop biting my lip?

Dad set the timer on his camera and accidentally farted as he ran back to take his position.

The last picture with the Newquay family before we set off to New Zealand.

I was amazed when the *Shazam!* team said I needed cards to send out to fans. It never crossed my mind.

Sitting in one of my favourite places, at the decks of Radio Hauraki in Auckland.

The first picture of me taken in the broom cupboard. The view behind was what I could see as I sat behind the desk.

Messing about on a *Going Live* photo shoot with Sarah Greene.

Dressed up for a spot of ballroom dancing on *Going Live* with Sarah.

I loved the tradition of signing autographs after a Radio 1 Roadshow. For years I had stood in the queue to get an autograph, now it was my turn to sit in the window.

Who would ever believe I'd get there! The crowd at the Newquay Radio 1 Roadshow was vast. Oh, and Jason Donovan came too.

Cheeky snog in the hall with Steph at our house in Chiswick.

Our wedding pic taken by the fireplace in the Great Hall at Ackergill Tower in Wick.

With beautiful Steph on our wedding day. The papers insisted I wore a kilt.

Pictures all taken by our official photographer my brother Tim. Steph's brother Tim's job was to do the video.

Molly's first trip to visit Mum and Dad in their cottage in Trerice, Newquay.

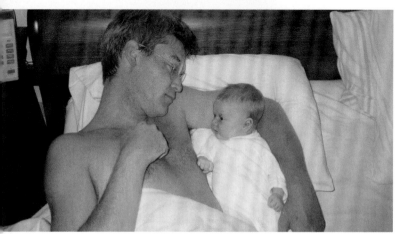

nuggled up with Molly in bed in our new house.

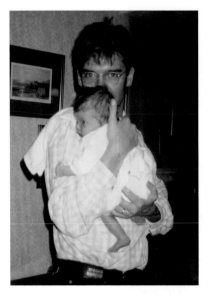

Our family is complete, Ruby has arrived.

On stage at the London Palladium with *Joseph* and wearing the coat that ended up in the boot of my car.

The world's most sophisticated simulator at the time. Learning to manoeuvre Concorde at Filton in Bristol.

he had seen the sign. Would I please write back so that we could arrange to meet? I was mortified. I would like to take this opportunity to apologize that I never did write back.

Each afternoon I replenished a cardboard box with letters and pictures that had been sent in. That box was a very important safety blanket. If a programme we were showing was on film and the film snapped down in the basement transmission suite, it could take a minute or two to fix it. For those two minutes, I would be expected to fill the time, which I did with letters and pictures from the box I carried from the office to the booth every day. It was also vital every Monday and Thursday when *Blue Peter* was being transmitted from downstairs in one of the big studios. The presenters didn't wear earpieces back then so timings could be extremely haphazard. They could over-run, and we'd be frantically dropping everything we were going to do, or they could under-run and I would fill the spare time they had given me with letters from the box. The only hint that they were finishing was when the presenters all sat together on the sofa.

'They're gathering, here we go,' our network director would say in my ear.

One afternoon they dropped short by seven minutes and I read every letter in the box. Then I went to find the legendary and formidable editor of the show, Biddy Baxter. She was leaving the gallery and I caught up with her in the corridor. Biddy was incredibly short-sighted and I was practically nose to nose with her before she recognized me.

'Dahhhling,' she said. 'You were magnificent.' My irritation subsided at the praise from a BBC icon.

'Is there any way you can help me out here, Biddy?' I said. 'Can I have any stuff from the show that would help me fill the time if you drop short?'

'I would love that, darling. You'll be like a fourth presenter.'

Pat was extremely concerned about that final comment. I should have been, too.

From then on, twice a week, a runner dropped off pictures, props and miscellaneous bits and pieces that I could use in times of emergency. Other shows saw what was going on and began to provide content for us to use around their shows, too. The only show we ever upset was *Play School*. In an act of extreme trust, they sent over their legendary character toys from the programme – it was as if royalty had arrived. In a carefully carried box were Big Ted, Little Ted, Humpty, Jemima and Hamble. We used them that afternoon. Unfortunately, the runner arrived earlier than expected to our office to collect them and was met by a very disturbing sight. I had arranged the toys for the amusement of Ian. Big Ted was 69ing Hamble while Little Ted, Humpty and Jemima were involved in a passionate threesome. The runner was not amused, and they were never allowed to visit us again.

One afternoon, the box of letters saved me from almost certain dismissal. There were huge benefits to presenting on TV in the eighties. No mobile phones to screenshot, no ability to live-pause and rewatch, no internet to send whatever you saw viral.

I still occasionally smoked, and though, now, it seems unthinkable on so many levels, it was perfectly acceptable for me to smoke in the Broom Cupboard. Every programme had an accompanying picture that could be put onscreen if it broke down; unsurprisingly, it was called a breakdown slide. When I was on air, they were fairly redundant: if something broke down, I would be there to fill the time and there was no need to use them. Nevertheless, they were still loaded into the system each day and I had access to them via a button on the desk in front of me. During a long cartoon, perhaps *Dogtanian* or *Phileas Fogg*, I would switch the booth output from the camera to a breakdown slide so that if the gallery cut to me, my output would be the slide and not the camera. Essentially, I was temporarily hiding behind a picture that would give me enough time to put my cigarette out so as not to be caught smoking in front of the nation's children! I could safely watch the cartoon, or phone my friends from the booth phone beside me, kick back and have a smoke. Though the breakdown ruse was never used, I was still very nearly the instrument of my own demise.

In front of me were two cartridge machines. I could use them to play any music I might need on air, and the top made a useful shelf on which to place pictures, toys or props. The shelf was closer to the camera, so anything on it was nicely visible. One afternoon I had gone through the 'I'm having a smoke' routine during a cartoon. I finished my smoke, cut the camera back to output and waited for the cartoon to finish. I linked into *John Craven's Newsround*, then looked down at the shelf. My heart nearly stopped and I heard the bang of adrenaline in my ears. There on the shelf, in full view of the nation during my entire link to *Newsround*, was my packet of B&H. I hastily removed them and looked through the glass into the gallery. They hadn't noticed. The phone didn't ring, so neither had anyone in the building. But what about the viewers? Had any of them noticed? I sat staring into space for a moment. I had five minutes to think of something before my next link. A light bulb went on in my head. I rummaged through the box of letters and found one written on yellow paper and carefully folded it into a similar size to a fag packet and placed it exactly where the B&H had been. *Newsround* finished, I did the link into *Blue Peter* as normal and hoped I'd got away with it. Any eagle-eyed viewer might have thought they'd seen a packet of cigarettes but, five minutes later, on closer inspection, ah no, it was only a folded piece of paper. Nobody wrote in. Nobody said a word. I've certainly never told. Until now.

That wasn't the only time I thought I might be fired. As I've mentioned, I sat behind a fully operational and rather complicated television mixing desk. I had become pretty comfortable with the areas of it that I was allowed to use: I could play music, I could mix through slides of the pictures that had been sent in and I could cloak myself if I wanted a smoke. I steered clear of the forbidden areas: the clock, the spinning globe and the 3 OS buttons. 'OS' stood for 'Outside Source', and the buttons were usually linked to the VT machines downstairs. Though the gallery next door to me was responsible for starting all the programmes, in theory, if needed, it could also be done from the desk in front of me. Perhaps, if for any reason the gallery became incapacitated, the announcer could take over and 'play out' the content for the network.

One Friday afternoon, I made a simple error that led to a meltdown. During the final long link of the day I was playing music and mixing through slides. When I cut myself back into vision, an anomaly on one of the faders caught me out. I started to speak and the gallery shouted, 'We can't hear you!' There was instant confusion. Was it a problem with them or with me? It was very much with me. I had never been shown that I could mute my mic or been told how to rectify the problem if it happened. I had opened a fader too far and, though I only spotted it afterwards, a little blue light above it had illuminated. If I'd pressed that button, all would have been well. As it turned out, that was the only button I didn't press.

I mouthed, 'Can you hear me?' to Great Britain. 'No!' shouted the gallery. I panicked and, for whatever reason, I played the desk like a piano. I pressed every button. There was the spinning world, there was the clock, then I worked myself down to the OS buttons that were linked to the three VT machines downstairs, all under the supervision of one man. I had no idea that when one of those machines was live and its VT (as Keith Lemon would say, 'That stands for videotape') was playing out on the network, an on-air sign lit up above it.

The operator was checking the machines that would play out programmes and trailers after the news. As he checked everything downstairs, my stabbing finger was getting closer to the OS buttons upstairs.

I hit the first button. From his end, the on-air light burst into life: his machine was live on BBC1 for no discernible reason. He yelped and jumped back to the second machine, by which time I had pressed the button for that one. The on-air light leapt from the machine he had jumped away from to the one he was now standing beside. He screamed and leapt to the third machine and, upstairs, I followed him: that machine was now also briefly live. As he backed over to the second VT unit, I had begun to work my way back up the desk and the process was repeated. He was allegedly heard to cry out, 'Christ, it's me! Every time I go near them they go live! It must be my static. I've gone fucking electrical.'

Unaware of what I had done to the poor man, and unaware of the investigation that would follow, I waved a silent goodbye to the stunned public. Then I waited. There was silence in the gallery. I just stared at the desk in horror. What had I just done to this proud department? The silence in the gallery was broken by the sound of the door opening and heavy footsteps heading my way. The door to the booth burst open and the Assistant Head of Presentation stood looking at me, seething.

'Come with me. Malcolm wants to see you.'

Malcolm Walker was the Head of Presentation, an imposing Scottish gentleman who I had only met once before, when he welcomed me to the department. I stood and then walked from the Broom Cupboard behind his second-in-command as she led me through the silent gallery. She didn't say a word to me as I was led to the sixth floor, but I could tell that she considered this presentation experiment to be over. We had had our fun and now I'd sunk the ship. Pat was going to go nuclear.

This spiky Canadian with a very pinched expression stomped in front of me as we got to the door of Malcolm Walker's office. My head was down, a condemned prisoner led to the gallows.

'He's here,' she spat.

'Come in,' said Malcolm.

I walked into his office and stood before his desk, alongside my Canadian escort. He leapt to his feet.

'Dear boy!' he bellowed. 'That was magnificent! My God, you just made me laugh. That's the second-worst moment in the department's history and I loved every moment. It shows we're live, it gives us an edge. Just don't do it again.'

I'm not sure who was the most stunned, me or his deputy. Her face was a picture.

I had achieved the second-worst moment in Presentation's distinguished broadcasting history? Then what was the first? Apparently, that honour went to one of my favourite announcers, Malcolm Eynon. *The Last Night of the Proms* had fallen off the air, for a long time! Malcolm was on duty in the booth as the announcer for the evening. He valiantly tried to fill in by attempting to read out what was to come on BBC1 for the following few days from the *Radio Times*. However, unknown to him until he opened the magazine, the *Radio Times* had just changed the format of the way it listed the programmes. Malcolm couldn't find anything, and all the viewers could hear was the frantic turning of pages and a very lost announcer.

My mishap didn't go unnoticed within the building. It was a Friday, so I'd hoped to slink off into the weekend. Noel Edmonds had other ideas. At the time, he was presenting *The Late Late Breakfast Show* on BBC1, which was huge. One of the items in the show was the presenting of the 'Golden Egg Award', given to people who had cocked up big-time. His production team had been watching. The phone rang: would I like to go on the show tomorrow evening to relive my humiliation and to collect the award? *Absolutely!* I was overjoyed, and more than happy to laugh at myself. Plus, I got the chance to watch my TV idol working and be on the biggest show on the box. I still have my Golden Egg Award and I'm still proud of it.

Noel's *Multi-coloured Swap Shop* had come to an end and its successor, *Saturday Superstore*, hosted by Mike Reid and Sarah Greene, ably assisted by Keith Chegwin, was reigning supreme on BBC1. Chris Bellinger was still the editor and had been keeping an eye on me in the Broom Cupboard. I was asked if I'd like to help out on a couple of the outside broadcasts with Keith and, of course, there was no hesitation. What a dream to be working with that team, and Keith was so kind, a genuine delight to be around. I adored him, and the whole team. After the long, hot summer of 1976, when Cornwall nearly ran out of water and I had the best tan ever, along had come October, when I watched the first-ever *Swap Shop* broadcast live from Television Centre. I was captivated, and from that moment on, to present on Saturday mornings was the absolute, ultimate goal. Even though I was engrossed in the success of the Broom Cupboard, I'd kept one eye on Saturdays, and it was beginning to look like a possibility.

However, I had one massive hurdle to overcome. I was about to be aggressively headhunted for another famous show.

Pat Hubbard knew what my dream was – I had made no secret of the fact that Saturday mornings on BBC1 was my goal – so it was with a grave face that he said, 'Biddy Baxter wants to take you to lunch. It will be long and difficult. Don't say yes to anything.'

I had no idea what he meant.

Biddy was (and still is) a legend in children's TV. She had been a producer on *Blue Peter* since 1962. She came up with the idea of the highly sought-after *Blue Peter* badge in 1963 and became editor in 1965. Much of what the show is today was born out of the values that she and her deputy, Edward Barnes, had instilled. As a child, Biddy had written to Enid Blyton on two occasions and was disappointed that she received the same reply to two very different letters. When she took over stewardship of the programme, she introduced a card-index system to ensure that the correspondence of every child was logged and that every letter they received in return was pertinent to their question and personal.

Biddy Baxter was also formidable. The desks in the production office were arranged so that they all faced her desk in a classroom-type formation. Valerie Singleton has said of her time on the show that the presenters were treated like children. It was rumoured that, in the gallery, Biddy Baxter would have her own monitor of the show's output in front of her, and if a presenter was caught looking at the wrong camera, she would take off her shoe, bang the side of the monitor with it and shout, 'Over here, you stupid girl!' So, a forceful woman with very clear ideas of what she wanted and, right now, it turned out she wanted me.

I was enthralled to be in a cab with her on the way to a fancy restaurant in Holland Park. She was a hero of mine, regardless of reputation. Pretty much everything *Blue Peter* was was down to Biddy.

The conversation was light and easy both in the cab and at the start of lunch. Was I enjoying my job? Did I like the challenges? Was I fulfilling my ambitions? Didn't I feel that I could do so much more? She made it clear that she had been watching me very closely and liked what I was doing. I was flattered. Gradually, over lunch, an imperceptible switch occurred. She was clever, and at first I didn't spot it. I soon recognized, though, that the game had changed.

She told me that I could be whatever I wanted to be, I could embrace my interests, I could be part of a bigger production and that I 'had to join *Blue Peter*'. However, much as I admired Biddy, her team and the show, I knew it wasn't for me. There was no grey area here: it was too controlled, too managed and there weren't many times when they seemed to have a bloody good laugh. I was polite – extremely polite, in fact. I was well aware in whose company I sat. I was respectful, but I had Pat's words ringing in my ears: 'Don't say yes to anything.'

Wouldn't I love to be part of a flagship brand?

I said that it was indeed a brand to be proud of.

Wouldn't it be fulfilling to be part of the most respected children's programme ever in Britain?

I replied that anyone who worked on the show benefitted from it.

Wouldn't I thrive from being able to fulfil all my ambitions?

I was happy with the way my career was going.

She switched up a gear.

She could send me anywhere in the world that my heart desired. I could meet the world's most interesting people. I could handle forbidden and priceless artefacts. I could realize all the hidden sporting dreams I had. That one made

147

me smile inside, because I knew how unsporty I was. Think TVNZ charity football match and you have my sports interest in a nutshell.

The assault continued. It was kind, but also incredibly powerful and compelling. I was being offered the world.

She 'could tell' I wanted to be on *Blue Peter*.

I had literally no idea where that came from, because I didn't, and for the first time, over that lunch, I told her that I didn't want it.

She asked why I was resisting.

Because I don't want to do it.

She said my destiny was to do the show.

I told her it was not. I said I wanted Saturday mornings, and she told me that my ambition was 'frivolous'.

'Come to work with me.'

'Thank you, but no, Biddy.'

'I know you want to.'

'No, I don't.'

'You have to.'

'I don't.'

'You'll regret it.'

'I won't.'

We left the restaurant, and the pressure all the way back in the taxi was relentless.

'No, Biddy' . . . 'You can't make me' . . . 'I won't do it' . . . 'Absolutely not' . . . '*No!*'

As we got out of the cab she continued: 'I *will* change your mind.'

'*You absolutely will not.*'

I walked back to the office flattered but battered. I had never encountered anything like it before. From being desperate for work a few months earlier, I had spent two hours trying to escape Biddy Baxter's sticky web.

The next day, Roy Thompson, who was the Assistant Head of Children's Programmes, called me.

'How was lunch with Biddy? She seems to think you left it quite open . . .'

It was never mentioned again, by anyone. I had turned down Biddy Baxter, and I'm sure that didn't happen often, but there was never a moment of regret. I knew what I really wanted. I just had to be patient.

It was approaching the Christmas holidays. I had Christmas itself off, but I had to work the few days between Boxing Day and New Year's Eve. I drove to Newquay to see my folks, who by now had restored a beautiful cottage on the outskirts of the town in Trerice.

Trerice Mill was their greatest accomplishment to date, peaceful and tucked away. We had many, many happy times there – myself and my parents, with Tim, then later with Steph, and when they came along, the girls. When they were a little older, we used to play Pooh Sticks on the footbridge that spanned the Forde by the cottage. We made sloe gin and one year picked such a huge crop the gin we made lasted for five years.

My mum's sister, Diane, lived a few minutes away in Newquay with her family, and we were all very close. Diane was more like a sister to me than an auntie; she was hilarious and very loose on the rules. From being a small child, I loved sitting on her shoulders and being carried around. Diane also shared the same sense of humour as me, Dad and Tim. We were all prone to hopeless giggles and all quite irreverent.

One of our family traditions was to go to St Michael's Church in Newquay for the Christmas Eve service. I should state here that, though I do understand the peace and solace found in all faiths, I am not religious. One Christmas Eve the

My mum's sister Diane, my awesome auntie.

vicar showed off his new-found love of the trumpet. As he started to play, Diane and I tried to stifle our giggles. He disappeared from the pulpit then reappeared moments later from a door high in the roof and started to play again, then he disappeared once more, only to re-emerge from another door behind us, where he started to play again. He was like a trumpet-playing cuckoo clock. We were in screaming hysterics.

That Christmas, we went over to see Diane and her family to give and receive our presents. We opened them all and said our thank-yous. Then Diane remembered that she had one 'joke' present that she had forgotten to give me. She left the room and returned with a small parcel. As I opened it, she explained. She had been to a local market and seen them on a stall, and they seemed quite fun. She knew it was random but thought it would make me laugh. Inside the wrapping was a small, golden-coloured hand puppet. It had long arms that you could wrap around your neck and a fairly annoying squeak. We all had a play with it, and I thanked her and put it to one side, thinking no more about it.

It was time to return to London. I packed my bags, kissed the family goodbye and started the drive that I have done hundreds of times over the years. On my way to my folks it was always joyous to pass the sign that said 'Welcome to Cornwall', but it was always sad when it flashed by on the other side of the road on the way back to London and I knew I had left my family and the county.

Work was quiet. Ian had now moved on and my producer was a compact bubble of blond energy called Tim Robinson. What should we do on air in these dead days between 27 December and the thirtieth? I decided to take in the silly golden-coloured hand puppet. Maybe it would be fun.

I played with it for a couple of links and then Tim decided that, in order for me to have both hands free, he should operate it. That seemed like a reasonable idea. It was brilliant chaos. Tim was bringing it to life. In the first link of him operating it, the puppet knocked over my tea and soaked my lap. It needed a name. During a cartoon, I set about thinking, and by the end of the cartoon I had thought of one. The silly Christmas present from my auntie had become Gordon the Gopher.

At that moment, neither of us realized what we had done or how far it would go. Certain subtle changes had to be made to the puppet so that we didn't infringe copyright. His legs and arms were shortened and he was given red hands, and that seemed to cover the problem. In the days that followed he became a star in his own right. The kids were unhappy with the fact that he was naked, so families up and down the land knitted him clothes. Later, on *Going Live*, record companies soon cottoned on to the fact that although I probably wouldn't wear their promotional T-shirts, the

Gopher, who was a freebie tart, would wear anything. His clothing progressed from T-shirts with 'T'Pau' on the front to the most beautifully stitched leather jacket commissioned by Adam Ant's record company and signed on the inside by the man himself.

As his popularity grew, it became clear that there was a potential business opportunity here. I phoned the department in charge of licensing and asked if they would be interested in mass-producing Gophers. They couldn't have been less interested. The gentleman on the end of the phone said he needed to look into it and would call me back. Later in the week he called.

'I've been looking into this Gary the Gaffer. I'm afraid the BBC aren't interested in any marketing.'

'Would you mind if I pursued this myself, then?'

'Be my guest, but from our point of view, we believe there will be little commercial interest.'

Gordon went on to buy a sizeable proportion of my house in Chiswick and sent Diane and her family on the trip of a lifetime to Disneyland Florida. Marketing were considerably more alert when Ed the Duck came along after Gordon and I left the Broom Cupboard.

Each producer that looked after the Broom Cupboard also had to have a hand in Gordon, so to speak. It was fascinating how he magnified their characters. With Tim, he was mischievous; with Sue Morgan, he was outrageously dramatic; with Mike Harries, he was wistful; and with Paul Smith, he was dry and cynical. I'm sure the others won't mind me saying so, but Paul became the spirit of Gordon the Gopher. In fact, I just WhatsApped him to tell him that I was writing this book and he has just told me that he has Gordon in his office at this very moment, down from his Perspex box in Salford, wearing that very jacket because 'the

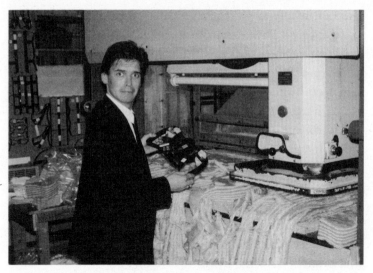

Cutting out Gophers for manufacture.

Paul Smith and Sue Morgan, two Gopher wranglers.

Observer wanted a pic for an article'. The Gopher lives on, and we are all powerless to stop it.

I had to invent an entire back story and a family tree for Gordon when Jeremy Swan asked if I'd like to do a mini-series of Gordon 'sitcoms' with him and Paul Ciani for CBBC. Jeremy had produced *Rentaghost*, *Galloping Galaxies* and *Jackanory* and was a gentle, kind producer with a soft Irish lilt. I created Gordon's girlfriend, Glenda, most of his family from back on the Prairie, and the fact that he owned and ran a cactus-juice farm. Paul and Jeremy created a whole world for Gordon under my flat. It was the first time I'd had to learn lines and act, and I had a ball. My now-grown-up girls were watching it the other day and it was a good sign that it wasn't too embarrassing.

These days, if I'm asked where he is, I usually say he's in rehab.

One afternoon, as I was sitting in the booth and watching *Blue Peter*, a new presenter was introduced. I sat up. Caron Keating was welcomed to the team, and I was instantly entranced and set about orchestrating a meeting. We had a few drinks and ended up going out for a while. How to describe Caron? Beautiful, artistic, stubborn, wild, unpredictable and one of the world's greatest party animals. Caron would leave a black-tie event and insist she knew a short cut out. Thirty minutes later, we'd be lost in the kitchens of the Grosvenor House and sitting with the staff, drinking whisky.

If I went out with her for a quiet, romantic meal, by the end of the evening we were sharing our table with thirty drunken revellers and someone had invariably found a fiddle to play.

It was great fun, brilliantly chaotic, but not easy to understand. We parted the very best of friends and, one day on a train, Russ nervously asked me if he could ask her out. Would it break 'the lads' code'? 'Absolutely fine by me, mate. You're perfect for each other. I'm thrilled,' I said.

And they *were* perfect for each other. They had two wonderful boys in Charlie and Gabriel. Along with Steph and our girls, we all went on holiday together. My mind always goes to the memory of Caron and I dancing round the pool table to 'Fairytale of New York'. Caron was a wonderful friend to have, a shining light in all our lives. Russ was indeed the perfect man for her. He tenderly and selflessly cared for her as she fought breast cancer, and he was devoted to her right up to the moment she tragically succumbed to it. Her boys are a constant credit to her.

Another person in the Presentation gallery who had become a very good friend was Stephanie Lowe, a very pretty network assistant and, I would discover, without doubt the kindest, most devoted soul I will ever have the good fortune to meet. To be honest, I think it was fair to say that she spotted me first. I walked through the gallery, said hi to the team then set up in the booth each day, but I had caught her eye. Quite what Steph ever saw in a lanky bloke in highly questionable jumpers, I have no idea, but thank God she saw something.

We got to know each other over time because we shared the same circle of friends so we were often out together. Nights as a group to the cinema, big, raucous dinners, evenings in the BBC club. One afternoon, Steph was the production assistant on a film I was making with Gary Numan. I finally plucked up courage at the end of filming to ask her out. She went to work the next day in the same clothes as the day before. I know she would agree that I wasn't the perfect boyfriend. If I'm honest, I was totally wrapped up in my job and extremely reluctant to commit, but she played the long game beautifully.

Things were moving rapidly at work. I had been asked to present *Take Two*, a sort of kids' *Points of View*, and I was also presenting *Song for Christmas*, where I introduced a young singer-songwriter who was appearing on TV for the first time. He obviously had a very promising career in front of him. Yes, Gary Barlow was very good on the show that night. In fact, Gary and I would meet again twice in the future, before the world fell at his feet. I was hosting a promotional tour for Coty, who were launching a new fragrance called Exclamation. Part of my job was to introduce new bands. One afternoon, I introduced a new group who bounced enthusiastically on to the stage in one of their first-ever try-outs. Both Russ and I thought Take That were really very promising, but Russ thought they should ditch the leather. Which they had, by the time they appeared as a warm-up act on my Radio 1 Roadshow in Falmouth. Shortly after that they became international superstars.

Aside from waking with a hideous pain in my groin in April 1987 and the doctor coming around to my flat to confirm that I had appendicitis and needed to be admitted to hospital immediately, things were going well. I was doing more and more for *Saturday Superstore*, and things were looking increasingly promising.

I had fought off Biddy Baxter, and I had been in the Broom Cupboard for two years, earning my stripes and having more fun than I could possibly have imagined. The phone rang.

'Hi, Phillip, it's Chris Bellinger. Would you like to come and play on Saturday mornings?'

The 'Hallelujah!' choir in my head burst forth once more.

Leaving the Broom Cupboard was going to be a wrench. I had started it, we had built it up, and we were all incredibly proud of how much a part of afternoon life it had become. There was so much to be proud of, so much I would look back on with such fondness. I was a kind of older brother to the viewers. I felt protective of everyone who watched. At one point, there had been a spate of cruel chain letters going around that threatened death to anyone who didn't forward them, and the kids watching were terrified, so I told them to forward them to me so I could tear them up. Doreen and I tore up hundreds. I'm still alive, guys!

I had launched an afternoon sing-along, sent out lyric sheets to any viewer who wanted them, and we all belted out the theme to *Mysterious Cities of Gold* together. We had also pledged to get Petula Clark's 'Downtown' back in the charts. The devoted afternoon club loved it, and Petula charted triumphantly once more. About two months ago, Petula appeared on *This Morning* and asked why I'd picked that song all those years ago. I told her that it was the song that me and my friends had belted out one night as we walked down Ealing High Street, full of exuberance and wine and the joy of life.

Michael Grade was Controller of BBC1 at this stage of my career. He had a particular quality that I've seen in few bosses I've had since. Michael would arrive in his office after watching a day's television and write small notes to some of those on the channel. I know this for two reasons: firstly, because for a time Steph was one of his two secretaries and would send out the notes he had written while sharing a Mars Bar with him; and secondly, I know because I was sent one.

He would drop a note to anyone and everyone, from executives to researchers. Imagine the power of a little thank-you note arriving randomly in the internal mail. He would watch a music show and congratulate the sound team, or a documentary and compliment the work of the research team, or a drama and send a 'well done' to the lighting crew.

One afternoon I opened my mail and on headed paper was the handwritten note:

I watched you yesterday afternoon. You really made me laugh.
Thanks for all the hard work, Michael

The power of those words was astonishing. Here was a kid who had studied Television Centre as if I was swotting for an exam, who had had seemingly wild dreams of some kind of broadcasting future, and now I had got a note from the boss. For me, it was a great place to work and, in my eyes, everyone working at the BBC wanted to make him proud. It's a great example to all bosses: a little unannounced thank-you note has immeasurable weight. My ITV boss does exactly the same now over text.

As my last afternoon in Presentation arrived, my final producer there, Paul Smith, and I decided to ask Michael if he would record a little sketch to send me on my way. He

Outside my spiritual home.

happily agreed. We arrived in the boss's office on the sixth floor with our camera crew. Paul would, as usual, produce and direct, but also have his hand up the Gopher. We ran the idea we had had past Michael, and he loved it.

And so, my farewell to the Broom Cupboard was Michael Grade, Controller of BBC1, sitting jacketless in his chair, red braces resplendent, cigar in hand, thanking me for all my hard work but saying it was time for me to move on: he had secured a position for me in the post room.

'Now, Gordon,' he said. 'I see great things ahead for you, a really promising future. Perhaps we could talk contracts? Would you like a cigar?'

I backed out of the Controller's office and left the Gopher to it. I left the Broom Cupboard in the capable hands of Andy Crane on 21 August 1987. I was moving downstairs to TC7. In a month's time, *Going Live* would take its place in the roll call of Saturday-morning shows.

All the Children's BBC presenters together.

5

The roster of artists on the books of James Grant Management was growing. Caron Keating had signed up, then Mark Goodier, Simon Mayo and Anthea Turner. The management team had also grown. A young, eager guy from Bolton called Paul Worsley joined in 1987, and in 1990 Darren Worsley (no relation) would join to sort out the accounts because Russ had a habit of rounding everything up! Darren also became phenomenal at firmly but fairly negotiating contracts. With Daz's arrival, so was formed my closest group of friends in the world, the people I trust with my life and whom I adore. Pete, Russ, Paul, Daz and me are 'The 5'. They are the friends

My besties. Paul Worsley, Darren Worsley and Peter Powell.

who would guide me through my life, help me negotiate my career, keep my feet on the ground, make me laugh until I ached and, much later, guide me through the most difficult decision of my life.

Either Russ or Paul or both drove me the length and breadth of the country for personal appearances. There were usually a couple in the diary each week, and we travelled for miles. I had put together an hour-long show of games and competitions, and they were always great fun to do. It was a fantastic way to meet the viewers. If we could, we'd stop off at Watford Gap services for breakfast; we called it a 'train wreck' because it was a disaster on a plate. In all the many, many miles we drove, we only nearly fell out once. Paul, Russ and I were all on the way to Nottingham, where I was to turn on the Christmas lights. Russ was driving my car. The traffic was hideous and it was becoming apparent that we were going to be late. We phoned ahead. 'No problem,' said the organizer. 'We have friends in the police force.' They phoned back ten minutes later. As we came off the motorway, a police car was waiting at the junction under a bridge. We spotted it and pulled over.

'Okay, guys,' said the officer. 'Switch on your headlights and your hazards and stick very close to me.'

'Russ, I want to drive,' I said.

'No, it's okay, I've got this.'

'Please swap seats.'

'It's fine.'

'Russ, I want to drive behind the police car.'

'It's okay, Phil, I'll do it.'

'No! It's my car! *I want to drive.*'

'It's fine, mate. Look, it's too late, he's setting off.'

The police car burst into life, a cascade of blue flashing lights and sirens. Russ drove behind as the cars parted to let us through. Wrong side of the road, through red lights, we scythed through the traffic jam. I looked at Russ's face. He was smiling with glee. I was furious, and dripping with envy. I phoned Pete back at the office.

'Russ won't let me drive.'

They all, quite rightly, burst out laughing.

I've only had that opportunity for a police escort on one other occasion: leaving Windsor after Harry and Meghan's royal wedding. A very kind police officer said that it would take hours for me to get out of the town and that he would escort me. With almost uncontrollable excitement, I got into the car, turned on my hazards and headlights and set off behind him. There was absolutely no traffic on the road. He turned off his lights, I turned off mine and we drove sedately to the M4, where he cheerily waved me goodbye. I was gutted. The first time I had had an escort, I wasn't driving; the second time, when I was, there was no traffic to clear.

The first transmission date of *Going Live* was getting closer. I knew most of the team from my guesting on *Superstore*, but this was very different: this was now our show. I'd spent some time with a Gopher as a partner, but now I had my first real co-host, in Sarah Greene. We hit it off immediately. We had the same sense of humour and the same very naughty streak. Thinking about it, I didn't know I had a naughty streak until Sarah let it out.

Our office was on the twelfth floor of the now-demolished East Tower beside TC. The lift only went up to the eleventh floor, so we had to walk up the final flight of stairs to the twelfth. Sarah and I soon discovered how great the acoustics were on that walk. A tiled concrete staircase with a drop of twelve storeys was joyously echoey. As we belted out song after song, our voices reverberated down to the ground floor. We'd sing until someone on the staircase below leaned over

With 'Greeno'.

the banister and looked up to see where all the noise was coming from. Every annoyed face was a point.

Chris Bellinger headed the team. The colour of his jumper and socks always matched, which was immensely endearing. Chris was assisted by Cathy Gilbey and Angela Sharp. They were a dream team. Chris knew exactly what worked and what didn't; after all, this was the man who had created *Swap Shop* and *Superstore*. He was kind and fun, but firm when he had to be. On numerous occasions on the studio floor in the future, as Sarah and I were getting naughty, Chris would just say, 'Stop it,' into our ears and we instantly obeyed.

We all visited Studio 7 on the Wednesday before the first live show to look at the set. On the Friday we returned and recorded the opening titles and promotional trailers. Trev and Simon had been booked as a comedy duo and had made us howl with their left-field humour. Chris had suggested

The mighty Chris Bellinger with Pete.

Gordon came with me from the Broom Cupboard and Paul Smith had agreed to continue as his operator.

I went to bed on that Friday night and couldn't sleep a wink. From the day I had watched the first ever *Swap Shop* launch in 1976 to the night I lay in bed on the eve of presenting *Going Live* was eleven years. It was a dream about to come true.

I got up on that Saturday morning way too early, I drove to Television Centre way too early, I was in TC7 way too early, but I was determined to make this day last for as long as I could. I wandered around the set, chatted with the crew, drank endless cups of tea. Sarah Greene (now Greeno to me; even all these years later, she is still saved as Greeno in my phone) arrived in Make-up and made me laugh to put me at my ease. We were buzzing. I was very nervous. The titles ran, the transmission light outside the studio went from 'rehearsal' blue to 'transmission' red. Sarah and I walked from behind the scenes and on to the studio floor to unveil the new set.

Friday night *Going Live* script study in the Chiswick kitchen.

On 26 September 1987 *Going Live* was live for the first time, and would be for another joyous six years. In my career, the first time I do something huge and new it usually goes by in a blur. I'm concentrating so hard on making it work I don't tend to allow myself the luxury of enjoyment. The two hours flew by, and Sarah and I instantly worked well together as a team. As the show finished we looked at each other and laughed and hugged – it had worked. Sarah had been a main presenter on *Saturday Superstore*, the predecessor to *Going Live*, so everyone knew that she was a safe pair of hands. The unknown quantity was me! But Chris Bellinger was thrilled and the team were quick with their congratulations. I had done it: the show I'd wanted to do since I'd seen the first *Swap Shop* eleven years earlier was mine. The following week, and the weeks after, I could relax and enjoy myself. If Television Centre was my spiritual home, TC7 was always its heart to me. I loved every moment in that studio with those wonderful people. When the centre closed down in 2013, a friend of mine, Ray, was in the building late at night. People were taking souvenirs, much to the annoyance of the bosses. Ray called me.

'Phil, I've got you a souvenir from TC.'

'Oh my God! What did you get me?'

'I've been up on a bloke's shoulders to prise the studio sign of your favourite studio off the doors.'

'Jesus. Really, I can't believe you thought of me. Thank you so much.'

'No problem. TC6 looked really empty and sad.'

'TC6?'

'Yes! Your spiritual home.'

'Amazing, mate. Thank you so much.'

I didn't have the heart to tell him that the one I wanted was on the studio next door. Nevertheless, it's still a pretty cool souvenir to have. It's beside my EMI 2001 camera. I hope the fact that I've told this story doesn't mean that someone is going to want it back. If you do, I'll swap it for TC7.

We used every part of the building, inside and outside, while filming the show. I was outside the front of the building one Saturday waiting to present an item, and Sarah was inside interviewing the band 5 Star. I was listening to the studio in my earpiece and Sarah was taking questions for the band. Eliot, who was about sixteen, came on the phone to ask one. There was a dog barking in the background, identified as Tammy.

'Do you have a question for 5 Star?' asked Sarah.

'Yes, I'd like to ask them why they're so fucking crap,' said Eliot.

'Right,' replied Sarah calmly. 'I'm sure Tammy would have made a lot more sense. Let's move on to line 3. Do you have a sensible question?'

As calmly as it was handled on air, we were all affronted.

A *Going Live* phone-in.

You couldn't call in without giving your number and being called back, so we had his number. It was handed out to a few people and for a few days we dialled the number and hung up. Gentle revenge was very satisfying as we occasionally got him out of bed and, better still, he didn't know who it was.

Gordon the Gopher was still an important member of the team. By now, he had his own signed cards to send out to his fans. Paul Smith was so perfect in the way he brought him to life. Especially as Gordon was, essentially, just a squeaking sock, I was always in awe of the expressions and moods Paul's hand could get him to show. Anger, hurt, cynicism, defiance – all were part of Paul's repertoire. Although the Gopher was now part of the show, Paul was still a very busy producer upstairs in Presentation, so he continued his work there alongside working the puppet. One Saturday, we had just shown *Thundercats*. The cartoon finished and I picked up to read out some letters. The world was so much slower back then: Gordon and I had two seven-minute slots to read out letters and basically muck around. No one's attention span would accept that now and, besides, no one writes letters any more!

As the Gopher sat beside me, I started to read out some funny notes we had been sent, but the Gopher was silent, refusing to react. I always knew where Paul was going with a joke – we could read each other – but I couldn't understand where he was going with this. I cracked jokes; the Gopher refused to engage. I asked if he was okay. He wouldn't answer or look at me. I asked if I'd upset him. Nothing. Well, whatever Paul's gag was, I didn't think it was particularly funny. Then I looked up and, standing beside the camera, waving his arms and ashen-faced, was Paul. He had been in his office, lost track of the time and hadn't returned to the studio before *Thundercats* finished. The Gopher beside me was empty. I almost burst out laughing. I scooped up the lifeless Gopher, saying, 'Well, if you're in a mood, go and sulk somewhere else,' then I turned around and put him behind the sofa. No one was any the wiser. Paul was never late again. I was never left with just a Gopher carcass.

Paul took his puppeteering incredibly seriously. One morning, I was cooking on the show with Emma Forbes, who was our resident chef. These segments were always chaotic affairs. I had already lost my grandad's ring in a mountain of minced beef as I was making burgers. The Gopher was squeaking happily beside us. Paul was under the desk with his hand through a hole, watching a monitor and bringing Gordon to life.

Above the desk, some kitchen roll had caught fire. On the telly, the Gopher was trying to attract our attention. The fire grew, getting closer and closer to Gordon. It looked as if he was going to go up in flames, so he was squeaking multiple alerts.

Underneath the desk, Paul was laughing. This was hilarious on the telly – the Gopher was going to get singed. Paul continued to laugh, lost in his role. Until he realized, 'Shit, my hand's in there.'

It was a plaintive yelp of 'Fire!' from under the desk that alerted me above it. Gordon was saved, and so was Paul's arm.

The puppets were being mass-produced by this time and, through constant use, the one we had for the telly would begin to wear out. We'd have to break in a new one. Before the old one was retired to the archive, we had to 'dirty up' a new one. The new fluffy ones didn't look anything like ours until they got dirty. So, for a week before the swap-over, anyone with grubby hands would 'rub the Gopher'.

As a new partnership, Sarah and I were invited to turn on the Christmas lights in Belfast. I have always loved the city. Even staying in the Europa was a strange thrill. It was known as 'the most bombed hotel in the world' after suffering thirty-six attacks during the time of the Troubles. The welcome in the city had been warm when I'd been once before, to appear in a televized discussion with my boss, the Head of Children's Programmes, Anna Home. Anna had managed to get herself into a pickle, when she appeared to say to the attentive audience of children that Father Christmas didn't exist. I could see the headlines: 'BBC Children's boss in "There's No Santa" storm'.

I jumped in with, 'I think what Anna means is . . .'

Afterwards, she thanked me profusely and, from then on, although she was always rather stern, I think we had a bit of a bond.

Anyway, this time we were in Belfast to turn on the Christmas lights. As Sarah and I left the Europa, we were dismayed to see that the streets were pretty much deserted. We both voiced our concern to the Royal Ulster Constabulary (RUC) guy that was driving us. Had there been a problem? None that he was aware of. Maybe the people of Belfast weren't that bothered that we had come to town, I thought.

As we got closer to City Hall, we turned into a street and could only see the backs of people. We tried another route: more backs. Another: the same. It seemed the good folk of Belfast were indeed interested – they had arrived in their thousands. Our RUC escort was getting nervous. How was he going to get us in? We abandoned the car, met more of his colleagues and ducked our heads as we were smuggled in through a secret back entrance in Donegal Square. We met everyone inside, and they were extremely jittery because of the size of the crowd. All apart from the mayor. He was perfectly happy: all would be well; 'the crowd would listen to him'. Sarah and I looked at each other with an element of scepticism. Would they? Really?

Outside the building, it was rammed. There was a huge crowd hemmed into the square. Out in the middle of the crowd was an open, wooden shed that had been temporarily built to house the button to switch on the lights. We had to walk from the main door to that shed in the middle of the crowd. 'They will listen to me,' reiterated the mayor.

It was time to go. The RUC officers were not happy at all, and the organizers were aware that the crowd was much bigger than they had expected and were also unhappy. The mayor was thrilled.

We all assembled just inside the big doors and our orders were barked at us. We were to obey instructions for our own safety. It was all very serious and carried out with military precision.

'We are going to form a tight circle around you. Phillip,

Sarah, Mr Mayor, you are to remain in that circle. Do as you are instructed and listen to the team leader. If we have to abort, we will "extract" you.'

It was a bit intense, but bloody exciting.

'We will count this down. Ready yourselves,' came the order.

The mayor, resplendent in his red tunic and gold chain, put on his huge tricorn hat topped with a spectacular black feather. The protective circle was formed around the three of us and the doors were opened just enough to let us out. A huge cheer erupted from the crowd. Our tight formation began to move through the sea of people like a boat in a storm. I heard the mayor shouting, 'They'll listen to me. Stand aside. Let us through. *Stand aside!*'

The crowd pushed forwards as we were slowly advancing in our tight circle, protected by the iron ring of the RUC, towards the shed. And then, just for a moment, the circle broke and Sarah and I watched as the mayor got sucked out of the break and into the crowd.

'Stand aside!' I heard him cry.

'Man down!' I called.

The last time we set eyes on him, he was drifting helplessly out into the crowd, the black feather of his tricorn hat like a mighty sail on a lost galleon. Sarah and I started to laugh, heads down in this closed circle. We couldn't help it. At no point did we feel anything other than warmth from the crowd. They were exuberant and entirely friendly. There were tears rolling down our cheeks. Then . . . the Belfast City Christmas lights came on.

'The lights are on!' I shouted to Sarah in our circle.

'What?' she shouted back.

'The Christmas lights have come on.'

We were helpless with screaming laughter. Someone had

spotted the mayor adrift in the crowd and panicked. They had hit the button and turned on the lights.

Sarah and I made it safely to the shed, gave a speech of thanks . . . and turned off the Belfast Christmas lights.

The RUC weren't the only ones protecting me. James Grant were doing a pretty comprehensive job as well. At that time, and probably now, to a lesser extent, children's presenters were expected to be squeaky clean. To live pure, saintly lives. I couldn't be bound by those restrictions. I was by no means reckless, but my friends and I were all having a ball. A few magazine articles described me as 'beige' because I never seemed to do anything reckless. That always made us roar with laughter. The secret was not to go into the centre of London but to stay within the confines of either Chiswick or Ealing, where, back then, no one could be bothered to look. Everyone was protective of us. We knew all the bar staff and all the restaurateurs. Not one of them ever ratted if we had a raucous night out.

The thing is, if I'm honest, I have never felt 'famous' or understood the term 'celebrity' if it is apportioned to me. I didn't feel it then; I don't feel it now. Perhaps it's because I was never in it for the recognition. Being recognized was an unnecessary by-product of the job I loved to do. Instead, I loved it because I loved discovering the art of communication. The way to address a camera, how to throw it a glance, like a cheeky friend. I realized that just a look could be enough to tell the filthiest joke. I suppose that has become 'my thing', a casually thrown, knowing look. It can say, 'Is she mad?' or 'I disagree,' or 'Yes, I'm sure we all agree, this man is a twat.' It just happens. I don't think about it. The camera can be a very watchful, knowing accomplice.

Far from feeling famous, I couldn't feel more ordinary in my head. I like to think I'm good at what I do, but I don't successfully guide planes into Heathrow or fix a leak, and I certainly don't fix a brain. We have a very strange job, which gets more recognition than it deserves. At a Pride of Britain Awards ceremony, I met Sir John Sulston, part of the British team who mapped the human genome. Bill Clinton described their work as 'the most wondrous map ever produced by mankind'. In comparison, I will never understand why, very occasionally, I have been called 'a legend'! And while I don't do it for recognition, I don't mind that my job brings attention. I have always doubted those in my profession who get frustrated at being recognized. I've always thought, give them a week without that and they'd soon be paranoid that it was all over!

Russ lived in Drayton Avenue in West Ealing at the time with his flatmates and his brother Craig. I will describe Craig as . . . untamed. He was a genuinely good soul and a kind man, right up until his sad death only a few weeks ago, but he loved to party.

When it came to the parties I went to, my drug of choice has always been alcohol. I've never really been interested in dope because, as I've mentioned, I'm really not very suited to it. Though, one day in Drayton Avenue, Gary, one of the gang, sparked up a joint as we were watching TV. An ad for a Cadbury's Caramel bar came on the telly. The animated bunny was quite large and then, with a puff of dust beneath her, suddenly got thin. Gary said, 'My God, she just farted herself thin, mate,' and we laughed for four hours. That was the last time I touched it, because in between laughing, I was also being sick. Alcohol has always been enough for me.

We had such fun together and we did some crazy things. On bonfire night, we all trekked around the district picking up boxes and crates. The bonfire we built in the back garden was certainly too large to be safe, but when it started to die down someone unscrewed the kitchen door and threw that on. The cupboard doors followed.

Pete's advice was always the same: be dignified in public, don't let yourself down, always leave the BBC bar before everyone else, don't show yourself up. So I never did, or at least I was never caught. But if you lived in Ealing or Chiswick at the time and you saw us out, thank you for not telling.

For all the advice about being dignified and staying safe, the gang very nearly killed me on two occasions.

Pete had a boat, a Sunseeker he kept moored in Poole. One sunny Saturday after I'd finished on *Going Live* it was suggested that we all drive down to the boat to go water-skiing.

It was a glorious day out on the water, but quite chilly. Russ had decided he was going to mono-ski. He couldn't quite get up out of the water on one ski, so he got up on two then kicked off a ski and carried on with just the one. When he tired, we had to go in search of the ski he had dropped, which could have drifted anywhere in quite a wide area. The search was on. As it was chilly, I stood on the bow of the boat, still in my telly clothes from the show earlier, wearing a thick coat and my glasses. I wore contacts or glasses for years until, for a *This Morning* film, I had my eyes lasered. I haven't needed glasses since.

The boat was pounding across the Solent in search of the dropped ski, and our eyes were peeled, scanning the sea.

'There it is!' someone called.

Pete snapped the boat round forty-five degrees. I wasn't holding on.

I left the boat at around thirty knots, flying in a perfect arc over the water. I had enough time to think, 'I'm going to lose my glasses,' so I put my hands to my face as I flew. It was like hitting solid concrete as I smashed into the water. Every bit of breath was gone, leaving me completely winded. My thick coat filled with water and I began to sink. At that moment, I was done, no breath or energy to swim and no inclination to try. I felt my glasses slide down my nose and drift down into the depths. I was perfectly happy to follow them. By now, everyone on the boat knew that I was gone from the bow and the focus of the search changed from the dropped ski to me. I was quickly found and, as my head sank below the water, I felt Russ grab the neck of the coat and pull me to the surface.

My second close shave with death was in the Alps.

The gang loved to ski, and Pete was particularly good.

'Would you like to come skiing with us, mate?'

'I can't ski.'

'Don't worry, we'll teach you.'

It had snowed heavily in the south-east, so we piled into our cars and headed for Box Hill in Surrey. It had a particularly useful slope. Most often used for sledging, it also offered a reasonably acceptable training slope. I was put on skis and given about a half-hour lesson before the others got bored and started skiing themselves.

A couple of weeks later, in Méribel, high in the Alps, we kitted ourselves up and set off. At the top of my first-ever run, I certainly looked the part: all-in-one outfit, mirrored shades. I mean, how hard can this be?

The guys produced a set of walkie-talkies.

'Right, we're going to ski halfway down, then we'll stop. Put the headphones in and we'll talk you through the moves. Remember what we told you about putting a turn in and snow-ploughing?'

'Er, yes, I think I remember.'

'Okay, then. Just listen to the instructions and you'll be fine. Good luck. Enjoy.'

They skied off down the mountain. I waited at the top.

Eventually, the headphones crackled into life.

'Can you hear me, over?'

'Yep, loud and clear, over.'

'Good, so, point yourself down the mountain and you'll start to slide, over.'

'Okay, over.'

I pushed off and felt my skis start to glide. I tried to put in a turn, but my skis just wouldn't obey. I tried the other way, but my skis still didn't comply.

'Okay, Phil. Looking good, mate. Put in that turn now . . . Phil, you need to put that turn in now.'

'I can't. They won't turn.'

'Can you sense that you're beginning to pick up speed now, mate? Put that turn in. Phil, make a turn. Seriously, you have to turn *right now*.'

I was flying down the mountain in a perfectly straight line. Out of instinct, I crouched and tucked my arms in. I'm also pretty sure I closed my eyes.

'Phil, turn! Turn, mate . . . Fall, Phil! Fall! Just lean backwards and fall on to your back.'

I shot past them in silence. No yelling, no screaming, just an uncontrolled spear streaking downhill.

They stood in horrified silence, the useless walkie-talkie hanging limply in their hands.

A stranger came to a stop beside them.

'He's good,' said the stranger. 'How long has he been skiing?'

'First time.'

'Shit.'

I hit the ground so hard my ski flew for about thirty feet, away and up, hitting a sign that pointed the way back to Méribel, turning it forty-five degrees in a different direction. It took two days of people skiing in the wrong direction before someone got a ladder and turned it back.

Skiing with Peter Powell, apparently without poles!

Skiing became one of my favourite pastimes, followed closely by scuba-diving. Once, the gang all decided to travel to Antigua to take our open-water certification. On our first dive together, we realized that the faster you breathed, the quicker you used your oxygen and the sooner you had to return to the boat. The competition was intense; nobody wanted to be first back to the boat. It probably helped us enormously: we were all instantly calm and serene divers, and there was no way I was going to be first out. I spent most of the dives with blue lips.

It's a source of great joy to me that both of my girls have taken to diving. The family holidays with the four of us diving in formation are very special. They were all with me when a barracuda fell in love with me and stayed beside me for a whole dive. Those family holiday memories are twenty-four-carat gold to me.

As a group of friends, one of our most serene trips was

our annual trip to Loch Goil, on the Cowal peninsula in Argyll, Scotland. Our mate Gary had a boat – well, his dad did. Russ, Gary and I would fly to Dundee and then drive to the loch, where we'd meet Gary's dad. We stayed in Loch-goilhead, which, you won't be surprised to hear, was a tiny collection of houses at the head of the loch. The Bouquet Garni was the only restaurant and the guy who ran it would put a blackboard outside announcing who had made a book-ing that night. He had some sort of radar because, as we arrived, he would write on the blackboard 'The Southerners are back.' It was always a mad, furious dash from our accom-modation to the restaurant because the midges were furious and it hurt like hell when they swarmed on to our heads and hands and bit us in their hundreds! We'd all stand at the door, waiting to open it and make the frantic run to the restaurant.

'Is everyone ready? Remember, there's no going back if you've forgotten something. Right, ready? Three, two, one: *ruuuuuuunnnnn!*'

Everyone who arrived at the restaurant did so in the same way. There was a huge bang as they hurled themselves in through the outer porch door, arms wheeling above their heads and hands desperately patting at their faces.

The reason we made the journey north was because of the fishing. If the weather was nice, it was utterly sublime. In the morning, we'd be picked up by the boat and spend the day out on the loch, fishing for mackerel. At the end of the day we beached the boat, fired up a disposable barbecue and cooked the freshly caught fish, eating them with our fingers. I loved every second. It was calming and peaceful, life was slower, and it reminded me of Cornwall and of going out with my dad to fish for mackerel on the rocks in Newquay.

On one of the trips, the weather was roasting, so we all

stripped off to our pants and dived into the cool, clear water for a swim. Out of nowhere, there was a very strange swell. There was obviously something *huge* under the water! The three of us panicked and made for the boat, flailing our way through the water to escape the beast beneath us in the briny waters. What the hell could be so big to create such a swell? We got to the ladder of the boat and fought each other to be first out. All dignity had escaped us. As we lay panting on the deck of the boat, Gary's dad stood over us, looking down, tears rolling down his cheeks. He could hardly speak for laughing. We were affronted that he wasn't taking this encounter with a creature of the deep seriously. When he had composed himself, he explained.

'Aye, that's the funniest thing I've ever seen. Three grown men escaping a submarine!'

A *what* now?

It transpired that, as the loch was open to the sea, submarines would creep in unnoticed on training manoeuvres and, as they turned to leave and head back out to sea, they always kicked up a swell on the surface. I'm not sure that any of us were comforted. Which was worse? A mythical monster or a bloody massive submarine with gigantic spinning propellers silently turning beneath us!

We developed one quaint tradition on the day of the Oxford v. Cambridge Boat Race. Pete lived by the rowing club at the end of the race, where the boats were hauled ashore and the interviews were given. I'd been live on TV for two hours that morning, Pete had been live on the radio for two hours, yet we all gathered at his house to watch the race. He always recorded it. As the race drew to a close, we all ran up the riverbank to stand in the back of shot while the interviews were taking place. We then went back to Pete's and rewound the VHS to see if we'd made it on to the telly.

Every time we could identify one of us in the background, we had a drink.

Our nights out very seldom had any discernible effect on our broadcasting abilities, except maybe Peter's. After very heavy nights, when we'd all got into a bit of a mess and finally found our way to our beds, we would try to wake up to listen to Pete's opening link on the radio. He was presenting the weekend breakfast shows on Radio 1 from eight till ten. If he was in a bad way, two things would happen: firstly, he would say only 'Good morning,' in a particularly gravelly and pissed-off voice, then promptly play five records in a row. Then, if we were lucky, his 'neat freak OCD' would kick in. At home, for him, everything was/is always in an orderly pattern – even his cigarette stubs were arranged in a straight line. Sometimes, if he was hideously hungover, it would cross over into his show. Pete would look at the mixing desk in front of him; he liked all the faders to be in a straight line. Trouble was, if one was up on its own, the chances were, it was playing something. We knew that if the radio suddenly went silent, he had put all the faders in a neat line and taken himself off air. The screams of laughter from our individual flats could be heard all across West London.

My diary was filling up with personal appearances and other TV work. I was presenting *Take Two* and I was a regular presenter of *Disney Time*, which, in the days before subscription telly, was the only way to watch Disney clips without buying the VHS. I was happy to work whatever hours were necessary. I was mostly living the dream, but there was one gap: I missed radio.

It was proving tricky to get back on air because Doreen Davis, who at the time was a senior executive at Radio 1 and, no matter how hard Peter tried, wouldn't have me on the station. She always said: 'He's very good on television.' As long as Doreen was there, I didn't stand a chance – but then, she retired!

Johnny Beerling was the new controller of Radio 1 and, without Doreen as a barrier, things were much easier. I went in to see Johnny and he asked why I wanted to be on the radio when TV was working so well for me. I told him about the Fistral Roadshow, my obsession with radio, the 'Enter' sign in Broadcasting House. He smiled and said, 'Ah, I see, this is more than just ambition, this is destiny.' Johnny hired me, and I will love him for ever for that.

Radio 1 had, sadly, moved buildings by this time, so I didn't ever get to press 'Enter' as a DJ. It had, however, only moved next door, to Egton House, and was now in its own building. My life was literally complete as I walked through the doors for the first time, just across the road from All Souls Church, where my dad had sat on the steps when I had my booking-clerk job interview. I walked on to the floor that housed the studios: two Radio 1 studios, or 'cons', with their accompanying control rooms, overseen by the engineer and producer. The red, white and blue colours of the station were everywhere. I'm pretty sure the studios were Con K and Con L, but that's the geek in me. I make no apologies.

DJ Mark Goodier taught me how to use the desk, and I was ready to go. My first show on the station was on 29 August 1988, the summer bank holiday. I'd been allocated legendary Radio 1 producer Chris Lycett (his wife, Annie, is now a great friend at the Prince's Trust), and Louise Musgrave was shadowing, because she would produce my upcoming shows on Sunday afternoons and Thursday evenings, starting in October that year.

It was absolutely everything I had ever wanted it to be. Not only to be a part of the team, but also get to count the DJs of

My Radio 1 colleagues at the time.

the time as my friends: Steve Wright, DLT, Simon Bates, Mark Goodier, Simon Mayo and the legendary Alan Freeman.

I would be setting up my Sunday show in one studio and 'Fluff' Freeman was next door presenting *Pick of the Pops*. The joy of watching him through the glass, saying, 'Greetings, pop pickers' and 'Not arf' was supreme. What a wonderful man he was, and he swore better than anyone I've ever met. Getting Fluff to laugh and tell me to 'Fuck off' in that legendary voice was a delight.

Thankfully, there were still great 'old school' characters at the station, and reigning supreme among them was producer Malcolm Brown. Middle-aged and with crazy hair, he was talented but also hilariously eccentric and brilliantly bonkers. If he was thinking, he made a grunting 'muh' sound before he spoke. One Christmas, we were all in the offices above the studios. Cathy Mellor had become my programme secretary and we were working through the show. Malcolm was holding court. A record company had sent in sides of smoked salmon for everyone and one of those cards which, when you opened it, played a Christmas carol. We were chatting and eating salmon when someone wondered out loud whether, if you swallowed the card mechanism, the carol would continue to play.

'Muh, well, I expect so.'

Malcolm carefully dismantled the card to inspect what made the carol play: a battery, a couple of wires, a small printed circuit and a little speaker. He looked it over, took a piece of smoked salmon, wrapped it round the gubbins and popped it in his mouth.

'Noooooooooooooo!!!!' we all yelled in unison, and leapt forward. Too late. He opened his mouth, and it was empty. He had swallowed the card mechanism. One by one, we listened to his stomach. Cheerfully playing inside him was 'Good King Wenceslas'. It was reckless and dangerous and apparently played for two days.

Times were changing for Radio 1. New FM transmitters were opening up all over the country, the station was moving from the old, poor-quality 275/285 frequency on medium wave to a brand-new, high-quality stereo frequency on FM. It was a big deal, so the DJs were expected to take part in the switchover, which was slowly being rolled out across the UK. We were dispatched all over the country each time a new FM transmitter was activated. After a successful switch-on in Plymouth, I was dispatched to Southend with Malcolm Brown as my producer and Cathy Mellor as production secretary. We all arrived in the white Radio 1 Range Rover, resplendent in its station branding. The plan was simple. Simon Mayo was in a helicopter and had been visiting various switch-on sites around the country. The helicopter would land, Simon would jump out, a DJ would be there with local dignitaries, we would press a fake button and the FM signal would burst forth. We were on about the fifth switch-on of the day and they were running late.

Malcolm, Cathy and I arrived at the designated playing fields, cleared a space for the helicopter, set up the fake button, met the Lord Mayor and Lady Mayoress, said hi to the gathering crowd and waited . . . and waited. Mayo was late, and getting later. Malcolm's phone rang as he sat in the Range Rover and I stood beside it, looking at the sky.

'Muh, they're not cummin'.'

'What?'

'They've run out of time. We've been dropped.'

I looked at the expectant crowd. What were we going to do? What would we say?

I then looked into the Range Rover for help from the man in charge. Cathy was sitting in the back with the door open, watching us both.

There then followed the most bizarre set of instructions I had ever heard, and the most extraordinary executive decision, bearing in mind we were all representing Radio 1.

'Muh, get in the car, but not fully in the car, stand on the outside step with the door open, but don't make it look like we're leaving, make it look like we're arriving.'

'What do you mean, Malcolm?'

'Make it look nonchalant, like nothing is wrong. Cathy, dangle your legs out of the open door . . . Remember, we're just arriving.'

'But Malcolm, we're already here!'

'Just stand on the side of the bloody car . . . Oh, and look up.'

I did as I was instructed. I stood on the running plate of the Radio 1 Range Rover, smiling and looking up. Malcolm slid the gearbox into reverse and slowly, so very slowly, we backed away.

Further and further away. The assembled dignitaries were still watching the sky as we retreated.

'We've left the fake FM button.'

'Muh, sod it, can't be helped.'

As we reversed out of the gates of the playing fields and on to the road, Malcolm shouted, 'Now!! Get in!'

I slipped into the passenger seat and slammed the door. Cathy drew in her legs and slammed her door, too, and we drove off! I looked questioningly at Malcolm's face as we raced off down the road, all those eager faces still staring at the sky.

'And that,' he said, 'is how you make an exit.'

Southend had its revenge some time later. I'd been asked if I'd do a wing-walk for *Going Live*. I'm not easily scared, and there's not much I won't try. I drove to Southend airport with a crew. I was going to fly over the south coast on the 'Crunchie' biplane. It was pretty well known at the time because, being in the orange colours of the chocolate bar, it was pretty easy to spot. There wasn't much instruction required. I just had to stand, strapped to the wing – that was basically it. When I got to the airport I was met by the owner/pilot. He said that it would be pretty cold up there so I'd need to wear leathers. Unfortunately, his leathers were unavailable so I would have to wear his wife's. I don't know to this day if they were winding me up.

So it was that I stood on the wing of the biplane in a tight purple leather jumpsuit with tasselled fringing on the sleeves. We pulled over at the end of the runway to let a passenger jet go first. I love planes, as I've said, and I looked over to the cockpit window of the jet. The pilot, who was going through his pre-take-off checks, looked up, our eyes met, him inside a passenger jet with his shades on, me strapped to the wing of a biplane in a leather jumpsuit. As he taxied into position he showed me the internationally recognized sign for 'wanker' and took off. I was crushed.

I was becoming a bit of a daredevil, happy to take on most challenges (except any more charity football matches). Would I be winched from a military helicopter on to Brighton Pier to meet up with Jackie Brambles, who was broadcasting live? Of course! On the day, I was driven to the huge helicopter, which was waiting in a corner of the airfield. After the introductions were made it was explained that we'd perform a couple of dry runs before we flew out to Brighton. The helicopter lifted vertically about a hundred feet into the air. I sat at the open door with my legs dangling out. The winch man stood facing me, a leg either side of me. Was I happy? Everything okay? As the rotors beat their steady, thunderous roar, I gave him the thumbs-up. I slid forward and out, and he cast off at the same time. It takes a bit of skill to get the ropes exactly the right length, taking into consideration both the winch man's height and mine. Anyway, work needed to be done because, as we slid out of the helicopter, his face disappeared out of view and mine jammed into his crotch as we descended! I couldn't move my head because of the rope tension, and I couldn't breathe. I was seriously suffocating, totally jammed against his package! As we got to the ground, my feet touched first, then my head was released from the grip of his groin and his body slid down in front of me until we were face to face. The helicopter roared above us as I looked at him, stunned by this forced intimacy.

'All okay?' I think he yelled, above the roar of the hovering helicopter.

'*No!*' I shouted back 'The rope length isn't right!!' He couldn't hear me and signalled that we were going back up.

'*No!!* I can't breathe! I was suffocating.'

It was useless. Neither of us could hear each other. He looked up to the crew and signalled that we were ready to be lifted.

His face lifted out of view, his chest passed by and then, *whoomph*, the rope tightened. I tried to turn my head: no chance – my face was pulled back towards his groin. I took a deep breath and, again, the world went dark, as we were lifted skywards. Nothing was ever said, but the ropes were adjusted and I was winched down to Brighton Pier in a much more dignified fashion. I was dropped off and the helicopter soared away. When I told my mates what had happened, they couldn't breathe for laughing, and the 'winch man's bollocks' story has been regularly retold.

Sometime afterwards I was asked by the *Going Live* team if I would like to fly with the Red Arrows.

'Absolutely, yes,' was my obvious reply. Since childhood, as I've mentioned, I'd had a fascination with aircraft, and this was one of those incredible 'money can't buy' opportunities that I was not going to miss.

I had no idea it would end in disaster.

Every summer in Cornwall, the Schofield family drove to St Mawgan for the airshow. It was one of the highlights of our summer. The Red Arrows were always the stars of the show, but we also loved the Vulcan Bomber, because when it was being built and still highly classified, my mum was involved in printing up all the top-secret information on it. My grandad also shaped many of the copper pipes in the bomb bay. When the Vulcan soared overhead, it felt like the screaming roar could pull your soul out of your ears.

One of the other treats of the day was watching the Nimrod

fly overhead. St Mawgan was a military base with a runway long enough for Concorde to land. In the sixties and seventies it was home to a squadron of Shackleton long-range maritime patrol aircraft. The droning noise that the Shackleton made was the best sound ever! They were replaced by Nimrods and, because of my job, way off in the future, Dad, Tim and I would get to go on a top-secret patrol out in the Atlantic on board a Nimrod to find a rogue Soviet fishing boat.

After seeing them so many times as a child, now I would get to fly with the Arrows. That was an unexpected dream come true.

The crew and I drove to their base at RAF Scampton in Lincolnshire, where my training began. Firstly, I was told how to operate the Martin Baker ejector seat in an emergency. The *Red One* pilot at the time was Squadron Leader Tim Miller. I would be flying with him. He pointed out that in an emergency he would say, 'Eject, eject, eject,' and on the third 'eject' he would be gone, up and out of the red Hawk

About to experience my Red Arrow shakedown flight.

188

jet. I could, he said, choose to stay in the plane and attempt to land it. If I was successful, I would be an RAF hero. However, he suggested that if he couldn't land it, it would be unlikely that I could. I agreed to follow him out of the plane in the unlikely event of a disaster.

After the briefing, I felt confident that I could safely attach and detach myself from the seat and eject if I needed to. Next came the shakedown flight. This was Tim and me in *Red One* going through the manoeuvres that I could expect in a full-on display. Months before, a journalist who wanted to write a piece on the team had visited them. He had been taken out over the North Sea to experience the thrill of aerobatics. He panicked and, for no understandable reason, the pilot heard an almighty bang and the journalist was gone from behind him. Without warning, he had ejected. Other than a very

The closest I ever got to *Top Gun*.

expensive shattered canopy, no one was hurt. The moment the seat separates from the jet, a tracker beacon is activated, so the hapless journo was quickly found by a search-and-rescue helicopter, bobbing in the North Sea. I clearly understood the importance of a shakedown. An idiot ejecting during a display was something no one wanted to witness.

It was orgasmic! Tim put the plane, me, my nerves and my stomach through our paces and I was ecstatic with undiluted joy and awe. We rolled, we dived, we twisted, we spun and we turned.

The pilot and any passengers have to wear a special jump-suit to counteract the high gravitational forces – 'pulling Gs'. It inflates when necessary and exerts pressure on the legs to stop the blood from leaving the brain and gathering in the lower extremities. When we hit 7Gs, I was happy to be wearing it. Otherwise, I would certainly have passed out.

'Right,' said Tim in clipped tones over the radio. 'You've passed the shakedown. Let's have some fun.'

He dived the streaking red Hawk jet down to ground level. We followed the twisting track of the North Yorkshire Railway as it wound through the beautifully rugged scenery. As it flashed past, we snapped left and right to avoid the rocky terrain on either side. At the end, he pulled back on the stick and we went vertical, straight up like a launching rocket, up to the perfect, fluffy cumulus clouds. He gave me my instructions.

'It's your turn to fly now. I want you to imagine that these clouds are as hard as the hills below. Fly around them, through the gaps. Think, if we go into a cloud, you'll kill us . . . You have control.'

'I have control,' I replied, attempting to sound cool.

I gingerly moved the joystick left and right, missing the gaps and flying through the clouds.

Every time it went misty white around us Tim shouted, 'Dead!'

'Dead!'

'Dead again!'

I was being too careful, too cautious. He had had enough of my fannying around.

'You will *never* get this opportunity again. You will *not* break it. Now *fly the bloody thing*.'

That was all I needed. So began the most exciting twenty minutes of my entire life. I snapped the stick left and right and we darted through the gaps: round, over, under. I saw the clouds as solid objects as we tore through the sky, a tiny red dart weaving through huge, white, bubbling clouds. I didn't kill us again and my exhilaration almost made me cry with emotional triumph.

The next day was the display. To make sure of coverage from all angles, the usual nine red Hawks of the display team were joined by a tenth, an identical jet equipped with cameras. Our camera crew positioned themselves about halfway down the runway. All ten Red Arrow planes positioned themselves perfectly in formation at the end of the runway. We started to roll. I have no idea what went wrong.

We gently lifted off. The wheels retracted and, at that exact moment, the jet behind me and to my right got out of position, dropping back as I watched. The pilot overcompensated and the plane leapt towards us. The nose of the jet was so close to the cockpit I gasped and pulled my right arm in beside me. The pilot overcompensated again by pulling back on the power. It all happened so fast. The jet dropped back but lost height and slapped back down without wheels on to the runway, where the diesel tanks filled with fuel and the dye for the trademark coloured smoke ignited in a fireball. The pilot ejected. As the wheels had been retracted, the stricken Red Arrow briefly slid down the runway, leaving a fiery trail behind it, then veered off into the grass, to where the crew were filming. Some of the other jets had briefly scattered to get out of the way. What the *hell* had I just witnessed?

Over the radio, to the pilots under his command, Tim was incredible. Calmly, he said, 'Battle formation,' and the nine planes regrouped. We performed a circuit of the airfield. The runway was damaged, so returning to base was impossible. We were diverting to RAF Conningsby. If he was calm over the radio to his team, he was anything but in the cockpit, with just me to hear. He was absolutely steaming with fury, his language varied and ripe in the extreme. I wasn't really listening as I was distraught about the crew. Were they okay? How was the pilot?

As we approached to land at Conningsby, he reminded the pilots to check that their landing gear was down. It hadn't occurred to me to think that, although every one of them was highly trained, after witnessing an accident and not knowing how their colleague was, they might also need to be reminded how to proceed. Tim Miller pointed out that very few civilians approached Conningsby in this way and that this was highly irregular. He also instructed me not to disclose what I saw. So I won't.

The Red Arrows landed perfectly and all taxied into a perfectly straight line. Tim slid back the cockpit canopy and made sure I could remember how to unplug everything and get out without ejecting myself. I assured him I could. He said he was going to talk to the pilots and I was to join them when I could, and with that he climbed out and was gone. I made sure everything was disconnected correctly, then climbed out. The tinted sun shield was down on my helmet, so you couldn't see my face. As I stood by the plane, the ground crew arrived.

'Good morning, sir. Don't often see you here, sir,' one of them said to me.

'There's been an accident,' I replied. 'One of the planes has gone down.'

One of the crew stood back, looked down the line and actually counted! As if a mistake had been made.

'You've got nine, sir.'

'We left Scampton with ten. One of these is the camera plane, and you can stop calling me sir. I'm a civilian.'

All protocol was dropped as he exclaimed, 'What the *fuck* has happened?'

By the time I got to the group of shaken pilots, I was told that my TV crew were all fine and that the pilot was also unhurt. Although he may have ejected directly into a desk job.

The footage filmed for *Going Live* was used that evening on the *Nine o'Clock News*.

Because of what we'd all been through, a few months later I was invited back to Scampton for a dinner. Those guys partied *hard*. Sometime after that, I finally took part in a complete display.

On Monday 3 October 1988 I was on the twelfth floor of the East Tower at TV Centre for a *Going Live* production meeting. Chris Bellinger had a TV tuned to ITV in the corner of the office. There was a new show about to launch that he wanted to watch. At ten forty we all stopped what we were doing and gathered around the TV. Broadcasting live from the Albert Dock in Liverpool, *This Morning* took its place in the nation's lives. I could have no idea how important it would become to me.

I suppose part of writing a book like this is that you tell stories that make you wince, especially when you see them written on paper. I have always had the greatest respect for our emergency services and I try to make time if they need my help in promoting any schemes or initiatives they launch.

The Northumberland Police asked if I would help to promote a new scheme to get young children to talk to adults if there was anything worrying them. I travelled to the launch and was happy to take part. A few days later, I was caught speeding on the M1. Not excessively, but enough. The James Grant office called to warn the chief superintendent in Northumberland that this had happened and that we were sorry if this had caused any embarrassment. He surprised us by saying he would look into it. A week or so later I got a letter from the police in Hendon, where the speeding offence had happened. The chief inspector told me that in light of the fact that I was currently working with the police, and to prevent embarrassment, he would on this *one* occasion overlook the offence. However, if my name *ever* crossed his desk again (it never has), he would without question come down on me in the fullest way possible. I wrote, 'Yippee!' on the letter and drew a car with speed lines around it and 'Vroom' coming out of the exhaust. I drove to the office to tell Russ and Paul. They were both out. My intention was to copy the letter once and place the copy on Russ's desk. I accidentally made ten copies. I stabbed at the copier in a frantic attempt to make it stop, but it wouldn't. I left one copy on Russ's desk, put the remaining nine copies in my bag and went to work at Radio 1.

By a stroke of sheer misfortune, that evening at the studio a particularly clever thief managed to get in. He left with a reasonable haul of wallets and cards, and my entire bag. I called the office to explain that I wasn't bothered about anything inside the bag, it could all be replaced. The thief had, however, got the nine copies of the 'Yippee! Vroom' letter. I was mortified, and the office, who were becoming increasingly adept at putting out media fires, said that I had been stupid to make the copies, but thanked me for owning up. They would be ready if the thief decided to sell them.

Nothing happened. Silence. I thought nothing more would be said on the matter.

About six months later, two police constables from Chiswick Police knocked on my door. They had arrested the thief, who turned out to be a criminal very well known to the police.

My bag had been returned intact, with most of the items in it. Did I want to check? I did just that. Everything but my wallet was there, including the 'Yippee! Vroom' letters. I discreetly counted them: damn, only eight. My heart sank. I thanked the constables and showed them to the door. As they were leaving, one of them turned to me and said, 'If you were wondering why there are only eight copies of your letter, we've got one on our noticeboard at work.'

I've had my share of over-zealous fans. One thought we were getting married and booked our wedding venue then sent me tickets to New York for our honeymoon. And one was obsessed by the secret messages I was apparently leaving for her in the *Radio Times*. But by far the most peculiar was the Chinese lady who took to jumping out at me with her camera at the ready. It didn't matter where I was in the country or what time of the day or night it was, she always seemed to know where I'd be. I would walk past a bus stop, a billboard, be parking my car in a multi-storey . . . I never saw her coming until she was in front of me. She would jump out and shout, '*Yaaaaa!*' I would scream in surprise and, at that moment, she took her photo. I had my very own Cato from the Pink Panther movies. Somewhere, there are about thirty photos of me, trapped in a moment in time, with a look of abject terror on my face.

In November 1989, Pete, Russ and I were all sitting in the

office watching the news. The Berlin Wall was being besieged, and the soldiers on both sides of the wall were watching it happen and not firing on the crowds who were gathering. They were climbing it; they were taking hammers and pickaxes to it. The atmosphere was jubilant, euphoric. We couldn't believe what we were witnessing. Russ had a thought out loud:

'We should go.'

'Huh?'

'We should go! We should go, right now!'

He looked in my diary. 'You're not working tomorrow. Let's go now.'

'Okay,' I said. 'I have to go home for my passport. I'll meet you at the airport.'

Just forty minutes later, we were at Heathrow. At the ticket desk, we were told that if we ran we could get the flight that was about to board. We ran.

Three hours after watching the news, we were in Berlin and approaching the Wall. Old ladies were sobbing, hitting it with anything they could find, in some cases just their shoes. The bits of concrete that were chipped off were being handed out as souvenirs. A guy lent me his hammer and I chipped some of it off for myself. We climbed a ladder and stood on the top, looking into no-man's-land and the darkness of East Berlin beyond. That vantage point, only days before, would have got me arrested, or worse. We walked to the Checkpoint Charlie border crossing and found, to our astonishment, that it was open and, with the proper paperwork completed, we could cross into the East for a few hours. The walk through the checkpoint and into the East was, even for us, emotional. As we stood in East Berlin, we saw how profound the difference between the two sides of the Wall was.

The sky of the West was lit by the glow from neon signs and we could hear the noise of horns and the bustle of busy

The Berlin Wall comes down.

lives beyond. Walking into the East was like stepping back in time, or on to the set of *The Third Man*. Very few streetlamps lit the shadows; the buildings were dark and brooding. There was no traffic, and the roads and pavements had dry grass growing through the cracks. We walked aimlessly for about thirty minutes, then spotted bright lights in the distance. The source of the light was a grand hotel. Although its best days were behind it, it still had a faded magnificence. A hotel stopped in time offering the only light in the dark streets.

We walked through the doors, and back about sixty years. Crystal chandeliers sparkled above the old guy in a suit playing a grand piano. Only a handful of people sat in the bar. They were furtive, their conversations spoken into hands covering their mouths. On the bar was a huge ice bucket filled with bottles of Dom Pérignon champagne and beside that a huge bowl of caviar. The opulence inside compared to the forlorn and gloomy streets outside was shocking. We sat at the bar in stunned silence. What conversations had been had in this bar over the years? Probably quite a few like the one we were about to have.

'Hello, boys,' said a husky female voice with a heavy German accent. 'Would you like to buy us a drink?'

The woman with her asked, 'Maybe you'd like a little fun tonight?'

The two 'professional' ladies were very beautiful and excellent company. I should say immediately that our time with them remained in the bar, on four barstools!

They drank champagne and told us about their lives. Both had young children and struggled to keep them fed. 'Business is slow,' they said. They asked why we were there and we explained that we had just walked through Checkpoint Charlie. They were captivated. Was it easy? Could anyone cross? What was it like on the other side? We answered their many questions and reassured them that the border was open, the Wall was coming down. Did we think they could cross? We said we were sure they could. They said that they were extremely scared. Perhaps we could cross with them?

We agreed!

Both girls raced from the bar, assuring us they would be back in twenty minutes. Their mothers took it in turns to watch the children as their daughters went to work. About half an hour later, they returned, each with a small bag and their passport. They had also brought their car.

At about 3 a.m. we drove through Checkpoint Charlie in a Trabant with two East German hookers. They kissed us on the cheeks as we sent them, wide-eyed, into the bright neon lights.

Things were marching along at a substantial pace back in London. Kenneth Williams had asked me out (I declined) and Bob Monkhouse had said to me outside TC reception, 'If I had ever had another son, I would have liked it to have been you.' I only include that because it touched me deeply at the time, and still does. Bob was an ever-smiling gentleman and a TV icon.

So, everything was happening – all fun, some bizarre. There were only two things left to be ticked off my teenage wish list. And then Johnny Beerling, the Controller of Radio 1, called me into his office and I ticked off one of them.

'I wondered if you would like to do a week on the Roadshow?'

The chorus in my head played yet again.

I was teamed with Roger Pusey as my producer, and I asked Cathy Mellor, who was production secretary on my Radio 1 shows, to come on board too.

Roger Pusey was literally the perfect pairing for me. Looking like a handsome Captain Birdseye, he was the best fun, totally lovely, a wonderfully dynamic producer and he loved all

Cathy Mellor and Roger Pusey.

On stage at the Roadshow and swinging my pants with Trev and Simon.

the daring 'adventure' stuff that I did. To complete the party, Trev and Simon from *Going Live* made up the joyous team.

I was part of the best travelling circus of my life, with the best radio family. We'd roll into a town, perform a live radio show for two hours and then move on. It was so big, I even had my own bodyguard. Jerry Judge was a big guy, and the most well-known 'personal protection' in the business. He was someone that you wouldn't mess with – a 'unit'. He was also a very kind and lovely man and was the only person who could get Frank Sinatra out of a bar and up to bed. Jerry had protected them all, and would continue to do so until his death in 2019. The showbiz world was so sad to lose this giant of a man who had kept us all safe.

I'd phone Steve Wright on his afternoon show from a secret location – 'the farm shop by the phone box on the A171 between Scarborough and Whitby' – and wait for the scores of Radio 1 fans to arrive. We did the Roadshow from the south-coast leg, to the North-east, to Northern Ireland. I was totally in my element. By now, Peter Powell had left Radio 1 and I asked him if I could have his legendary 'Summer Radio' jingle. He was chuffed. We had it remade with my name, and playing that jingle from the stage of the Radio 1 Roadshow was the absolute epitome of summer to me at the time. Everything about it was special – Smiley Miley giving away merchandise, me sitting backstage listening to the crowd as I waited for my introduction, the games I played in the warm-up before we went live, the GMT 'pips' signalling eleven o'clock and the start of the show, the roar as we went on air . . . All, literally, a dream come true.

And then, in 1990, the final tick.

'This year we thought you might like to do the final leg of the Roadshow season, the South-west, finishing in Newquay.'

No 'Hallelujah!' chorus could ever play louder in my head.

Cath, Roger and the team knew how special this was to me. They made that week one of the best of my broadcasting life. The unadulterated jubilation has never quite been surpassed.

Roger Pusey went to town. The Red Arrows flew over the stage in Plymouth for us, I was air/sea-rescued from Falmouth Harbour and broadcast all the way from bobbing in the sea to inside the helicopter. An RAF Nimrod flew over us and I could talk to the pilot. In a genius, makeshift invention, our engineer had sent the crew a small radio receiver, no bigger than a packet of cigarettes, and told them to hold it up to the cockpit window . . . it worked! The crowd loved it and, somehow, we got away with it on the radio, even though the listeners couldn't see a thing. All of those complicated and technical live links were achieved by the Outside Broadcast Department; the brilliant engineer on site with us was Dave Broomfield. It was a magnificent twist of fate. I had booked Dave out on to jobs when I worked in that department at the

On the roof at the Roadshow with Steph and Anthea Turner.

age of seventeen, and now, here he was, making sure I could be heard as I was bobbing in the sea. I would find out from him that to waterproof a mic, you popped a condom over it! Safe sound.

Kylie Minogue was the guest in Plymouth. Steph stood with me on the roof of the Roadshow stage on the Hoe as we watched the Red Arrows fly above the crowd. My thoughts drifted back to my days in that city with the Hospital Radio gang. That night, Steph and I stayed on Burgh Island. She told me later that it was there that she realized that, if I didn't feel the same way about her as she felt about me, she was in trouble. Thankfully, I did.

The night before the final Roadshow season of 1990 I stayed with Mum, Dad and Tim in their cottage in Trerice. We had a barbecue and the whole team came, even Johnny Beerling, the boss.

In the morning, I was picked up by a police car driven by

A quiet break from the Roadshow.

one of Tim's mates, a police constable called, coincidentally, Philip Schofield! He drove me through the town and out to the lawns of the Headland Hotel, where the Roadshow was set up. However, that wasn't the first time I had made the trip that day. The first time was in the dead of night to play a trick on the team.

The roadshow weeks were famed for their practical jokes, and Tony 'Smiley' Miles was usually the ringleader. I had sunk him in a rowing boat on a lake, had a sack of lion shit delivered to his merchandise truck and had him marooned on Lundy Island. At a show in Cleethorpes, they had all been in on a big trick to get me. I had been told that a local magician would be part of the warm-up and that the local news would be there to cover the show and his act. It seemed like a good idea. He

Another Roadshow prank with 'Smiley Miley'.

performed a few tricks for us and about ten minutes before we went live, I crouched down to put my head into a guillotine so he could 'chop my head off' in front of the crowd. He secured my hands in place with padlocks. The guillotine dropped, my neck was intact, the crowd went wild. As he undid the first padlock he snapped the key inside it. I was locked in. No matter how hard the team tried, they couldn't get me out. I was, at best, rather peeved! Not only because I was on my knees and trapped, but also – and I didn't tell anyone at the time – I had split my knee on the metal steps earlier in the warm-up and it was incredibly painful. The show started, with me on my bleeding knees. I asked the audience to be doubly loud because I couldn't do my usual dancing around to whip them up. It was during those deafening cheers that Noel Edmonds walked unseen from backstage. To the delight of everyone, he was carrying a 'Gotcha' – another of his awards, this time for his

House Party TV show. The camera was for him, and not the local news. It was a brilliant stunt, and I had been totally 'got'. I added his 'Gotcha' to the 'Golden Egg' I'd been awarded in the Broom Cupboard. It was never possible to get him back – he was way too wily – but I had decided I would have my revenge on the team . . . in Newquay.

As the production teams and DJs either drank or slept, the drivers and engineers arrived at the next location to set up the show. They usually rolled into town at about 2 a.m.

With the help of a friend of my folks, Frank Wilkinson, I had organized the entire 5th Newquay Scout troop to be camped on the exact spot the roadshow was to be set up. Tents, canoes, cooking utensils and, of course, Scouts. Cathy Mellor, my dad, Tim and I were all hidden in a tent as the circus arrived. The huge articulated truck hissed to a stop and the other vans pulled up behind. Driver Richard Greaves got out of his cab and walked over to the encampment. Frank emerged from a tent in full Scout leader regalia and played his part beautifully. Driver Greaves was stunned but calm.

'Mate, you can't camp here! I've got the entire Radio 1 Roadshow to park on this spot.'

'I don't know what you mean. We have written permission.'

'For tonight? It's not possible. We've had this spot booked for years.'

'Well, I'm sorry, but I'm not going to wake everyone up. You'll have to go somewhere else.'

'Somewhere else?! Where do you propose I drive all this kit?'

'Well, I don't know. Try another beach.'

The stand-off continued, until talk of the police crept in. It was time to come clean. We all emerged from hiding and the look on the faces of everyone on the team was spectacular. The impromptu camp was quickly dismantled and the Roadshow trucks rolled in. I had had my revenge.

Whipping up the crowd on the Roadshow roof.

Now, in the daylight, I was being driven back to the site in a police car to fulfil a childhood dream. As I was introduced to the 25,000-strong crowd, I could barely speak. What was happening to me was sinking in. How was this possible? How had this dream come true? All I could say was, 'My God,' before emotion made me turn away temporarily. My folks were there. I played my games in the warm-up. One of the games featured speed-drinking. Three blokes were brought onstage, all thinking they were going to get a free pint of beer, but by the end of the game they were drinking a pint of Coke through each other's socks. I matchmade a couple and made sure they stayed together by tearing a tenner in half and giving them half each. The day had started off a bit drizzly, but as the clock ticked towards 11 a.m., the sun started to break through. Amazingly, it's all on YouTube.

A VERY proud moment: Mum and Dad on stage at the Newquay Roadshow.

And then, it was eleven o'clock. The 'pips' pipped, the jingle played and Adrian Juste's voice boomed over the crowd.

'Today, the final summer roadshow, from the Headland Hotel lawn, North Fistral beach, Newquay with . . . Phillip Schofield!'

The cheer seemed to last for hours. I tried to speak, but the emotion was caught in my throat. The first song was Craig McLachlan's 'Mona'. I danced with the crowd. Everywhere I went, they screamed. Jason Donovan arrived in a Sea King helicopter. I put my brother on the radio to play 'Bits and Pieces', the guess-the-song game. It was the best moment of my life.

I looked into the front row, and there I was, looking back. Eleven years old and smiling. 'You did it.'

That was it, then: the final tick was ticked. Anything that happened from here was a bonus.

Then Andrew Lloyd Webber called.

6

One weekend, soon after the roadshow, I travelled back to Cornwall to do something else that no member of the Schofield family had ever done: I bought a brand-new car. Every car that I or anyone in my family had ever owned had been second-hand. On the forecourt of the garage, my dad put his arm around me and said how proud he was. My black XR3i was knackered with all the miles it had been asked to travel, so I'd decided that I'd buy a brand-new Volvo 480. It wasn't a sports car, so the insurance wasn't prohibitive, but it did have pop-up headlights, which looked cool. It was the worst car I have ever owned. In fact, the first one died very quickly so they swapped it and I got another one. It was just as bad. I was constantly talking about it and how it had gone wrong again, so much so that my mates said that if I ever sold it I would lose half of my conversation. One of the headlights regularly refused to come up so I often drove through London with a winking car.

I was filming *The Movie Game* in Milton Keynes. I never understood why we shot it there, in the Open University studios. The camera crew were very old and kept nodding off. We had to retake a link because one of the cameramen yawned so loudly. Anyway, in the car park, before setting off for home, was the first time the car caught fire, which it did on a number of occasions. The final straw was as I drove past the Royal Albert Hall. I pulled over the heater slider and the entire unit fell out of the dashboard and on to my feet, jamming my leg on the accelerator. I was out of control for about ten seconds on Kensington Gore. That was it. The car had to go before it killed me. Thankfully, I wasn't going to need it because I was about to record a series of programmes around Europe, but my schedule was going to end up making me cry!

On top of all the other shows I was doing at the time, in 1991, *Schofield's Europe* sent me to an amazing set of destinations. When it was announced that I would be doing it, I got a very sweet note from Alan Whicker (the presenter of *Whicker's World*, which had run for a groundbreaking thirty years). He said he was prepared to lend me Europe if I let him keep the world. I met witches in Barcelona, filmed in the cathedral-like sewers under Vienna and had a naked sauna in Finland with the rally driver Ari Vatanen. That day of filming required an enormous amount of trust in Chris, the director, and our cameraman and, as a result, I let them show my bum on telly. We filmed in Poland, Switzerland, Iceland, Greece – it was fascinating, but relentless. We did a week's filming, came back for a day, then went off again. And when I returned home at the end of the six weeks' filming, I had to immediately set off to record something for *Going Live*. It was too much.

I called Anthea Turner, who was going out with Peter at the time. She was the organizer of our group and then, as now, a fixer of domestic dilemmas.

'I don't have a single item of clean clothing and I have to go filming. I'm so tired and so hungry,' I sobbed.

Anthea jumped in her car with hot food and did my washing, as only she would.

Going Live continued to be a dream to work on. If Dawn French and Jennifer Saunders were filming next door in TC6, they would wander in wearing whatever costumes they had on and just mess around with us. In the course of working on the show, I had skydived from a plane with the Red

Devils and been met on the ground by a wing commander who bellowed into my ecstatic face, 'Now you know why the birds sing.' We had broadcast live from a train that had been evacuated by a bomb scare, and I was the only one who didn't know. I wondered why it was so quiet, and it was only the horrified face of the guard at the window that alerted me to the fact that I'd been left behind.

Judi Dench had come on the show after nearly pulling out the night before because she didn't think anyone would call in. It was the busiest our phone lines had ever been. I have always been Judi's greatest fan, and she is something of a fan of mine. I have a framed signed picture she sent me when I was in the Broom Cupboard which reads, 'From your most ardent admirer'. It's one of the few possessions I would save if the house burned down, along with my signed Katharine Hepburn picture – but that's for a bit later. Judi may be a fan, but I have yet to persuade her to sit on the *This Morning* sofa.

My idol . . . Dame Judi Dench.

Steph and I had been going out for a few months and were seeing more and more of each other. I suppose the one thing that is rare and commands a very high price in this industry is trust. I'd had friends who had been the subjects of 'kiss and tell' stories in the newspapers and it made me incredibly wary of trusting anyone. I knew I could trust my friends with my life. I've always said I could win 200 million quid on the lottery and trust them to go and pick the money up for me, but trusting my love to someone was new, especially now I was quite well known. It was obvious, though, that Steph was the one to trust with my heart. It helped that we were in the same industry and shared the same friends. It also helped that we were falling in love. I loved her voice and her blue eyes, her blonde hair and . . . if I'm honest, she had, and indeed still has, great boobs. I felt utterly comfortable with her and totally safe, and my friends adored her.

I continued the tactic of staying out of central London, and we ate our way up and down Chiswick High Street under the protection of the local restaurateurs: Barry in Haweli if we fancied a curry, Jack in Sabai Sabai if we went for Thai . . . it's safe to say I didn't cook very much.

By the time the next series of *Schofield's Europe* came round I asked Steph if she would like to house-sit for me. She was living with her lovely sister, Georgina, in White City, so it would give both of them space. The house on Netheravon Road had four bedrooms and a lovely kitchen and garden. It would be perfect for her and she could keep an eye on it for me.

I returned from filming slightly less stressed than after the last series. Steph thanked me for the use of the house; she had loved being there. We went out for dinner, and the next day she began to pack her little Fiat Panda with her belongings. As she closed the hatchback and prepared to leave, I was standing on the front doorstep, watching. As well as watching, I was also thinking – thinking about us, about how much fun it was being together, thinking that I loved her in every way. She was beautiful that day and has been every day since. I was captivated by her dancing blue eyes (I'm definitely an eye man) and melting smile. We clicked on every level – tastes, humour, interests. Yup, I'd fallen deeply in love, and she was so small and so damned cute.

'Don't go,' I said from the step.

'What?'

'Don't go. Unpack the car and stay.'

'Okay.'

I'm eternally thankful that she did.

At the time, she was having a nightmare with her bank manager, a very unsympathetic man indeed. She was waiting to be paid, but he was giving her a hard time and was sarcastic to boot. She explained that in a couple of days there would be more in her account; he 'hoped there would be'.

I think it was his tone that got my back up. It was time to teach him a lesson.

I transferred every pound I had in the bank into her account. Steph phoned him to check it was there. He was 'delighted' and spluttered his 'surprise'. 'Good,' said Steph. 'If you had been more courteous, I might have kept my account with you. A bank should be there in good times and bad. I shall now be closing my account.' Which she promptly did, even though he tried so hard to backtrack. She opened another account elsewhere and gave me my money back.

Matt Goss was going out with Melanie Sykes at the time and the four of us would occasionally meet up for dinner. Matt would also pop over to the house for a chat once in a while. I always knew when he was arriving. I'd hear his car parking, followed by about another ten cars arriving in the street. Matt couldn't go anywhere without his convoy of fans behind him. I always figured it must drive him mad until, one day, he arrived and was a bit flustered. He came into the house as his posse parked up. They were always very polite in the street.

'You okay?' I asked.

'Yeah,' said Matt. 'Just had a nightmare on the Hogarth Roundabout.'

'Oh! What happened?'

'I lost the bloody fans. Had to drive round three times until they caught up.'

One of the magazines I loved being interviewed for was *Smash Hits*. It was always a bit random and bonkers, but great fun. They decided to launch a big awards show to be shown live on BBC1, and I'd been asked to host. The *Smash Hits* Poll Winners Party had arrived and it was just as random and bonkers as the magazine.

Each year, there was a different theme. One year, it was 'underwater', and Janet Street Porter was producing. I arrived in the morning to rehearse. The show that year was sponsored by Skittles sweets. Onstage was a huge submarine painted in the Skittles rainbow. The PR company executive employed to promote Skittles was overjoyed – he couldn't believe what he was about to get away with on national television. He phoned the head of the company and told him he should watch the show for a great surprise. His job done for the day, he left the arena. Janet Street Porter arrived.

'What the fuck is that?!' she said.

'It's the Skittles submarine.'

She weighed up the advertising issues an enormous, branded submarine would throw up and after a moment's thought picked a colour.

'Paint it red, *now*.'

Another year had an Indiana Jones theme, so I was dressed

as Indy. Two of our mates were dressed in suits of armour behind me. Carter the Unstoppable Sex Machine were on the bill. The show was over-running and Janet was scything through the running order in the truck out the back. She said she was going to start fading tracks out, but that was really going to piss off the artists. Funnily enough, I asked her not to fade Carter because it wasn't a long track to start with and I liked it. She faded it anyway. The band were rightly angry. Carter threw his mic stand and I watched it arc perilously through the air and skewer the ground between two girls who were dancing in the front row. I said, 'That was clever.'

Carter saw red and ran at me. To be honest, it was a brilliant rugby tackle. We both disappeared from frame. Janet must have been looking down and missed it because in my ear I heard her exclaim, 'Where the fuck has he gone?'

What made us all laugh as we watched it back were the two guys in the armour who were standing behind me. They both clanked forward to help me, then realized that neither of them could bend over so they were going to be of little help, so they both turned around and left me to it. One of them was Roger Wright, who went on to have his own very successful singing and acting career, including the lead in *The Lion King* in the West End.

Jason Donovan was appearing one year, and he told me he had a secret and I couldn't tell. I pride myself on being the very best secret-keeper. People have always confided in me and I would never betray a confidence. Okay, so what was the secret? He told me that he was going to be in a musical. It hadn't been totally signed off, but he was going to be Joseph in a new stage production.

'That's amazing,' I said. 'We did it at school, but my music teacher wouldn't let me be in it because he didn't think I had a good enough voice.'

It was soon announced that Jason would be appearing in Andrew Lloyd Webber's brand-new production of *Joseph and the Amazing Technicolour Dreamcoat*, directed by Stephen Pimlott, at the London Palladium. It sounded like a great idea. I'd definitely have to go to watch.

After *Joseph* had been running for a couple of weeks and after I'd heard how good it was, I bought tickets so that Steph and I could see what all the fuss was about.

Jason and I shared the same kind of fan base so when we arrived and took our seats it caused a bit of a stir. In the interval we were whisked out to a private room because it was getting a bit out of control, and at the end of the show we had to be fully rescued. The production was every bit as good as it had been made out to be. Stephen Pimlott's direction was brilliant. It was clever, very funny, colourful and short! The perfect night's entertainment – a real feel-good show. Everyone leaving the Palladium had a smile on their faces. I was really pleased for Jason: he was in a major West End hit. Whenever any friends came to town, we always took them to see *Joseph*. Though I thoroughly enjoyed watching West End shows, I had absolutely no thought, desire or ambition to actually be in one!

I got a royal seal of approval for *Going Live* that thrilled the team when, at a lunch, I was introduced to Princess Diana. I don't often get starstruck, but that was a big deal. She was absolutely beautiful, with stunning sapphire-blue eyes – yes, I'm definitely an eye man! She turned to me and smiled, and I thought I'd better tell her who I was.

'Your Royal Highness, I'm Phill—'

'I know who you are!' She laughed. 'You and Sarah keep me and the boys entertained every Saturday. We sit on the floor in our pjs and have breakfast. How's the Gopher?'

I never told Gordon. He would have been intolerable.

I may also be the only person to have said no to Margaret Thatcher and live.

I was asked to present some children's awards, I think at the Guildhall. As soon as I arrived I knew something was going on. There was extra security on the door, sniffer dogs checking the place out. Someone famous was obviously coming. I knew better than to ask, though. I'd be told in good time, and if I wasn't told, then I'd see them in the audience as I hosted the ceremony.

With about half an hour to go before the event started, one of the organizers came up to me and said, 'You may have spotted the extra security.'

'Yes, I did notice.'

'You should know who your co-host is today.'

'My co-host?! I thought it would be someone in the audience.'

'No, no, your co-host will be Margaret Thatcher.'

'Oh, right.'

I heard the police whistles outside as her car pulled up. The doors opened, and in she strode, handbag in hand. She took the seat beside me and said hello.

'Do you know what I'm expected to do?' the Prime Minister asked.

'How much do you *want* to do?' I asked. 'Do you want to share the links, read out the names?'

'I don't think so, do you?'

'Perhaps not. How about I actually start it, I read the names, you hand over the awards and then perhaps say something at the end?'

'Yes, that will be fine.'

It was time. After I'd introduced the event and thanked everyone for coming, including the Prime Minister, I read out the first name. It was a young and particularly accomplished

The Cabinet Room at No. 10 and a PM.

girl who had cerebral palsy. As I read out her name, the audience clapped and she stood and began to walk towards the stage. Her steps were very slow, but solid and unfaltering. We all waited for her to make her way to us.

'I'm going to go down and help her,' said the steely voice beside me.

'I don't think you should,' I said to Margaret Thatcher.

'She needs help.'

'No, she doesn't. She's doing fine.'

'I'm going to go down to meet her halfway.'

'No, don't!'

'What?' She turned to look at me with a smile that could have blinded a snake.

I stood my ground.

'This is her moment. She has won this award because of what she has overcome. A walk to this stage is the least she deserves. She's perfectly capable.'

Margaret Thatcher looked directly into my eyes. I thought I might turn to stone. She was thinking, and her eyes softened and she said, 'You're right. Thank you.'

My heart resumed its steady rhythm.

I was sitting in the kitchen of my house in Chiswick one day when the phone rang.

'Hi, mate,' said Russ. 'Bit of a weird one. I've just had a call from the Really Useful Group, asking if you can sing.'

'I dunno! I sing in the shower and in the car, but I have no idea if it's any good. Why do they want to know?'

'Well . . . Jason is taking six weeks off *Joseph* and they're wondering if you'd be interested.'

I burst out laughing.

'Russ, it's a wind-up. Phone the number back and see who picks up. It'll be a bloody sex hotline.'

He dialled the number back and heard a cheery 'Really Useful Group' at the end of his phone and hung up.

'Shit, mate, it's really them. What do you want to do?'

'I suppose we'd better meet up and find out if I can sing!'

Russ called them back. They were deadly serious. A meeting was set up. It was to be totally secret, and could I learn 'Any Dream Will Do'?

On Friday, 1 November 1991 I was in the *Going Live* production office on the twelfth floor of the East Tower. Sarah, Trev and Simon and I had all spent the morning messing around. In the afternoon, we'd wandered over to TC7 to run through anything we needed for the show the next day.

That lunchtime, I excused myself. I met Pete outside the building and he drove us the ten minutes it takes to get to the Lyric Theatre in Hammersmith. A door had been left open for us. We walked into the auditorium and waited. What the hell was I doing? Why was I even taking this seriously? Was

I really about to sing for Andrew Lloyd Webber? If it hadn't felt so surreal, I think I would have laughed, but my overriding emotion was confused disbelief. It was too soon to feel out of my depth, but the water was about to rise. Five minutes later, a guy who introduced himself as Paul arrived. He said he'd be playing piano for me and would I like to warm up. Warm up? What did that mean? A workout? A Jane Fonda-style exercise class? I obviously looked even more bemused, and he explained a vocal warm-up to me. I explained that I genuinely had no clue how to do one and Paul said we'd better leave it then.

Sir Andrew Lloyd Webber (the Lord came later) slipped in through the doorway. We all said our hellos. We had met once before on *Going Live* when he appeared as a guest. He wasn't mucking around and asked me to go onstage to sing.

'Where would you like me to stand?'

'In the middle might be a good idea,' came his voice from the darkness of the stalls.

I looked to the back of the theatre. Pete has always rubbed his hair when he's stressed, and he was vigorously rubbing his head now, as if trying to summon a genie that could help me.

I sang 'Any Dream Will Do', but I couldn't remember how to finish it. I went round and round a couple of times, Paul on the piano dutifully following me, until Lloyd Webber could take no more.

'Okay, thank you, you can stop,' he said, putting me out of my misery.

The clandestine meeting broke up, and everyone left suitable gaps before walking through the door, which had been left ajar. Pete and I left last. I closed the door behind me. What an utterly bizarre experience. We drove back to Television Centre and I carried on as though nothing had happened.

On Saturdays, when *Going Live* was on air, I usually got up at around 7 a.m. Work was only twenty minutes away so it was all nice and leisurely. I'd get up, get dressed, have a cuppa, pad around for a bit, then go and do a couple of hours of telly. At about 7.30 a.m. on this particular Saturday, I heard the tell-tale roar of Pete's Porsche in the road. He'd never driven over on a Saturday morning before. Why was he here? Surely there was no way he would give me bad news before I was about to go on TV. The rule was simple: you always got shit news as you came off. He walked up the path and I opened the front door.

'You got it.'

'Got what?'

'Mate, you're going to be bloody Joseph!'

'*What?*'

Not for one second did I think I would get the part. After the mediocre audition the day before, I'd moved on in my head. Now the entire world stopped for a moment as I absorbed this news.

What did this mean? How would I fit into the world of theatre? Oh God, I didn't know anything about it! I'd be a big pretender, they'd hate me. What if I cocked it up? The day before, I had auditioned out of simple curiosity and nothing more. The only 'theatre' I'd ever done were the annual school pantomimes. I had the first panicked 'What am I getting myself into?' moment. If I didn't feel out of my depth yesterday, at this moment the water was up to my very tight throat. I let out a kind of strangled 'sheeeeesh' as I leaned back against the open front door, staring into the sky.

'Bloody hell, Pete, this is *huge*.'

'Yes, it is, mate! It's massive. You're going to be on the stage of the bloody Palladium.'

The water rose to just beneath my nose. Should I stop this right now? Put an end to this madness before it got out of hand? Pete left and I ran upstairs to tell Steph what had just happened on the doorstep. As I had to leave for the studio, I woke her up and garbled the conversation I had just had. For someone awoken from a deep sleep, that must have been a particularly bizarre moment. By the time she had fully woken and come to the conclusion that she hadn't in fact been dreaming, I was on my way to *Going Live*. I fretted about it for the full show, not breathing a word to anyone in case I changed my mind and pulled out. That afternoon, back in Chiswick, as we sat in the kitchen drinking tea, Steph said something profoundly true: 'All you have to do is agree to take it to the next step. *They* will decide if you're shite.'

We continued to keep it under wraps. I went to meet Mike Dixon, the Musical Director for the show, in the Really Useful Group (RUG) offices for the first time. Mike, alongside so many people I was about to meet in this entirely alien world, would become a friend for life.

Mike asked me to sing.

'Okay. Not bad. We can work with this,' he said afterwards.

'Well, that sounds reasonably encouraging,' I replied.

'You'll be great.'

There was plenty of time, surely? It was the beginning of November and I wouldn't be onstage until January. I had two and a half months to learn an entirely new set of skills.

When I told my family, they were a little stunned but, as always, totally supportive. I think they always relied on the fact that I must know what I'm doing! My brother just burst out laughing, which was a very grounding, brotherly reaction. We were certainly not the Von Trapps and seldom sang with each other, unless we were singing along to a song on the radio.

A few days later, the press release was sent out. Now there was definitely no going back. Everybody knew.

Twice a week, I was sent to Mary Hammond in North

London for singing lessons. At the time, she assured me that what happened in those lessons was between us: every bum note stayed within those walls. She admitted years later that as soon as I left her house she was straight on the phone to Really Useful to tell them that I was going to be fine. Of course she was. I was naive to think that a singing unknown would be put onstage to front a multimillion-pound production with a million quids' worth of advance bookings and that someone wasn't going to reassure them that their money and reputation were safe. A few people I came into contact with were less enthusiastic. After one singing lesson with Mary, I climbed into the back of a black cab. We set off down Camden High Street and the driver looked in the mirror and did a double take. He then actually pulled over and stopped! He turned around to look at me. He had obviously read the announcement in the papers.

'What the actual fack are you doin', mate? You are so goin' to arse this right up!'

He roared with laughter, but when I got out he wouldn't take my money and thanked me for the laugh!

I was really self-conscious trying to learn the songs. I made Steph turn her back so she couldn't see me as I sang. She was so encouraging as we sat on the sitting-room floor in Netheravon Road. When I look back at moments like that, I can't help thinking how complicated our heads are. I can present in front of millions of people without a twitch, I can make up an instant speech off the cuff in front of Royalty and actually enjoy myself, but at that moment I was so embarrassed to sing out loud, sitting back to back with Steph. She kept reassuring me: 'You'll be fine, you have a lovely voice.'

It didn't help that I couldn't belt out the songs because I knew I'd annoy the neighbours, so one Saturday night I put the cassette that Mike Dixon had recorded for me in the car and set off down the M4. On my own, I could let rip with no embarrassment. I drove to Bristol, did a couple of circuits of the city centre and then drove back. Just enough time and distance to get it in my head. If I thought it would have taken longer, I would have driven to Wales! By the time I arrived back in Chiswick it was 3 a.m. and I knew every note, every song and all the colours of Joseph's coat.

I know there are actors who take on a role and, in a very thespian way say, 'Dahhhhhling, I haven't watched any other production or anyone else in the role. I want it to be authentic and pure, with no outside influences.' Well, *sod that*! I was constantly at the Palladium. I knew nothing of theatre life, and I didn't want any surprises. I learned the thrill of the backstage Tannoy calls:

'Ladies and gentleman, this is your half-hour call. Half an hour, please.' Then the quarter, and then, 'Ladies and gentleman, this is your Act I beginners call. Beginners to the stage, please.'

I got confused by that one and asked Jason if that was for show newbies. He laughed and explained it was everyone who should be there as the music started. It all seemed so polite and everyone was incredibly kind to me as I hovered backstage. I also wanted to watch everything, multiple times. Every night I'd see the show from a different vantage point, either in the wings or hidden in the auditorium. It was all sinking in. I knew myself well enough to understand that I *had* to have it absolutely committed to memory by the opening night, because I knew I would be galvanized with fear otherwise. I learned very quickly that there is a huge difference between the nerves at the start of a new TV show – nerves that I'm used to feeling – and the nerves before you launch yourself on to the stage of the London Palladium with absolutely no theatrical experience in front of 2,500 paying customers in a show with an unblemished track record. This was becoming terror on a scale I had never experienced before.

I hope Jason won't mind me saying that those weren't his most 'lucid' years. Onstage, he was triumphant every night. Offstage, slightly less so. We'd have lunch and, the next day, he wouldn't remember that we had. Or we'd get to the end of lunch and he'd say, 'I made sense today, didn't I, mate?' and we'd both burst out laughing. I think the correct and kindest phrase to use would be to say that for a fair proportion of the late eighties and early nineties Jason was 'chemically assisted'. He lived in Holland Park, just a couple of miles from my home in Chiswick. Each night after I'd been rehearsing and watching the show, I'd drive him home.

One night in January it was particularly cold. I had a convertible BMW 325i at the time and because of the soft-top, it got very cold inside. Jason finished the show, signed autographs at the stage door then jumped in the car. I'd been waiting for a few minutes and was warming it up. As I set off past Liberty's, Jason dozed off, as he tended to do. I was listening to the radio.

Suddenly, he woke with a start.

'Oh. Shit, mate, I'm so sorry. I think I've pissed myself,' he said.

'What the hell? How have you managed that?'

'I don't know, but my arse is warm.'

'Go back to sleep, ya twat, I've turned your seat heater on.'

JD was more open, honest and giving than he needed to be. He warned me that in Act II there was a moment by the giant corn one-armed bandit where the spotlights on you are turned off briefly as the corn spills out. It's the only time in the show that suddenly you can see the audience. The rest of the time, all you see is velvety, smoky blackness as you look out.

Jason warned me that at that second when the spots go

out it's such a shock to suddenly see 2,500 people on your opening night. The first time, he jumped and nearly swore.

Also in a moment of extreme openness, Jason told me how much he was paid each week.

My jaw hit the deck. This was 1992, and these figures were the equivalent of footballers' wages. It was an astonishing piece of information. I passed it on to Daz, who had started work on my contract. He was, as ever, firm but persuasive, and negotiated the same fee for me. I told you earlier how I retired my dad and bought him his dream Hasselblad camera. Now you know how.

My dad was, as usual, doing some DIY in the Chiswick house for me. He, Mum and I were chatting. I was in the bedroom; they were in the bathroom. All their lives they had put me and Tim first. They had gone without things so that we could have them. We had both had perfect lives because of them. I couldn't have been more grateful for the net of safety, support and love that they always had ready in case I needed to fall into it, and it was my turn to repay that. My dad was saying that he had a big job coming up and that he was knackered. The timing was perfect.

'Don't accept the job.'

'I have to accept it, we can't afford not to.'

'Yes, you can. As of this moment, you are retired. I'm paying your wages from now on and always will.'

Their faces were a picture. It was a nice feeling to be able to do it for them, but then I said, 'But please finish painting my bathroom before you down tools.'

Even though I lost my dad in 2008, I still keep my promise to Mum.

My opening night was getting closer and I had hit a minor snag. I can't dance for shite! I spent my days with Assistant Director Nichola Treherne, who was teaching me the part, and occasionally Anthony Van Laast, the choreographer, would pop in. It became obvious pretty quickly that if a singer, dancer and actor was a 'triple threat', it was quite apparent that I was only ever going to manage a double threat at best. At the end of Act I, I had to walk across the stage, and the moves were a simple 'step, clap, step, clap'. On my opening night, they both presented me with a leather keyring that said 'step, clap, step, shit!'

I'd started having regular anxiety dreams. I'd wake up sweating in the night, having just dreamt that I was standing on the stage of the Palladium in front of 2,500 people and, when I opened my mouth, nothing came out. Some nights I dreamt I'd forgotten the words, and one night I dreamt I was naked!

The big day finally dawned on Monday, 13 January 1992. I was about to be the lead in a West End musical, just about the last direction I had ever expected my career to take. There were a few moments during the day that I just stopped to think where I was. It was all quite difficult to process. At about

My name in lights . . . at the London Palladium!

midday, I understood what I was thinking: it was grown-up! I had the reputation of the show, the cast, the theatre and Andrew Lloyd Webber in my hands – the responsibility was very bloody adult. I think the word to describe it would be 'exposed'. On TV, if something goes wrong, it's seldom a calamity. I try to seamlessly cover it up, or my usual reaction, if it's appropriate, is to point out the mistake so that the viewers feel involved and included. That tactic would *not* be available to me here! If I screwed up on my opening night, there would be no covering it up and no laughter to be had.

Thankfully, any worry or concern that I had about being seen as an imposter, proved to be totally unfounded. The West End, in its supportive entirety, was achingly wonderful. All the other shows sent huge bouquets of flowers – *Cats*, *The Phantom of the Opera*, *Blood Brothers*, *Miss Saigon*, *Les Mis*, *The Mousetrap*. The cards attached to them said things like 'Welcome to your new West End family,' and 'We're all cheering you on.' The office had to go out and buy monster vases to accommodate them all.

Inside the Palladium, the atmosphere was equally supportive and loving. Linzi Hateley was the super-talented narrator, and I was in awe of her and the entire company.

It had been decided to give Piers Morgan preferential treatment, as he had been very supportive of James Grant and its stable of artists. If he was allowed in to watch the dress rehearsal, he would have the steal on everyone else and could write his review for the *Sun*. In the afternoon, I did my first full run: costume, wig, make-up, full cast, company and full orchestra. To sing with a live orchestra is one of life's great experiences: full-on spine-tingling goosebumps. Piers was sitting in the auditorium. He and I have had a couple of bumps in our friendship over the years, but the review he wrote that day for me was immensely kind.

It was 7 p.m. 'Ladies and gentlemen, this is your half-hour call. Thirty minutes, please.'

I could hear the bustle of the auditorium filling up as I sat waiting in my dressing room for the evening performance. This hallowed space had been home to some of the biggest showbiz names on the planet. The dressing room had two areas, a sitting room complete with a coffee table made by Ronnie Barker and an area with the full-on lights-round-the-mirror vibe. There was a jacuzzi in the bathroom which I'm sure, if you turned it on, bits of Tommy Steele would come out. The rooms were full of the heady scent of flowers and there were cards by the hundred. Steph and my family had taken their seats. Pete, Russ, Paul and Daz had done the same. Pete was a nervous wreck – there was a lot of hair-rubbing going on. All my friends were in their seats. If I did indeed arse it up, as the cab driver had suggested, I didn't know how I'd ever recover from it. To mix metaphors, I had stuck my head above the parapet and I risked being holed below the waterline.

Before or since that night I have never felt that level of fear. Shaking hands, dry mouth, rapid heartbeat. This wasn't fear, this was full-on fight-or-flight terror! Why? Because I wasn't in front of the glassy black eye of a camera, I was in front of 2,500 real human eyes – 5,000 if you count both eyes – right in front of me, watching, appraising, and what's more, the bodies that those eyes lived in had paid £27.50 for a ticket.

The cast, the crew, the band were popping their heads through the open door. 'Break a leg, Phil.'

'Ladies and gentlemen, this is your fifteen-minute call. You have fifteen minutes, please.'

Jason's dresser, Tina, had stayed to look after me, and she was doing a good job of preventing me opening the secret back door from the dressing room and bolting down Great Marlborough Street.

'Ladies and gentlemen, this is your Act I beginners call. Act I beginners to the stage, please.'

I looked at Tina with unblinking, scared eyes. She smiled and said, 'You'll be fine, you know it back to front. Just sing the right words, in the right order and in tune. Oh, and try to stand in the right place. That's all you need to do tonight.'

'Yeah, okay, right,' I mumbled.

We walked out of the dressing room and down the 'donkey run', the large corridor that led from big double doors at one end; that opened on to Great Marlborough Street, directly to the wings of the stage at the other end. If indeed you needed a donkey, that's how you'd get it to the stage. It was rumoured that during his run in *The King and I* Yul Brynner was so vile to the company, as he walked down the donkey run barefoot he was very likely to stand on a tack or two that had been 'clumsily dropped'.

At the end of the donkey run, on the left-hand side, is a huge and very famous mirror. I looked into it and checked myself before I turned and walked into the darkness of the stage, as had been done by so many before me: Bing Crosby, Bob Hope, Judy Garland, Danny Kaye, Nat King Cole, Shirley Bassey, Sammy Davis Jr. I walked on to the stage of the most famous variety theatre in the world, my head screaming, *'Pretender!'*

The prologue music had started on the other side of the curtain, and the stage manager walked over to me with a small torch, which she shone through the swirling dry ice so I could see the circular, dinner-plate-sized break in the yellow carpet of the stage. I stood in the centre of the circle, she tapped my shoulder and said, 'Enjoy it.' Then she spoke into her mic and the hydraulic lift I was standing on rose fifteen feet into the air. I couldn't run for it now, even if I wanted to. I was totally alone, elevated above the stage in the darkness with dry ice swirling beneath me. My legs were shaking uncontrollably. Linzi Hateley had started to sing. I was moments away. I looked high up into the flies, where the scenery hangs before it drops in. There was a spotlight that had been dimmed down so it was only a faded ivory disc, and the operator leaned forward and put her hand in front of it. The last thing I saw before the curtain lifted was a thumbs-up on that faded disc.

'. . . In the story of a boy whose dream came true, and he could be . . . you,' sang Linzi.

'Any Dream Will Do' began, the curtain flew out, I was blinded by multiple spotlights pointing at me. The hydraulic lift travelled forwards and down, carrying me through the swirling mist to set me and my cowboy boots gently on to the yellow stage. I was sure most of the auditorium were desperately on my side, but there were certainly a few who would delight in saying that they were there the day Phillip Schofield arsed it up on the stage of the London Palladium.

Just get the words right, just get the words right, big . . . deep . . . breath . . . and . . .

'I closed my eyes, drew back the curtain.'

That first show flew past. There was no time to really enjoy anything; I just had to get the mechanics right on this show. There would be time to enjoy and fine-tune in the next six weeks. I stood in the right place, I sang the right words at the right time in the correct key. I thought: *I may very well get away with this.*

In the interval, ALW sent back one scribbled word on a torn-out bit of paper: 'Superstar.' The relief washed over me like the giant Cribbar surfing wave in Newquay.

Act II started. Here was the moment Jason had warned

me about. My spotlight went out and there, suddenly, was every face in the auditorium. I was so grateful he'd told me. I looked up to the front of the dress circle. There were Steph and my family, and they looked happy, certainly not hideously embarrassed. The spotlight burst back into life and they were gone.

If you saw the show in the West End, you'll know that at the end Joseph is once again lifted on a hydraulic lift, this time, at the front of the stage. I ran to it, two of the brothers made sure the safety clips were fastened and up I went, over the heads of those in the stalls, up to the dress circle, huge rainbow coat spread out behind me. I stopped and looked into the eyes of my family. They had tears streaming down their faces, my dad was punching the air and shouting, 'Yes!' That is a moment I can remember with total clarity, seeing their beaming, proud faces, and their tears of joy were all the reassurance I needed that the biggest gamble of my career had paid off.

As the last note was sung, the audience leapt to their feet: I was getting my first-ever standing ovation. I could feel the tears stinging my eyes as I fought to keep them in. All the anxiety I had felt evaporated. Someone told me that the ovation went on for minute after minute. I was lost in the moment and have no idea.

As the curtain came down, the wonderful cast lifted me on to their shoulders. Joseph's brothers really did feel like my brothers. We laughed, we cheered. The next time I faced a TV camera wouldn't be from behind a curtain of shame and embarrassment, after all. It's hard to explain how I felt at that moment. Definitely elated, pumped with adrenaline, massively relieved. I was proud that I didn't think I'd let anyone down, and I think I was also stunned that the audience had actually stood up. I hadn't even considered that reaction. I had

My last ever Joseph performance.

debuted on the stage of the Palladium and I hadn't made a tit of myself. I quietly thought, 'Up yours!' to the taxi driver.

There was a party afterwards in the Langham Hotel, opposite Broadcasting House, where the BBC club had been when I was seventeen. Sarah Greene and her hubby, Mike Smith, said they would take me to the party, but they had one thing they wanted to do with me first. I got into the car and, instead of turning right up Regent Street, Mike turned left. Through Piccadilly Circus, down to Trafalgar Square, past Downing Street to Parliament Square, then, turning left on to Westminster Bridge, he stopped halfway across. Even in 1992 you weren't allowed to stop on the bridge. I asked why we were here.

Mike and Sarah had been in a horrific helicopter crash during a series of *Going Live*. They were outrageously lucky to

Backstage after my opening night with Mike Smith and Sarah Greene.

survive. As a show and, as friends, we had waited daily for the updates by phone to see if they were going to be okay. Although suffering terrible injuries, they pulled through. Mike and Sarah then told me why we were on the bridge. When they were well enough to drive after the crash, they stopped on Westminster Bridge at about ten at night. There was the city stretching out in all its glorious 360-degree detail. In front, the Festival Hall, the River Thames flowing past the ITV Southbank Tower and down to St Paul's Cathedral. Beyond that, the skyscrapers of the financial heart of the City. Behind them, Big Ben and Parliament. The lights of the city reflected on the inky water. They wanted to scream that they were alive, and so they did, from Westminster Bridge.

Mike put his hands on my shoulders and looked me in the eyes.

'You will never have a moment like this again in your life. Nothing will come close to this moment. Tonight, the city is yours. Shout it out at the top of your voice.' And so we did – we bellowed to the city. The moment was mine.

And then the police car screamed to a stop beside us, blue lights flashing. Two policemen got out and walked sternly towards us.

'You *know* you are not allowed to stop on the bridge, so will you *immediately* . . .'

He saw me.

'Christ! It's you, Phillip. How did it go tonight?'

The papers were kind, though some felt my legs were too skinny, which I couldn't disagree with. I had actually joined a gym a couple of streets behind me in Chiswick. I went exactly once. I got the personal trainer to write me up an exercise regime, saying I wanted to concentrate on my Twiglet legs. We worked through weights and squats and crunches. He then set me up on the running machine and told me to do about twenty minutes. I was watching MTV on the telly in front of me and I was starting to sweat. The more sweaty my head got, the more my glasses slipped down my face. I had to keep pushing them up my nose and, momentarily, my coordination failed me. As Lyndon B. Johnson said of Gerald Ford, 'He can't fart and chew gum at the same time.' So, it transpires, I can't run and push my glasses up my nose at the same time! I shot off the back of the running machine and found myself upside down with my feet up the wall. The humiliation of the gym bunnies running to help me was too much. I left and didn't return. I still have Twiglet legs.

Those six weeks at the London Palladium were so much fun. I found out that I very much liked being part of a theatrical team. This was different to the teams in TV and radio. Eight shows a week, relying on each other onstage, singing together, in each other's dressing rooms in the interval, howling with laughter. That's the thing I remember the most – absolute and total helpless laughter, when your laugh goes up to a gear you hardly ever reach. Patrick Clancy was the baker, and one of the funniest guys I've ever met. He could get me into such a state of helpless laughter that I had to try very hard in the second act not to cough because of the damage he'd done to my respiratory system.

Once, during a Wednesday matinee, I got Joseph's two premonition dreams mixed up. My mind went racing forward: was I going to be able to make it fit? No, they were different lengths; it was going to come apart and I was powerless to stop it. I was standing, hands on hips, resplendent in golden crown and golden Timberlands. I was all-powerful, I was regal. I was also about to go down in flames! As I ran out of words, the brothers were all in a semicircle in front of me, grovelling, foreheads on the stage. What should have been 'How do I know where you come from?' . . .

Turned into: 'You . . . who are you?'

Nic Colicos, who played Reuben, shouted into the carpet, 'Tim Rice!'

I don't think that anyone who had paid very good money that day to watch the show would have noticed, but the brothers, Joe included, spent the show with shaking shoulders and wet eyes.

I also learned a very big physics lesson. In the second act, Joseph has to become regal, so in the wings I painted two green, Egyptian-style decorations on my eyes. One day I left the lid off the make-up and it dried out; I'd have to get some more. Tina ran out to Boots. When she came back she apologized. They didn't have green, I'd have to use blue. I didn't

236

see that would be a problem. I put it in position by the mirror at the side of the stage for when I needed it. At the appointed time, I ran into the wings, changed costume and then applied the make-up.

At the side of pretty much all stages, the lighting is blue. It's the least intrusive for the audience should they catch a glimpse of backstage. I started to apply the eye make-up in the mirror. It wasn't working – none of it was coming out. I tried and tried, but nothing was happening and time was running out. I'd gone beyond delicacy. I was desperately trying everything. I gave up and went back onstage. Here was my physics lesson. Blue make-up under a blue light is invisible, which is probably why it was green in the first place.

As the curtain lifted and I stood before the brothers, who were all ranged before me, there was pandemonium. This professional group of highly talented singers, actors and dancers completely fell apart. They were literally crying with laughter. Some couldn't even sing. I had no idea what the matter was. As they attempted to pull themselves together I could see Mike Dixon in hysterics as he conducted in the orchestra pit. They were obviously laughing at me. I felt on edge: was there a costume malfunction? Only as one of them ran past me and was able to say, 'Well, hello, Barbara Cartland,' did the penny drop. Every bit of blue make-up that I had applied and thought invisible was *very* visible onstage. What the brothers saw as the curtain lifted was a face that resembled a small child's when they have got hold of their mother's make-up bag. All around my eyes was completely blue; there were huge smears that covered my eyebrows, went to my ears, over my cheeks and on to my forehead. We all went to the pub afterwards and our sides ached for days.

Linzi Hateley and I discovered that we were both hopeless gigglers. It got to the point where we could barely look at each other in the final song because we knew we were going to laugh. One afternoon, the company manager called us both into his office and told us, thankfully while smiling, that we had to behave ourselves and that we weren't to laugh any more. People had paid good money and it was not professional that, on a regular basis, neither of us was capable of singing the final note. We both apologized and promised to do better. That evening as we came together at the end of the show to sing, neither of us was looking at the other. We looked past each other's heads, over each other's shoulders and up into the lights. On the last note, Linzi figured that it was safe to look into Joseph's eyes because we had been so well behaved. As she looked at me, I slowly closed my eyes. I had painted two big eyes on my eyelids. She fell apart.

I didn't want it to end. I had discovered something new and unexpected – a love of the camaraderie of theatre. I know of one 'stage star' who, when introduced to her new company, said, 'Don't bother with names, I won't need them.' I always thought what a terrible shame, she will spend her days alone in her dressing room, rather than throwing her head back in uncontrollable mirth.

On 23 February, my six weeks were up. I had laughed myself senseless, I had made new friends, and also, I knew I wanted to do more. Eventually, that wish would nearly destroy my TV career.

There had been one casualty during my six weeks onstage at the Palladium. Because I was onstage on Thursday evenings and Sundays had been my only day off, I had to make the unbearable decision to give up Radio 1. Something had to go, and I was distraught that it had to be radio. Before I left, I had a few weeks on the breakfast show, filling in for Simon Mayo when he went on holiday. Breakfast-show timings do not suit my body clock. Getting up at 4.30 a.m. proved to me that I didn't want to do it full time. One morning I was so tired that as I passed Stamford Brook Tube station and got to the right-hand turn on the Goldhawk Road, my hands slipped off the steering wheel and I thought, I literally can't be arsed to steer. Obviously, I did, but I realized that theatre suited my body clock perfectly. Get up whenever you want, work in the afternoon and evening and stay up late. Ever since I was a kid, I had hated going to bed early. The clocks changing in the spring were torture to me – I was sent to bed and it was still light?! I think that's when my FOMO (fear of missing out) started. I can't stand going to bed and missing out, and theatre was my perfect timetable. Which is funny when you think about it, considering I've spent the last eighteen years getting up at 5.30 a.m.

Sarah and I were also beginning to wonder if six years of *Going Live* were perhaps enough. We both wanted to be sure that we left at the peak, and we agreed that if one of us went, both of us would go. The show was still riding high. Anna Home, the Head of Children's, would still phone Chris and ask, 'Is there any possibility you could actually aim this show at children?' Among our team, we had no intention of doing that. It was the secret of all the BBC's Saturday-morning shows: make them for the family so everyone can watch; don't alienate anyone. It was also extraordinary how many restaurateurs watched. Sarah and I could always get a table in any restaurant.

The decision over when to call time on *Going Live* would have to wait, though. I had a party to host. I love fireworks. One thing better than watching other people set off their fireworks is setting off your own. It had become a tradition that I would host the bonfire-night party. The bonfire was always too big for the garden, and so were the fireworks! The house was rammed with all our friends, and this was the moment that Chris Bellinger drank overproof rum and, as he chatted to me with his back to the wall, began to slide down it. Andy Crane was out in the garden when I set off the fireworks. At the precise moment I lit a Catherine wheel and set fire to the fence, I also set fire to Andy. Thankfully, we put him out. Andy also went on to drink more overproof rum than is sensible.

When I woke up the next morning I looked into the spare bedroom. There was a mass of forgotten coats that would have to be returned. As I sorted through them, I yelped as I uncovered a pale and lifeless face. Oh shit, I've killed Andy Crane! Mercifully, that wasn't the case and, after a couple of cups of strong coffee, Andy was well enough to leave.

After another night, gathered around Midge Ure's kitchen table drinking Jack Daniels, the decision was made. This would be our last series of *Going Live*. At the time, Midge was married to Annabel Giles, who was one of the faces of Saturday mornings. Many of the wrongs of the world were put right around that kitchen table in their beautiful house by the river. Sadly, I could never remember the decisions we had made to actually make the world a better place. I'm pretty sure it involved pledging not to drink so much Jack Daniels.

Another consideration in my decision to leave *Going Live* was that Jason Donovan had decided his time as Joseph was over. My six weeks had gone well, so I was asked if I'd like to take on the role full time. There was no hesitation in my answer. On 23 May 1992, I became Joseph again, first at the London Palladium and then on the nationwide tour. I would go on to do 1,147 performances.

7

Life with Steph was enormous fun. We continued to eat our way up and down Chiswick High Street. We'd been on holiday to Thailand, the first of many holidays in our lives as we explored the world together. We were complete soulmates, and inseparable. Steph had also discovered a foolproof way to my heart: her ginger puddings are the best I've ever tasted. In fact, a few weeks ago, along with my girls, she made them for me again for my birthday. Still just as good. My family adored her, and there was no question I had fallen very much in love. From those days until now we have shared everything, and no man could be loved more than Steph loves me.

Steph has said in her own words that she was born to be a mum, and that is certainly true. As well as all her other accomplishments, our two girls couldn't have hoped for a better mum. She literally never puts a foot wrong, whereas I'm always the one apologizing and saying, 'Sorry, I could have handled that better.' However, at first it seemed that being a mother might cruelly elude her. Her doctor had said that having children may not be that straightforward. He said, 'Are you with the man you want to marry? If not, get rid of him and find Mr Right, because time is running out.' Thankfully, she stuck with me. If having children was going to prove difficult, then we'd better start trying even harder. In one of the greatest miracles of our lives, Molly proved remarkably easy to make.

I had found exactly the ring I wanted on Bond Street. Every year, I made an advent calendar for Steph, little boxes filled with bath oils or chocolates. In the box for 11 December (Steph's mum Gill's birthday) was the ring. As she opened the box and found the ring, I leapt starkers from our bed and proposed. We kept it mostly among our family and friends until, on *Going Live* the next day, Des O'Connor let the cat out of the bag. But we were happy he had.

I had been a guest at Sarah and Mike's wedding and, though it was a really beautiful day, the behaviour of the newspaper paparazzi was pretty intrusive. I watched as they got in everyone's faces and, as the married couple left, the paps were bouncing off the car. I vowed in my head that, on my wedding day, I wouldn't let that happen.

Organizing our wedding was a top-secret affair. I was onstage every night as Joseph, so timing was difficult. Marriage laws in England at the time prohibited weddings outside of a church, and I also knew a church would be a pap fiasco. We looked at flying somewhere romantic in Europe, but most countries required that the couple live there for a

My stag night.

week before the wedding, and I couldn't take that amount of time off. I looked into the laws in the wider UK. Scotland seemed to fit the bill – a plane ride away, and we didn't have to get married in a church. That might work! We set about looking for a castle. Russ found Ackergill Tower near Wick in Caithness. It looked perfect. Steph and Russ flew up secretly to check it out. It *was* perfect.

Saturday, 27 March was Steph's birthday. On that day in 1993 she and our immediate families and three of our best friends travelled in a coach to Luton airport. I had two shows at the Palladium, and Russ came to pick me up afterwards and we set off for Luton. We all met up at the airport and boarded a private plane I had chartered to carry us north to Scotland. A couple of hours later we were being picked up by a fleet of Land Rovers that pulled up next to the plane on the tarmac and we were driven the short distance to Ackergill. The driveway was lit by flaming torches, and the sound of bagpipes drifted across the lawn. The tower was built in the early sixteenth century and had a rich history, and we all fell instantly in love with it and its staff. It sits on the coast of Sinclair's Bay and its seaward wall drops straight down to the rocky shore.

The atmosphere at Ackergill was homely and informal, yet it was also sumptuous and grand. By the end of our stay, no one could find where they'd kicked off their shoes. We met the vicar, who was jovial and very easygoing. We would get married in front of the huge fireplace in the great hall and a harpist would play throughout.

Because of limited space, both on the plane and in the tower, our numbers were small. I had my mum, dad and brother, along with Pete, Russ and Paul. Steph had her mum and dad and her brother, Tim, her sister, George, and her best friends, two called Alison and one called Candy. Steph

On the way to Ackergill to get not-so-secretly married.

had gone to school with Candy at the age of nine and still works alongside her now.

Back in London, the only indication that anything was different at the London Palladium was a sign placed by the box office explaining that I wouldn't be appearing on Monday, 29 March due to 'filming commitments'.

However, some secrets are impossible to keep for long.

'Phil, there are photographers and journalists at the gate.'

Ah well, it didn't matter. The castle had been impregnable in battle over the centuries so I was pretty sure we'd be okay. It was cold and windy outside, not the best 'stake-out' conditions.

They tried everything to get in, but the staff were unbribable, the castle was locked down. I felt sorry for the paps and journalists shivering by the walls on the rocky shore so I sent down a bottle of whisky and some glasses. The Old Pulteney distillery is just up the road in Wick, and every time I see their whisky or drink it, it brings back a flood of lovely memories from very happy times.

One of the journalists said to Russ, 'If you don't tell us who is in there or what's going on, we'll just have to imagine.' Nothing was said to them, so their imaginations ran riot.

Apparently, I got married in a kilt, which didn't go down well among the Scots. I actually wore a blue suit. Noel Edmonds arrived by helicopter; Mike Smith and Sarah Greene were there, alongside Jason Donovan and others. Andrew Lloyd Webber also jetted in. It was hilarious to read their inventions. The reality was much lower key.

Steph was absolutely beautiful as she walked through the door to the great hall in her wedding dress. My heart melted. My mum made a speech, but was sobbing with such emotion,

'You may now kiss the bride.'

Mum, Dad, Stephie and I.

to this day I have no idea what she said. Steph's sister, George, was more coherent with a beautiful poem, and her brother, Tim, videoed the day so he ended up watching the entire ceremony in black and white on a tiny viewfinder! My brother was best man and photographer, and the harpist was so engrossed by the proceedings she forgot to play.

We went back to Ackergill a number of times in the coming years, filling it with family and friends. It was a very happy place. It has changed hands a couple of times over the years, but last year it was apparently sold to a millionaire as a holiday home. I was very sad to hear that.

It was a truly magical weekend, but we did lose a couple of friends, because they didn't understand why they hadn't been invited (after all, Jason Donovan was there and they weren't, if the papers were to be believed!). We both wanted to celebrate with a much wider group of friends and family so, two weeks later, Steph's mum and dad, my wonderful in-laws

John and Gill, held a huge reception on their lawn. Everyone could come to this one, and it was a joyous occasion. My nan got drunk on whisky and, as we left for our one-day honeymoon at Cliveden, I leaned down to give her a kiss.

'We're off now, Nan.'

'Oh, piss off.'

Such a charmer.

Another of my nan's perfectly placed and cruel putdowns involved a photo for *Woman's Weekly*. I was asked if I'd like to be on the front cover with my mum for the Mother's Day edition. We both agreed – it was a great idea. The photoshoot was lovely. They pampered Mum, full-on professional make-up and hair – she was having a ball. The selected photo was a beauty. Mum looked stunning.

Every Wednesday in Newquay, my mum would meet up with my nan for a coffee and to shop. The magazine was out,

The controversial cover. Nan: 'Well, it's a nice one of our Phillip.'

247

and obviously Mum couldn't wait to see it on the newsagent's shelves. They walked in, and there it was. Mum was thrilled. She looked at her mother and asked, 'What do you think of the picture?'

After a few seconds of appraisal, my nan replied, 'Well, it's a good one of our Phillip.'

Over the years, we'd had some pretty mad conversations in the office. I walked in one afternoon and Russ said:

'You'll never believe who just called.'

'Who?'

'Guess.'

'No, tell me.'

'Madame Tussauds. They want to do a waxwork of you.'

'No way! I don't believe you.'

'It's true.'

It was.

Tussauds said that they wanted me to be in the *Joseph* white linens, wearing the cowboy boots and, over that, a Technicolour Dreamcoat. Could I please go to the offices above the exhibition galleries on Marylebone Road and could I please bring a pair of small shorts and the cowboy boots. Intriguing.

The staff were delightful. The office had been asked what sandwiches I liked. Tussauds had been informed that I was happy with anything but egg, but I particularly liked prawn. Every time I stepped through the door there were always gorgeous prawn sarnies.

I was shown upstairs to a light, airy room that looked out over Marylebone Road. A camera was set up on a tripod. In the middle of the floor was a circular revolve the size of a dinner plate, similar to the hydraulic lift on the Palladium stage, but this one didn't go up, it went around. Could I please go into the changing room and just put on the shorts and the cowboy boots? As I was getting undressed and re-dressed, I was beginning to think it might be another wind-up.

I stood on the dinner plate in the centre of the room in only tiny shorts and cowboy boots. An assistant stepped forward and began to place small blue dots all over me, on my face, down my legs, just above my nipples and on my stomach. The photographer took his place behind the camera and in his hand was a remote with two buttons.

'Okay, I need you to stand very still and keep looking forward.'

He took a picture, then pressed the button on the remote, and the dinner plate on which I was standing turned by a degree clockwise. He took another frame, pressed the button and I went round by another degree. Those of a certain age will know what I mean when I say that I felt like Windy Miller in *Camberwick Green* about to go down into the music box.

As I went slowly round, I caught a glimpse of my reflection in the office window. Almost naked, covered in blue dots, my Twiglet legs in cowboy boots. Oh, bloody hell, Noel had got me again.

Except he hadn't. It was totally above board and taken incredibly seriously. They didn't laugh when I asked if the Queen had gone around on the plate in just her bra and pants.

The most fascinating part of the experience was the eye department. Drawers and drawers of eyes. I had no idea they went to so much trouble. Past the blue eyes and the brown eyes to green and then hazel. The drawer was opened. Hazel with blue flecks, hazel with green flecks. 'Ah, here we are, hazel/gold flecks.' I was staring back at my eyes.

The waxwork was impressive. It stayed there in the Dreamcoat for as long as I was in *Joseph* at the Palladium. When I went on the road with the tour, for a while I was in jeans, shirt and jacket. Then one day someone told me I had gone. I think they save the heads somewhere. I hope so, or maybe I could say to some other head, 'You've got my eyes.'

The last *Going Live* was broadcast on 17 April 1993. Another awesome adventure had come to an end, and it was extremely painful. Trev and Simon joined us for a final 'pant-swinging session', Sarah and I stepped forward, and we thanked everyone who had been so wonderful over the years. I kissed her on the cheek and had to turn round as the tears started. *Going Live* had ended. I would never work in TC7 again.

I was too distracted by *Joseph* and family to take much notice of TV opportunities. Jason's dresser, Tina, had moved on. I interviewed a few people for the job and gave it to a young woman called Petra Hodgson, who obviously loved the theatre. Petra fitted into the team beautifully and contributed to the laughter. She fitted in *so* perfectly that she later married my brother, Tim, and they have two terrific kids.

Steph was getting very close to having our first baby. The understudy was on alert in case I had to make a run for it. We had booked into The Portland, which was moments from the stage door.

We had both decided that it would be better to bring up a family a bit further out of London, so I had sold the house in Chiswick and we moved to a home in the country that needed an incredible amount of work doing to it but had huge 'potential'. We're still working on it now!

On Saturday, 10 July 1993 I had just done two shows at the Palladium and driven home. Steph was tired so had gone to bed. I decided to play with the flight simulator downstairs. I had just safely landed a flight from Heathrow to Edinburgh when she called down to me.

'I think my waters have broken.'

They had, and we jumped in the car and raced into

Celebrating my brother Tim's birthday at Cliveden.

With Emma Forbes, Céline Dion and producer Jeff Thacker on the set of *Talking Telephone Numbers*.

Emma and I had to be 'blown up' for a joke on *Talking Telephone Numbers*.

Two smilers, my dad and Ruby at my brother's wedding. He was utterly besotted with the girls

The last photo taken of my wonderful dad on the day he showed off his fly fishing skills in the garden, by casting his fly onto a plate.

With my gorgeous girls on a picnic.

Mum and Dad all dressed up in our garden ready to go to the Henley Festival.

In our festival finest with my mum and dad and Steph's parents, John and Gill.

The adorable Bernard Cribbins on a clay pigeon shoot. The only friend I had that my dad was in awe of.

Our clay pigeon shooting team for the day. With Sarah Greene and her husband, Mike Smith.

The five amigos off on a jolly: me, Russ Lindsay, Nick Alsopp, who also joined us for lunch, Peter Powell, Darren Worsley and Paul Worsley.

My gorgeous girls out for another family picnic. We used to drive to the field behind the house in case anybody needed a wee.

My beautiful, wonderful, one-in-a-million girl.

Whenever the family come over it's a tradition to take a group picture. This one has the whole clan.

Ruby hitching a lift on a holiday to Portugal.

With Ruby, endless sunny days in the pool.

Part of my 24-hour TV marathon. About 20 hours in I broadcast live all the way from ITV to Downing Street and back and interviewed then Prime Minister David Cameron.

With Holly on a photo shoot, they usually end up like this, make-up ruined and Holly on the floor trying not to wet her pants!

Me and my girls, all *Friends* fanatics, at the London FriendsFest.

London. Steph is good at pretty much everything, including having babies. She was amazing; it was a miracle to see. I did get shouted at, though, a couple of times; first, for interviewing the anaesthetist. When I asked, as the epidural was being administered, 'Is this classed as an invasive procedure?' I quite rightly tipped Steph over the edge. The second time was, as she was concentrating very intensely on actually giving birth, I sprayed her with water! I was feeling completely useless. Of course, in those circumstances, I *was* completely useless, just a bit part in a drama starring someone else who was far more important. I think, more out of pity than anything else, one of the nurses gave me a 'cooling water mist' spray. I could lightly 'mist' Steph's brow, should she start to feel hot. At a fairly crucial 'pushing' moment I sprayed her face. It went in both her eyes and made her cough.

'What the hell was that?'

'It's a misting water spray, it's rose fragrance.'

'Don't do that again.'

'Okay.'

Molly May was born in the early hours of the Monday morning. In that moment, Steph and I had gone from being a couple to becoming a family. I had never in my life seen anything more beautiful or realized just what fierce, protecting love could feel like. Molly had a touch of jaundice so looked a little tanned. She has always been organized; she became one of my managers for a while and was brilliant at her job. Her organization that day was a mark of things to come. She had arrived so perfectly, my schedule was unbroken. I didn't miss a single show.

Mike Dixon, the Musical Director of *Joseph*, knocked on my dressing-room door.

'Andrew would like you to record "Close Every Door" as a single.'

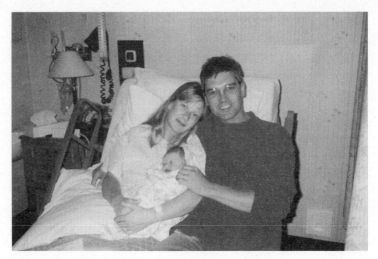

Hello Molly!

'Oh God. Okay, that scares me to death.'

'It's okay. There's nothing to worry about.'

The day of the recording, I had the beginning of a cold. I'd interviewed many stars in recording studios but, obviously, I'd never recorded a single. I seem to have a two-tiered nervous system. TV, radio and public speaking seldom ever make me nervous. On countless occasions, someone has come up to me and said, 'Would you mind saying a few words?' and I'm never horrified or scared. However, the minute I have to sing, it's an entirely different ballgame. I hated literally any singing performances I had to do on TV. I think it's because you can sing a song a hundred times perfectly in the theatre, but if you screw it up live on TV, it'll be on YouTube for ever.

So, I'm out of my depth in a recording studio. Mike Dixon, who was my rock to hold on to, wasn't there, there was no vocal warm-up and I was getting a cold. I sang it two or three times, and that was it!

A week or so later, I was sent the track. Halfway through the song, I knew I went a bit flat. I sang that song twice in every show – at that point, I had probably sung it over seven hundred times! I knew I could do it better. I knew I was never flat when I sang it. My office tried to get it re-recorded.

'It's fine,' came back the answer.

'No, it's not fine. It's not good enough. It'll haunt me!'

'Everyone says it's okay, Phil.'

'I have to do it again.'

When I first joined the show, Andrew Lloyd Webber had given me his personal number, saying, 'If you ever need me, this is the private number to my desk. If it's not picked up, it's because I'm not there. If you have any concerns or worries, don't go through the office, call me direct.'

I had never dialled the number, firstly because there had been no need and, secondly, because I didn't like to be a nuisance. Now, though, I had to dial. Andrew picked up.

'Andrew, it's Phillip. I'm sorry to bother you.'

'Hi, Phillip. I know what this is about, you're worried about the track.'

'I'm flat on it, Andrew. I have to do it again.'

'It's funny,' said Andrew. 'I've just put the phone down to Barbra Streisand. She's worried she's flat on something we've recorded, but she isn't. She's a perfectionist.'

'Andrew, there is a world of difference between me and Barbra Streisand, principally because I *am* flat.'

'Okay. If that's what you want, we'll re-record.'

'Oh my God, Andrew. Thank you so much.'

The phone call ended, and I was thrilled, but I later heard that Andrew had said straight afterwards, 'How the fuck did he get this number?'

*

Though I was loving being Joseph, I still had one eye on television. After all, that was my day job, and I didn't plan to stay in theatre full time. However, the BBC weren't being particularly dynamic with show ideas. Was there anything they were working on? Anything that might have my name on it? There really wasn't. The final show proposal that was pitched to me was 'Phillip cycles across the country, interviewing people along the way'. And so, another big decision had to be made. ITV had been circling for a while. I decided to change channels.

It would be a big psychological change for me. The BBC had been in my DNA since I was ten; it had never entered my head that I would switch channels. It was also quite a big deal for ITV, and they had some very interesting ideas. I was soon to say, 'We'll be back after the break,' for the first time. The channel switch was a big story in the press. ITV said they were thrilled to have me on board. Now, all I had to do was find a show to present.

Joseph was coming to the end of its run in London. It was to finish in October. I would miss the Palladium enormously; it had played such an important part in my life. I had worked on the world's most famous stage, but had got there completely by accident. What has remained is a wonderful legacy for me. If there is a documentary on the Palladium, I'm often asked if I'd like to take part, and I think I've said yes without exception. Those filming days are always such fun – I've swapped tales with Bruce Forsyth and Jimmy Tarbuck, Tommy Steele and Michael Crawford. In my mind, I will always remain the imposter, though.

I may have been signing off from the Palladium, but before I completed my West End run I agreed to sign up for the national tour. The last time I'd been part of a travelling team had been the Roadshow. Now I was going on the road with a huge West End smash hit.

My final show at the Palladium was on the evening of Saturday, 2 October, 1993, the day before I, sadly, attended the funeral of Pat Hubbard. The tempest would rage no more. At the end of the show, I hung up 'the Coat' and got changed. As I packed up my things I kept looking over at it. Every Joe had their own, and each was subtly different to all the others. I had worn this coat in the first dress rehearsal in front of Piers Morgan, and for every show since then. Up close, it was looking a little tired. What would they do with it? Where would it go? Storage? Would someone else wear it? Would it mean the same to anyone else as it meant to me? I kept looking at it. And then I made my decision.

It was coming home with me.

I am not a thief, but I am a bit of a magpie. I like keepsakes. Something to remind me of a place or a show, or a person or a moment. I'm hopelessly sentimental, but I was very aware that taking a Technicolour Dreamcoat was bigger than sentimentality. It was worth about twenty-five grand!

I rolled it up, packed it into a carrier bag and, when I left the building, I threw the bag casually into the boot of my car. If they kicked off, I would obviously give the coat back.

I turned to look at the Palladium. Briefly, it had been mine. Now, every time I returned in the future, it would be someone else's. I had been shown its secrets under the stage by the crew. The 'revolve' was controlled by a beautiful purple 'genie', like a light in a big valve, almost a living entity. I had been up to the fly floor and on to the roof. I might not have performed there as many times as all the greats, but I bet most of them hadn't been up to the 'spot box' or down into the hidden, dusty rooms below. And I bet most of their dads hadn't conducted the orchestra! Mine had. One evening, during one of my parents' visits to London, they came to see the show, again. Unbeknownst to me, a secret conversation had been had. My dad had been collected from his seat and taken to the orchestra pit. As I ran onstage at the end of the show, I looked into the orchestra pit and my dad was – briefly – conducting! I'm not sure who had the biggest smile, me onstage or him at the conductor's stand.

Goodbye, London Palladium. I know your secrets . . . Oh, and I've got a stolen coat in the boot.

The next morning, *it kicked off*!

The head of wardrobe (Sheila) had gone nuclear. Where was 'the Coat'?

Paul called me.

'Mate, hi, good morning. Er, well, I've got a bit of a tricky question. Sorry.'

'Hi. What's up?' I knew what was coming.

'Er, Phil, the Dreamcoat went missing last night after the show. I'm sorry to ask, but . . . do you have it?'

'Yes, I do.'

'Oh, shit, mate . . . you stole "the Coat".'

'In the cold light of day, I admit that it doesn't look good, but yes, I did.'

'Phil, they've gone bloody spare, mate.'

'Okay.' I sighed. 'Tell them I'm sorry. It's perfectly safe. I'll drive it over to them later.'

'Leave it with me for a bit, mate,' said Paul.

About two hours later, he called me back. A compromise had been reached. I don't know who was involved in this high-level 'Dreamcoat Summit', other than Paul, but the negotiations had gone well.

I was going to go on tour with a brand-new coat, which they wanted to keep pristine for the theatres. Obviously, there would have to be a lot of publicity photos. If I was pre-pared to use the coat I had 'liberated' for all the publicity shots, I could keep it. It was a genius compromise. Not only did I get to keep my Palladium coat, but its memory currency was also increased exponentially. All the shots of me outside wearing the coat on that tour were my coat. On the beach in Blackpool, by the River Liffey in Dublin, by the castle in Edinburgh. It is still a star and, when friends come round, everyone wants to wear it. It was last worn by Declan Donnelly and Holly Willoughby when we had a party at home.

After a successful run and to celebrate my agreeing to go on tour, Sir Andrew Lloyd Webber invited Steph and me, along with Russ, Pete and Paul, to his house in Eaton Square for dinner. Andrew and Madeleine were perfect hosts. It was pointed out that the beautifully patterned oriental bowls we were eating from had been purchased at auction and were part of the 'Nanking Cargo'. The intricate porcelain had been on board the Dutch East India Company ship *The Geldermalsen* when it sank in 1752 after hitting a reef in the South China Sea on its way to Holland. The huge haul had been rediscovered in 1985 and finally made the trip to Amsterdam to be auctioned. The bowls we were eating out of had lain, untouched, at the bottom of the ocean for 233 years. We were the first people ever to eat from them. I was suddenly terrified every time my cutlery touched the side. I can't imagine they went into the dishwasher.

During dinner, Madeleine had said that Edward might pop over with his new girlfriend.

Edward?

After dinner, Prince Edward and his girlfriend Sophie duly arrived and were both charming. I, however, used a word I'm not sure I've ever used before. The couple had just been out to dinner, and at any other time in my life I would have simply said, 'Lovely, where did you go?' Now, for whatever reason, I said, 'Do you have haunts?'

Haunts? What the hell did that mean? Why was I speaking

nonsense? Sadly, it got worse. Everyone there turned to look at me.

'Do you have haunts?'

'I'm sorry?' said the prince.

'Haunts, do you have haunts?'

The prince put both his hands to the top of his head and said, 'Not the last time I looked.'

Oh God, no! Not horns!

The first stop for the *Joseph* tour was Bristol. I didn't want to spend any longer away from Steph and Molly than I had to, and some venues, I could drive to, like Bristol and Oxford, but most of the others I had to be away for weeks at a time because there wasn't enough time to get there and back between shows. When I was in Edinburgh, we hired a lovely flat in the city and Steph, eighteen-month-old Molly and I were all together. Oddly, Steph was less enthusiastic about spending most of the winter in Blackpool, so I was on my own for most of that part of the run.

Whether onstage at the Palladium or night after night on a tour, I never found performing the same show even remotely repetitive. Firstly, there was always something that would make us laugh – a noise from the audience, a tiny mistake from someone, even though the audience never knew. Secondly, unlike TV, a nightly show that was essentially the same meant that I could play with each part of it, change it a little. I could work out whether, if I altered a move or a look, was it funnier? Could I get a bigger laugh? Rather than being bored, I was fascinated by the way I could concentrate on a different part each night to see if I could make it better. Every night, the roar of the audience let us know that we were in a great show and that they were going to leave feeling good. A standing ovation *never* gets ordinary!

Ria Jones had joined as the narrator and had the devastating skill of being able to make me laugh onstage without laughing herself. She can do an excellent impression of Shirley Bassey, and as we stood together singing the finale of the show, every so often I could hear Shirley belting out beside me. It would always make me laugh, and it got to the stage where the sound team on the mixer desk at the back of the auditorium fined me fifty pence every time I couldn't sing the final big note for laughing. You may have read recently that Ria was the understudy for Glenn Close as Norma Desmond in *Sunset Boulevard* when Miss Close went off sick. When Glenn's sickness was announced to the auditorium there were boos and catcalls and some members of the audience left and demanded their money back. Thankfully, though, the majority stayed and witnessed one of those rare fairy-tale moments when the understudy becomes a huge star. Ria was, as her friends already knew, astonishingly brilliant. The audience that had started out booing gave her a six-minute standing ovation at the end. I bet there was no Bassey in *that* performance.

Ria bought Molly a pair of tap shoes, which Molly called her 'tapping shoes'. We have the best video of a three-year-old Molly wandering naked up the patio, tip-tapping as she goes.

In a fantastic example of 'the show must go on', during a matinee in Oxford something happened that even those who had worked in theatre for forty years hadn't experienced before. Act I ended and the interval began. If you have been to the theatre, you'll have seen the safety curtain brought in during the interval. In the theatre, it's called 'the iron'. At various points of the show, that is, the start of the show, the beginning and end of the interval and at the end of the show, the iron would be flown in or out. As the interval in Oxford started, the iron was flown in. Backstage, we heard the most incredible heavy clattering and banging from inside the fabric of the building. One of the heavy chains to control this very heavy curtain had snapped, and it had then whipped up over the top of the upper pulley and crashed back down into the depths of its shaft. There was no way it was going to be fixed without serious heavy-lifting gear. A meeting was held backstage. We looked, unseen, from the wings, at the depth of the stage between the stricken curtain and the orchestra pit: it was about five feet. Could we do any sort of performance of Act II with us all onstage at the same time? We all thought we could. The company manager looked at me.

'You'll have to tell them.'

'Tell who?'

'You'll have to go out and explain to the audience that they're going to get a concert-style Act II. If they want their money back, they can leave, or they can stay to watch.'

Thus came true one of those 'panic dreams' you have before a big event or the start of a new job. In my career, I've had many such dreams, about not being able to speak in a big live show or things going hideously wrong during a theatre production. For me, they usually began as I started rehearsals. I have dreamt of hostile audiences, of getting things so wrong that I was booed off. Having to walk out and confront a potentially angry auditorium had been one of my panic dreams, and now I was about to do it for real!

I stepped from the wings on to the stage, and the buzz of the audience resuming their seats after the interval quietened as they looked at me. I explained the stuck curtain and said we were going to do a performance unlike any other we'd done before. It would be fun and very personal. Not one person stood up to leave. I think that second act was probably the most fun of any I've done. We all stood or sat together, dangling our feet into the orchestra pit. We acted as best we could, but we were all so close it just made us laugh. The cast loved it and, more importantly, the audience loved it. The show must go on.

I have always been absolutely aware of how lucky I have been, and I try never to take any aspect of my life for granted. There's no question that my career has given me some extraordinary experiences. One of those 'pinch me' moments was taking Steph to New York for a long weekend and travelling by Concorde. The upcoming tour was going to be long and there would be weeks away from home, so we decided to treat ourselves. The grandparents were overjoyed to have Molly for a few days. It was fantastic. I'd been in a plane behind Concorde as it took off at Heathrow and I'd felt my insides vibrate as it thundered down the runway with blue flames streaking out of the four engines. Being on board was like travelling on a luxurious rocket. In the loo, Steph marvelled at the fact that she was peeing at 1,300 mph. As she

walked out, she smiled at Dame Kiri Te Kanawa, who was waiting outside, also about to have a supersonic wee.

On the way back from New York, the pilot, who was called Martin Robson, asked if I'd like to go up front for take-off. I'm not sure I've ever said 'yes' to anything faster.

Sitting in the cockpit for take-off was one of the great moments of my life. I learned that the Americans were immensely jealous of the plane, so that made flying it into and out of New York very difficult. Noise-registering devices had been put up all over the place to try to catch it breaking the rules. This required some pretty deft flying. The passengers had been warned prior to take-off that we would make a very sharp, immediate left-hand turn as we lifted off. I sat upfront for the manoeuvre. As the wheels left the ground, the plane banked sharply. As it came out of the turn, Martin was peering out of his window and said to the co-pilot that we were 'bang on target for the car park'.

Excitement overload. On the flight deck of Concorde.

He explained that a particularly cantankerous old bloke lived on the flight path that Concorde took from that particular runway. If they flew over his house, he would complain. Every complaint was logged; too many complaints, and the jet could lose its licence to fly into the city.

The best way to keep the old guy sweet was to fly over the large car park of a mall further down his street. They also cut back on the power as they flew over in an effort to be quieter. This astonishing marvel of aviation technology was, briefly, under the control of an old bloke who lived near a car park.

There was no indication that we had gone through the sound barrier over the Atlantic, other than the passing of a black line on one of the instrument gauges. I was in raptures.

Martin had told me he lived in Bristol so, as I was returning to my seat, I said that to repay his incredible generosity, if he would like to bring his family to see *Joseph*, I could organize his tickets and give him a tour backstage. A week or so after we opened, Martin came with his family and they were given the full tour. He suggested that while I was in the city I might like to have a go on the Concorde flight simulator at Filton. He could book some time, if I was interested. Again, my answer was swift.

A week later I was sitting with him in one of the most sophisticated aircraft simulators ever built. I was lucky: it was a quiet day and we had it to ourselves. For the next few hours I was instructed in the immensely difficult job of piloting a supersonic passenger jet. We flew circuit after circuit of New York. I learned the importance of ten and a half degrees. As I was coming in to land, it was constantly repeated to me by Martin. There was a gauge indicating exactly 10.5 degrees, and it was a vital part of landing Concorde. At eleven degrees, the tail would scrape on the runway; at nine degrees there wouldn't be enough drag on the delta wings to slow it down on landing and we'd shoot off the end of the runway. It was incredibly realistic: I felt responsible for the hundred imaginary passengers behind me. *'Ten and a half degrees!!'*

Towards the end of the day, Martin suggested that because of the amount of simulator training I'd done on my PC at home, coupled with the training I had just received, I was ready to join a very exclusive simulator club. Because of the size and shape of Concorde's wings, it was one of very few large passenger planes that could fly between the Twin Towers of the World Trade Center. 'Obviously, only ever to be tried in the Concorde simulator', he said, laughing. Did I feel up to it? Absolutely.

I was in charge of nothing but steering. Martin controlled the power. We lifted off from JFK and I retracted the wheels. Off in the distance, I could see the towers. I turned to make the correct approach. The distance between the towers was about two hundred feet; the wingspan of Concorde was eighty-three feet and eight inches. If I got the approach right, there was plenty of room to spare. I levelled off at seven hundred feet, about halfway up the towers. My palms were sweating as I approached. The city flashed beneath me as the Twin Towers loomed ahead, closer and closer. I made tiny adjustments, but I was happy with my approach. 'Looking good,' said Martin.

It was perfect: we shot between the two buildings. I had joined a very elite club.

It feels uncomfortable to even write that story now. Little did I know that one day, I would stand horrified, watching a TV in another Bristol hotel room, because I would be back in the city appearing in *Doctor Dolittle*. Seven years after that day in the flight simulator, the Twin Towers would be gone.

8

At the same time as the *Joseph* tour kicked off, ITV had been working hard to find a show that would launch my new contract. It was going to be a very busy time. As well as doing *Joseph*, I would have to travel from wherever I was in the country to get back to the TV studios in London. A name and a company would become very important in my life. The name was Paul Smith (not of Gopher fame), and the company was Celador. Paul was in fact a TV executive who would soon become incredibly wealthy after he and his very talented team invented *Who Wants to be a Millionaire?* I wasn't going to make him quite that much. Paul is dry-witted, thoughtful, precise and uncompromising. He and his team,

Rehearsing *Talking Telephone Numbers*.

comprising Steven Knight and Mike Whitehill, along with David Briggs, had come up with an innovative programme idea that both Celador and ITV would like me to host, alongside Emma Forbes. Emma and I had had a ball cooking on *Going Live* so it would be fun to be teamed up again.

The show was *Talking Telephone Numbers*, and it would offer a prize of £10,000 and if you were prepared to gamble, a possible jackpot of £25,000. (I don't think anyone actually took that gamble because they were more than happy to have won the 10k. Minor format flaw there!) Just pre-lottery, this was the biggest prize that had ever been given out on a TV show. The premise was reasonably simple. Through a series of variety-style games, we would generate five numbers between 0 and 9. If those numbers matched the last five numbers of a viewer's telephone number, in any order, they could call in to one of ninety-six telephonists for a chance to win the prize. I should point out at this stage that the series was very successful. We made sixty-two shows and it ran until 1997, firstly with Emma and then with the equally lovely Claudia Winkleman. Having said all this, it was a totally new concept, partly live and got off to a rocky start. The huge prize money was its big selling point. On the first show, we failed to give it away; on the second show, we gave it to the wrong person! On the third show, one of the most spectacular cock-ups that I've ever been a part of took place on the nation's TV screens.

In the afternoon, we recorded all the games and generated all the numbers. In the evening, we opened the show live, then ran in the recording of all the numbers being generated, then we went live again to find the winner, which usually took about two minutes. Some huge stars performed on the show. When Mariah Carey came on, I realized that Paul Smith could only be pushed so far.

Mariah stood onstage, asking for lighting positions, camera

Emma Forbes and producer Jeff Thacker at *Talking Telephone Numbers*.

positions and light colours to be altered. No, still not right: that light up there, slightly to the left, a little lower. That one over there, a little higher, a little pinker. After about an hour of this, high in the gantry, I heard the gallery door open, then footsteps on the metal grid and down the spiral staircase. Paul Smith strode purposefully across the studio floor, stood in front of Mariah Carey and shouted, 'Miss Carey, please sing *now*!' He then turned and walked back across the studio floor.

She looked stunned for a second, then nodded and told everyone she was ready to sing.

The opening titles rolled, Emma and I said 'hello' live and introduced the first act. The VT recorded in the afternoon played and we had nothing to do until the live ending. The first part was seamless. Into the commercial break: no problems. Out of the break and part two began. Still all okay. As we watched the show going out from the studio floor, little did we know that a VT operator was about to sink the ship. For whatever reason, he hit the rewind button on the VT machine and the show spooled off.

Since the days of the Broom Cupboard, I have worn an earpiece on TV. Children's telly is a brilliant training ground in all aspects of apprenticeship, including talkback via an earpiece. There are two ways to listen to the gallery. The first is 'switched' talkback, which means you can't hear anything unless someone presses a key to talk specifically to you. The second way is 'open' talkback, which means that you hear everything in the gallery, all the time. 'Open' talkback is the way I was trained in the Broom Cupboard days, and it's the way I will present tomorrow on *This Morning*. People ask if it distracts me, but in fact it distracts me if I *can't* hear. I like to hear everything. That way I can hear a problem being born long before it's grown enough to affect the show. Over the years, I have heard some very funny things over talkback in my ear, some very sad things as news breaks, and some very panicked things. I was about to hear the last of the three.

Talking Telephone Numbers spooled off backwards and was gone. Most live shows with recorded content will have a back-up tape playing alongside the main one. As the show zipped backwards, the gallery erupted: 'Cut to the back-up!' The vision mixer did exactly that. In VT, the operator walked over to the now live back-up and hit rewind on that, too. We were off air. I ran from the backstage monitor I'd been watching to the set and stood in front of a camera. That was the moment I realized we hadn't generated all five numbers so couldn't play the game. I jumped from in front of the camera and hid – there was nothing I could do to help. It was absolute pandemonium. A sound recording of the gallery existed for a while, but I can't find it now. Sadly!

Finally, the show crawled back on the air, the team found a

place on the VT where all the numbers had been generated but a huge chunk of the show had been 'spooled through'. We were massively under time. Emma and I filled for seven minutes. No game on TV has ever been played more slowly. A strange serenity washed over me. It's happened since in complete technical meltdowns. It's best just to relax and do the best you can. Panic breeds panic. By the side of me for those seven minutes I could hear Emma's knee banging nervously on the lectern.

One Monday, as we were about to go live, I heard a yelp from the audience. A rather large lady had fallen, then rolled down the stairs and continued to roll out on to the studio floor. The cameras scattered out of her way. An announcement came: 'Three minutes to on-air.' The medics rushed over. The woman was okay but had hurt her leg and couldn't stand. There was no way we could open the show properly because she was halfway across the black, shiny floor. Five cameras were out of position. 'Two minutes to live.'

The floor manager knelt down and asked the woman's permission to roll her back behind the cameras. 'One minute to live.' She agreed to the indignity. Two cameramen and the floor manager unceremoniously rolled the lady, as if rolling a barrel of beer, behind the cameras. She was in remarkably buoyant spirits. In the first commercial break, the large scenery doors were opened and an ambulance backed in to take her away. At the end of the show a guy called me over and asked if I knew where the lady had been taken. I said I didn't know but I could probably find out.

'Why do you need to know?' I asked.

'She's my wife.'

'What? Why didn't you go with her in the ambulance?'

'Sod that, I've been looking forward to coming here for months.'

It was on that floor in Fountain Studios that Emma Forbes

and I nearly met our end. We were rehearsing for part of the show. Later, when we recorded, a remotely controlled 'drop box' above us would open and shower us with confetti. During the rehearsal, the drop box was triggered accidentally. It wasn't full of confetti. Emma and I were standing maybe a foot further apart than we would normally, and it was a miracle that we were. Inside the drop box were its usual contents of stored chains, large metal hooks and various parts of a dismantled winch. They hit the deck between us, missing us by about two inches on each side. The noise was deafening. If you know where to look, you can still see the gouges on the floor.

In the make-up room, getting ready for the show, Emma and I were chatting about our idols. I confessed to her that I only had one: Katharine Hepburn. I adored her sass, her no-nonsense approach to life, and the fact that her and Spencer Tracy's relationship was such a complicated but devoted Hollywood love affair. Elton John once told me that Hepburn dived into his swimming pool to retrieve a dead toad. She grabbed it from the bottom of the pool, surfaced and threw it into the bushes. When Elton said, 'Ewww, how could you *do* that?' she replied, 'Character, dear boy, character.'

When Michael Jackson came to stay with her, she berated him for not making his bed, and when he explained that he didn't know how, she marched him upstairs and taught him.

I loved her style.

Emma looked at me.

'You are joking?'

'No, I'm deadly serious!'

'She's a close friend of the family! My middle name is Katy.'

'No bloody way.'

She explained that her sister used to live with Katharine and, because of the actress's love of early nights and because she had incredibly keen hearing, Sarah (middle name Kate) would climb on every bit of furniture and avoid anything that creaked so that she could sneak out without waking Katharine up. She would repeat the whole exercise when she got back to the apartment and Ms Hepburn never knew Sarah had ever been gone.

I made Emma a big promise. Could she get me invited to tea with Katharine? If she could, I would fly us both to New York on Concorde, she could shop anywhere she liked all day and I would pick up the bill. My only request was to meet Katharine. Emma laughed. She really didn't think that would be a problem; she would ask her father if he could set it up. Emma's parents, Nanette Newman the actress and Bryan Forbes the movie director, were utterly delightful. I've had some wonderful days chatting with them both. Bryan had directed Katharine in *The Madwoman of Chaillot*.

I waited for the response. When it came, it broke my heart. Her age had, sadly, begun to take its toll. She was now too poorly to receive visitors; I had missed her by about six months.

A month after the news that I would never get to meet the one star I idolized, a brown padded envelope dropped through my letterbox. Inside was a photograph from Kate Hepburn. It was signed in her very shaky hand, 'For Phillip, All good wishes, Katharine Hepburn.' And that, along with my Judi Dench picture, are the things I will grab if the house burns down.

I was sitting in the *This Morning* Green Room in June 2003 when it was announced on the news that she had died. I made sure no one saw me cry.

Towards the latter end of the *Joseph* tour, ITV asked me to present another series. Michael Hurll was a huge name in television. He had produced *Top of the Pops* and *The Two*

Ronnies. He had worked extensively with Noel Edmonds and Cilla Black and had invented the British Comedy Awards through his new company Michael Hurll Television. He was known as something of a firebrand. People were scared of him. He came to us with an idea for a show. I loved the idea and I instantly liked Michael. *Schofield's Quest* was a live investigative show, but with an entertainment spin on it. We found people, we found explanations, we found reasons. On one occasion, we found trouble!

I'll be careful what I say here. A guy contacted us and said there was a set of steps at the bottom of his garden that he could see no reason for. At the bottom of the steps there was a door made out of metal. It was totally impenetrable. It didn't show up on any of his house details or on any local maps. I interviewed him and we asked the viewers if anyone had any ideas. Could it be a Second World War pill box? Following the show, we received a polite but uncompromising phone call from a brigadier in the 'security services'. We were never to mention those steps again. We didn't.

I also nearly presented the first link of one *Quest* without any trousers on.

I have worked with TV's most delightful dresser, Billy Kimberley, on many, many shows over the years and we've had a lot of fun. I think *Quest* was the first time we worked together. I had cut it a bit fine getting ready and putting on a new suit. Neither Billy nor I had realized the trousers needed turning up. I was already in a shirt, jacket and tie. I put the trousers on: way too long. We both ran into the studio, and Billy said he could turn them up in time for the live start. I sat behind the desk and took the trousers off and Billy raced away. I rehearsed the opening of the show in just my boxers as Billy worked madly at the sewing machine. 'Five minutes to on-air,' said the PA in my ear. I spoke to both Michael Hurll and the director: 'Guys, if Billy isn't back in five minutes, I'll have to do the beginning of the show sitting behind the desk.'

The crew and the gallery were in hysterics, and extremely disappointed when Billy ran in with a minute to go with perfectly turned-up trousers.

Years later, Billy was dressing me for a day's recording of *The Cube*. He was making me laugh by telling me about an opera singer he had worked with who kept losing their temper and throwing things at him. One day, the singer had chased Billy down a corridor, throwing shoes at him.

As Billy left my dressing room, I chased after him, shouting, 'And stay out!' as I threw various shoes in his direction, being very careful they didn't actually hit him. When I looked beyond the running dresser, I saw the *Cube* audience being led into the studio. We both tried to explain that it was a

Dresser extraordinaire Billy Kimberley.

joke, but I'm not sure anyone believed that I wasn't throwing a hissy fit (which, for the record, I have never done!).

Life was hectic, with TV and the theatre running concurrently. A simple question would reveal that life would be even busier, but in the best possible way.

'Would you like a cuppa?' I asked Steph.

'No, thank you, I don't really fancy one.'

We both looked at each other.

We are both committed tea drinkers. If I have coffee first thing in the morning, it gives me an instant migraine. A morning cup of tea, though, is an essential start to the day. The only time Steph had gone off tea before was the moment she became pregnant with Molly.

We bought the tester kit. We had been touched by another miracle. Steph was pregnant again.

When Ruby was born, I was in Oxford with *Joseph* and, in another remarkable example of organization, she arrived on

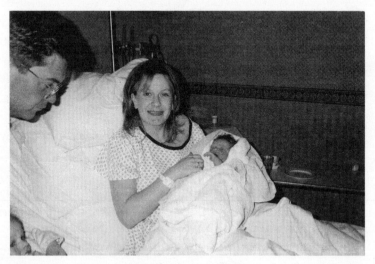

And then there was Ruby.

A very excited Molly with her new sister.

Sunday, 28 January 1996. With no show scheduled that day, the understudy was again denied the opportunity to perform.

As we set off for the hospital, Steph became upset. How could we possibly love another baby as much as we loved Molly? How was that possible?

Ruby was perfect – tiny and beautiful – and we realized that the heart has a remarkable ability to expand and accommodate equal quantities of endless love for each child. Molly fell instantly in love with her sister and was very protective, telling others to 'be careful' when they picked her up.

Ruby is the endless sunshine in all our lives. Only Ruby can make Molly laugh helplessly, and she has been doing that since day one. Molly always stuck by our side in the house. We were never out of her sight and always knew exactly where she was, so we got a hell of a shock when Ruby started to crawl and disappeared. We weren't used to *that*.

We're incredibly lucky. Both sides of the family get along and family get-togethers are always great fun. The Schofield/

A sunny holiday at Euro Disney with 'vanishing' Ruby at the front.

Lowes are a good team. When Steph and I decided to take the girls to Disneyland Paris, we took both sets of grandparents. At the end of a long day walking round the park, we were all relaxing in a little bar in the hotel. Molly was, as usual, by our side . . . Where was Ruby?

One moment she was there; the next, gone. We all split up. My mum stayed with Molly. Steph and I ran for the door, as did my dad and Steph's parents. We were distraught. We combed every inch of the hotel, every step more desperate. She couldn't have walked this far – had she been taken from under our noses? How could that be possible? Frantically, we called; desperately, we searched. She was gone. Tearfully, we gathered back in the bar. The park would have to be alerted, the police called. My dad heard a little giggle. There, wedged

Our gorgeous girls.

tightly between two chairs, perfectly hidden and impossible to spot, was Ruby. Hmmm. We knew then that we'd have to keep an eye on this one.

Having two young daughters was making life on the road very hard. I hated being away from Steph and the girls. As I set off for another week away one day, Molly ran out of the back door, grabbed my legs, wrapped herself around me and sobbed, 'Daddy, please don't leave me again.' It was time to hang up the Technicolour Dreamcoat. My final performance was at the Mayflower Theatre in Southampton. I had sung the show 1,147 times. So, yes, I can still remember the colours.

Steph organized an amazing 'end of *Joseph*' party for me. I was sad to finish, but so happy to be back home. We went for a walk around the garden. As Steph and I chatted, we realized Molly wasn't with us, which was, as you know, highly unusual. As we turned to run back and retrace our footsteps, Molly walked around the corner of the house. We asked

where she'd been and she told us she had been talking to the lady. Lady? What lady? We ran into the garden to search. It has an eight-foot-high brick and flint wall all round it. No one could get in or out. The garden was totally empty. Molly was adamant that she had spoken to a lady. We called the previous occupant, who had been an aged housekeeper and had lived in the house for many years. 'Oh, that'll be the Grey Lady,' she told us, an entirely benign ghost that patrolled that part of the garden and was only ever seen by children. We were told that Molly was lucky: sightings were very rare. That proved to be true. She has never seen the Grey Lady since; however, it has made for some great storytelling around the fire.

Up until about five years ago, all my diaries were big, padded Ryman 'week at a glance' ones. I still have them all and have been referring back to them for dates and memory jogging.

The first one was given to me by the band Talk Talk's record company. It's my 1986 diary and on the front is written 'Life's What You Make It'. It rang true then, and it rings true still. I've never kept a personal diary; these ones are all full of work things. Going through them for this book has been fascinating. There are entire TV shows I'd forgotten. *One in a Million* happened after the end of *Joseph*, as did *Predictions*. Apparently, I even wrote a book to accompany the *One in a Million* series: it seems to be on Amazon. I literally don't have a clue!

About five years ago, the office persuaded me to ditch the paper diaries and have the whole year on my phone. I was resistant at first, because in the cupboard where I keep my long line of diaries, mapping out my career like rings on a tree trunk, my life seems to stop in 2014.

I very clearly remember presenting *GMTV* with Emma Forbes for a few weeks, because we had a lot of fun, even though it was way too bloody early for me. I also remember *Schofield's TV Gold*, which I made with Paul Smith and Celador again. I mentioned their winning team earlier. Over the years, I've been lucky to work with many very talented writers, but Steven Knight and Mike Whitehill, who wrote *TV Gold*, were very special indeed. They probably don't remember, but I do. I absolutely loved delivering their lines. It came as no surprise that Stephen Knight went on to create *Peaky Blinders*, among other things.

In 1997, the TV series *Friends* was huge. Obviously, it still is today. I don't often use my name to get me in anywhere, principally because I'm always terrified the person on the end of the phone is going to say, 'Who?' But with *Friends* I was prepared to take the risk. In a stroke of sublime luck, one of the publicity team for the show was a Brit and a bit of a fan. If we were in Los Angeles, would there be any chance of watching a show being recorded? 'Of course.' Holy shit!

The timings worked perfectly. Steph's sister, Georgina, was producing David Bowie's fiftieth-birthday-concert film at Madison Square Garden. We found ourselves back on Concorde, only this time I stayed in my seat with Steph instead of going to the flight deck. After watching Bowie, we flew on to LA to watch an episode of *Friends* being recorded. I'd never seen anything like that scale of operation before. Even the warm-up guy was incredible. We were all served pizza, and that was even before the cast were introduced. As a telly geek, I was captivated; as fans of the show, we were beside ourselves. If a gag didn't get the laugh they'd hoped for, they stopped, rewrote the scene, learned it then ran it again. The episode we watched had Joey putting books that scared him in the freezer. Rachel suggests he reads *Little Women*. If you find the scene on YouTube, he delivers the line, 'These little women, how little are they?' It was a line that I loved. I burst out laughing, first and loudest. I knew that if they didn't re-shoot the scene, my laugh would be on *Friends*. They didn't, so it is.

The cast travelled to London to shoot a couple of episodes (Ross marrying Emily). They shot the interiors at Fountain Studios and Steph and I were once again in the audience. When Ross said Rachel's name instead of Emily's, he was standing on the chipped part of the floor where the drop-box nearly killed me.

My favourite subject at school was biology, and I studied hard because I was fascinated. I'm pretty handy in the 'human body' round in a pub quiz or, in lockdown times, a Zoom quiz.

So when I was asked if I'd like to present *City Hospital*

from Southampton General, I was all over it. The team was Suzi Perry, Nick Knowles and me. I absolutely loved it. Being behind the scenes at the hospital was amazing. Actually, I'm really good with someone else's blood, but terrible with my own. If I have blood taken, I have to look away or I will faint. I've fainted in front of many a medical professional over the years. I fainted when I broke my toe by catching it on a door frame. When I looked down, it was poking out to the side. That's where I learned the trick of 'going low'. Get as low as I can, then, when I, inevitably, faint, I don't have too far to drop. The last time I fainted was when I had a mole removed from my leg. However, I was lying down, so I fainted and recovered and they never knew.

There was no chance of fainting on *City Hospital*; it was all about other people. I loved the dark humour of the medics. One lunchtime conversation was about all the things they had removed from people who had 'accidentally fallen on them'! One medic told me he was removing a mobile phone and, just as they had successfully removed it from the gentleman's bottom, it rang. They handed it to him and said. 'I think it's for you.' One of the 'falls' must have been particularly acrobatic. The team removed Barbie and then, in a shock twist, they found Ken.

9

I had read the *Dr Dolittle* books by Hugh Lofting, and I'd loved the movie with Rex Harrison. I was about to be asked if I'd like to be the doctor in a brand-new musical. *Joseph* had been a wonderful theatrical experience, but I had taken over from Jason. Only the original actor gets to record the soundtrack album and be part of shaping the production, and that was an experience I was keen to have. The meetings began – it was going to be *huge*. At the time, it was one of the most expensive musicals ever staged. The state-of-the-art animals would be created by Jim Henson's Creature Shop. *Dolittle* was one of those shows that had had to wait for the technology to be created before a live theatrical production could really be considered.

The whole idea had come about when Roger Moore had appeared on *The Muppet Show*. He had asked Leslie Bricusse, who had written the *Dolittle* music and lyrics, to go with him. The two discussed a stage show of it, but Leslie conceded that, at the time, they couldn't make animals that were realistic enough. The innovations created by the Creature Shop had suddenly made such a production achievable. The genius of the animals was that they were realistic but also had character, and that made them immensely endearing. Wonderful Mike Dixon, who had nursed me through my terror in *Joseph*, was back as Musical Supervisor, with Mike England as Musical Director. Stephen Pimlott would direct. I'd worked with him on *Joseph*; now I'd get to see him create something from scratch. Mark Thompson would design, again ex-*Joseph*. This was going to be epic.

There was no chance I was going to learn this one in a round trip to Bristol. Leslie Bricusse didn't write one word when twenty-five would do, so learning the thing was going to be a slog. Later, when the show's producer, Adrian Leggett, asked if Leslie had written him a hit show, Leslie replied he'd done better than that, he'd written two! I set up a rehearsal room in the attic at home so I was well out of the way to learn my lines. I knew that this was going to be a challenge – the good doctor hardly left the stage throughout the whole performance.

Julie Andrews would play Polynesia the parrot, and even though she would record the part, she wanted to attend the rehearsals. That was a hell of a day when Julie Andrews as a parrot stood beside me for the first time. One of my most precious memories of the entire experience were the two evenings Julie and I spent in the studio recording 'Talk to the Animals'. She was so lovely. On one line, she made a small mistake and said, 'Sorry, I'm new in the business.'

Rehearsals were an absolute delight. The cast were wonderful and such fun. The team from the Creature Shop introduced us to the animals as they were finished, and the way they proudly unveiled them was so endearing. It was fascinating to watch everyone at work. I had never been involved in the process of building a show of this magnitude from the ground up. Watching Stephen Pimlott direct was like watching a masterclass. I marvelled at how he began to build the show, putting the flesh on the bones. Stephen was also a genius at teasing the best performance from his actors, and watching him direct a duck was a great moment. One day, over lunch, this Shakespearian director, a man who had also directed extravagant operas, looked up from his lunch and said to me, 'No, do you see? You have to quack as a question.'

He said that was the single most bizarre note he had ever given.

I had lessons in how to make the correct noises. The right depth of bark for conversing with Jip the dog, for example. And I worked hard on my duck and my pushmi-pullyu, which, it transpires, is very similar to llama.

As I stroked Polynesia, I was told that was the wrong way to stroke a parrot, and the doctor would know exactly the right way, so I was duly instructed.

Stephen Pimlott said one morning, 'Can I have the three principal actors over here, please?'

I didn't move. I had no idea I was a principal actor. I couldn't quite believe that I was any kind of actor!

By the time we got to the Apollo in Hammersmith most of the sets were completed. Mark Thompson had created something truly magical. Dolittle's study in Act I and his ship, the *Flounder*, were so beautiful I just walked around them in awe.

The Creature Shop were in full creative flight. It was clear that the animals were going to steal the show, and quite rightly. Day after day, they were introduced to us. The pushmi-pullyu was hard to control, with two operators inside, one moving forwards, the other backwards, in perfect, elegant synchronization. However, we were the ones to howl with laughter before that synchronization was perfected as we watched it trip up and fall over, to cries of 'I can't see a fucking thing!' coming from somewhere inside.

During rehearsals, and actually pretty much every night of the future performances, I loved watching Andy Heath control Gub-Gub the pig during the storm that sank the *Flounder*. Andy was lying, high up, in a tin bath with the pig on his arm, and what he managed to get that puppet to do was comedy perfection.

The only time I saw Stephen Pimlott come close to irritation was the evening during rehearsals when the curtain rose and we all saw the great pink sea snail for the first time. It was huge, with three people operating it from the inside. As Stephen valiantly attempted to concentrate on rehearsals, the expressions and noises they got out of it had the cast utterly helpless on the stage. As we all laughed, so did the snail, and we were all incapable even of breathing when the operators threw its head back and someone shouted, 'It's like a twenty-foot erection!'

'Ladies and gentlemen . . . and those in the snail, would you please try to focus!' called out the exasperated director.

As in *Joseph*, I got a fabulous finale, but rather than being lifted into the air trailing a billowing Technicolour Coat behind me, I flew above the heads of the audience in the cavernous Apollo sitting on a huge, flapping, giant lunar moth.

The production was spectacular on every level, including, unfortunately . . . length! As the first preview got closer, it was obvious the show was too long. There was a reluctance to trim it because no matter what was trimmed, something beautiful and expensive would have to go.

The night of the first preview had arrived. Some said it was the only show they had done that finished on a different day, it went on so long. As I ran up the stairs at the back of the auditorium to board the moth, I passed scores of people leaving, calling, 'Sorry, Phil, I've got work in the morning.'

The edit was swift and brutal. Whole swathes of the show which had been tirelessly rehearsed were chopped out. A stunning dream sequence with beautiful fantasy animals never saw the light of day. I can't imagine how much money was wasted.

That wasn't the only teething problem we had as the show started. 'If I Could Talk to the Animals' was a nightmare to learn. Julie Andrews had recorded the entire song, I had learned the entire song, so it was possible to keep changing who sang what. For example, 'I think we'll try Julie singing that line today, and you sing the two lines after,' or, 'It's better if you do those lines. The parrot can sing the one after.'

On my long dressing-room mirror, I had every interchangeable line on Post-it notes: I was blue; Julie was yellow. I could swap them over and then relearn the song. Sometimes I sang a different version in the matinee than in the evening. Each time I sang a new version, I felt like a train travelling down very rusty tracks. Eventually, I had to put my foot down. 'You have one more show to pick the definitive version,' I said, 'then that's it. No more changes.'

I think the final version was the best.

One of the other issues was the venue. The Apollo in Hammersmith was vast – the capacity of the auditorium was about 3,300 people. If you had tickets further back than halfway, the skilful acting of the pig and the subtle head tilts Iestyn Evans got from Dab-Dab the duck were mostly lost. There was no question, the show was spectacular, but it wouldn't really come into its own until we took it on the road to slightly smaller theatres of around 2,000-capacity. Only then could the true magnificence of the animals and the set be fully appreciated by everyone.

The huge lunar moth that I rode over the audience was very occasionally a source of concern. When I started the ride, the stage was a long way away. I could see the cast waving as the doctor made his triumphant return. One afternoon as I approached the stage I could see that the cast were faltering in their waves, and as I got closer I could see concern on their faces. As I came in to land, the closest cast member whispered, 'Get off! Get off quickly! It's on fire!'

'What?'

With Jo from wigs and dresser Angie. A guy in the pub said, 'You're
working in theatre now so you've gone from TV to nothing really.'

'There's smoke pouring out of the back. It looks like
you've been shot down over the bloody Channel!'

The batteries inside the moth didn't often short out but,
when they did, there were always a lot of Biggles impressions
on the stage. It reminded me of my summer in the tank range.

We were a very happy company and I made some wonderful friends. We also had an enormous amount of fun. Every
so often, the Creature Shop team would announce that the
animals were going to have a 'themed' day. No one watching
would have been aware of this. 'Angry Animal Day' was a
triumph.

The show was such a great spectacle for my girls to come
and see. They were friends with all the animals and, as a
present, the Creature Shop made them the most beautiful
mermaid tails Steph and I had ever seen.

One of the hardest shows I've ever performed was the evening show on Monday, 26 April 1999. Throughout the course of

Drunkenly watching the sun rise in Eastbourne.

the day, the news had broken that my friend and colleague Jill Dando had been shot dead on her doorstep just down the road from the Hammersmith Apollo, in Fulham. No one that knew her could understand it then, and still to this day no one understands it. The last time I'd seen her was outside the reception at Television Centre about three months earlier. We chatted for a bit and, as she walked away, she said, 'See ya later, handsome.'

For someone who is pretty good at spotting the unusual, thankfully, one evening I missed a huge set of clues. If I had questioned what I'd seen, I would have wrecked a very elaborate surprise and an incredibly well-kept secret. As usual, for the finale of every *Doctor Dolittle* show, I ran down the side of the building on my way to board the giant lunar moth. My route took me out of the stage door to the front of the theatre to a door that was specially opened so I could fly through it. I had to then run up the stairs of the theatre to another door that opened on to the roof, then I'd run across the roof (in all weathers) and down a set of steps into an old room that used to house one of the big spotlights. Now, one side of the room had been cut out and it acted as a kind of garage. Way above the heads of the audience and unseen, it housed the moth, hidden behind black cloths and ready for its descent to the stage. So that was the route.

Rewind to the start of that journey, to the moment I left the stage door and ran down the road beside the theatre. The secret clue I had missed were two unmarked TV vans, one of which had its doors open. If I hadn't been running at a sprint, and if I'd been more attentive, I'd have noticed the camera kit inside and, before the final bows, I'd almost certainly have asked backstage why the TV crews were here. And where were they?

Mercifully, none of that happened and, until Michael Aspel arrived onstage beside me, I was unaware that 'Tonight, Phillip Schofield, This is Your Life . . .'

I was totally lost for words. In conjunction with James Grant, Steph had played a blinder. I didn't realize that she, my mum, dad and Tim were standing at the back of the auditorium, ready for the moment when Michael surprised me. They then sped off to Television Centre to meet me when I arrived after getting changed.

'Phillip Schofield, this is your life.'

Most of the people there that night are mentioned in this book. They're the most special people in my life. How lucky I am to have a recording of pretty much the whole family, as well as friends I hadn't seen for so long: John and Mac from OBs; Louise Tucker, who I'd worn Hai Karate talc to impress, and failed; Bruce Connock, my careers adviser, who had sent me to watch the news at the BBC in Plymouth; Peter Grattan, my producer from New Zealand; David Rodgers, star of West Country TV and radio, who had become a life-long friend at Hospital Radio Plymouth. Paul Smith, my Broom Cupboard producer and master of the Gopher was there (Gordon also made an appearance). The cast of *Joseph* appeared and, obviously, Pete, Russ, Paul and Darren.

Then came Sarah Greene and Mike Smith, Caron Keating, Anthea Turner and Emma Forbes, followed by some of the friends I'd made at Radio 1, including Steve Wright and the man whose first ever Roadshow I'd watched when I was eleven, Alan Freeman. Steph was beautiful beside me and the best moment by far was when the doors opened and my two gorgeous little girls walked out, holding the hands of my dresser Angie White and the *Dolittle* cast.

I've always thought how lucky I was to have had my career celebrated in that way and, on reflection, it came early. The producers told me after the show that they had wanted to feature someone younger than the usual recipients of the big red book but who had still achieved enough to fill a show and had a family that spanned the generations. For me, it meant that I had two of my grandparents, my parents and my children all on one VHS. It is a beautiful living, breathing memento.

The year flew by in London, and it was time to take the doctor on the road. I was very much looking forward to seeing how the show went down in slightly smaller theatres. As

I'd hoped, it was a joyous transformation. All the subtleties that were missed at the Apollo could now be seen by every audience and the laughter rang out night after night.

I have so many happy memories of that two-year tour. We laughed a lot. We had poker nights and wine-tasting nights. We had long nights on the beach in Eastbourne when the most hardy of us drunkenly watched the sun rise out of the sea. Angie White was brilliant, hysterically funny but sensationally accident prone. As we unpacked after the move from one theatre to another, she asked if I fancied a cuppa – great idea. We were both horrified by the noise the kettle started to make. When we looked inside it, we discovered that she had packed all the cutlery, the corkscrew, a pan scrub and half a bottle of Fairy Liquid inside.

In Southampton, Angie and I stood on the roof of the Mayflower Theatre along with lovely Joe from the wig department and set off balloons with our telephone numbers on them to see how far they travelled. I got a confused call from Belgium. Was there a prize? No, sorry.

The relationship between dresser and actor can be a close one. Seconds before the curtain went up one night, Angie was with us all onstage, desperately trying to stitch a button back on to my crotch. But I think we laughed the hardest during a quick change in the pitch darkness when I accidentally rammed my finger up her nose. It was as if I was about to bowl her head down an alley. Those were very happy times.

Indirectly, the fact that I missed a performance of *Doctor Dolittle* in Plymouth was Jason Donovan's fault.

In the *Going Live* days, if ever we needed a guest, Stock, Aitken and Waterman would instantly fill any gap we had with one of their performers. We were constantly grateful. So when I was asked by them if I would record the links for a compilation video for all of Jason's hits, of course I said yes.

It would be a very easy afternoon in a studio. When they asked how much I wanted, I told the office that, as a thank-you, I'd happily do it for free.

That decision cost me a small fortune. I recorded the links and didn't think too much more about it until two cases of wine were delivered to my door in Chiswick. I knew nothing about wine at this point, so I bought a book on it, then another. I discovered that I had been sent twelve bottles of very good red Burgundy and twelve bottles of a very lovely white, with tasting notes. (I have kept one of the whites as a memento, and I will never open it.) I drank the bottles with family and friends. It was definitely the best wine I'd ever tasted. I bought more books, I joined the Wine Society, I bought a house with a cellar. I've now bought lots of wine – in fact, there are gaps on the wall where there should be pictures but, instead, I bought wine.

When the first one was full, my dad supervised the construction of another cellar to accomodate the overflow. That too is now full. I've often said I'd like to end my days in there with a corkscrew and a glass.

I met Stephen Browett through my New Zealand PA, Jo Hulton, and he introduced me to Britain's first female Master of Wine, Jancis Robinson, and from there my circle of wine friends grew wider and wider. They were incredibly generous, both with wine and in sharing their knowledge. I went with Stephen and Jancis to taste the year's new vintage in Bordeaux. I had lunch in Château Latour and I've been lucky enough to taste some of the best wines in the world.

Steph bought me an incredible present, a driving holiday in Bordeaux, which she meticulously organized with Stephen Browett. Now I could properly learn the geography. Stephen booked wine tastings in some of the châteaux and we ate lamb barbecued on vine sticks over a wheelbarrow at Château Cos d'Estournel. It was the best lamb I've ever tasted. After being shown around Château Margaux we had dinner in a very posh restaurant. I got cocky and, as I tasted the wine for our dinner, it went down the wrong way and I coughed. Both the sommelier and Steph were horrified by the two red jets of Margaux that shot out of my nose.

So, you see, I take it very seriously.

Anyway, back to that missed performance. Stephen Browett asked if I would like to go to a tasting of some really special wines they were having at their offices in Battersea. I decided I would. First thing in the morning I flew from Plymouth to Heathrow. I explained that I was onstage that night so I'd have to leave by about four. As we began our descent into Plymouth I felt the plane turn. The pilot came on the Tannoy. He apologized, but Plymouth airport was closed because of fog and we were diverting to Bristol. My heart was jumping out of my chest: I was going to miss the show.

At Bristol, I found a company that would fly me to Exeter, and from Exeter I got on the back of a motorbike that took me at terrifying speed to Plymouth. Just as I jumped off the bike and ran to the stage door, the show started. I'd missed it. If I hadn't done that free video for Jason, I wouldn't have been sent the Burgundy, I wouldn't have got into wine and I wouldn't have been at that tasting. See: all his fault.

The final city for the tour was Bristol, and it was lovely to be back there. I had a gorgeous suite in the Swallow Hotel, just across from the theatre. One afternoon I answered my ringing phone. It was Steph.

'Are you watching TV?'

'No?'

'Turn it on.'

As I turned it on, I stumbled backwards in horror to sit on the end of the bed.

Moments later, the second plane hit the Twin Towers of the World Trade Center. I had arranged an interview in a local wine shop that day. I was glued to the TV, but I didn't want to let them down, so I left the hotel room, dazed by what I had seen and trying to understand what it meant for us all.

We didn't talk much about wine in the interview. As I said my goodbyes and walked back to the hotel through the stunned streets of Bristol, my phone rang. Again, it was Steph.

'They've collapsed. Both towers have gone.'

I walked aimlessly through the streets. New York was the only city that I had literally dreamt of going to as a child. Steph and I loved our visits. We had both stood on the viewing platform at the top of the South Tower and been awestruck by the view over the city. I thought back to the last time I had performed in Bristol, my visit to the Concorde simulator and my success at flying the plane perfectly through the gap between the towers. We would visit New York a month later. The ruins were still smoking. A city had been stabbed in the heart. When I looked up from my thoughts, I was totally lost.

On 22 September 2001, I hung up my *Dolittle* top hat (actually, I put it in the boot of the car!). It was the last musical I did. I had got to know David Grindrod when he was the company manager on *Joseph*. He later left and became one of Britain's top casting directors. David and his partner, Stephen Crockett, have kindly offered me roles in many of the West End's big musicals but, sadly, the timings have never worked. I also wondered if my singing nerves had finally got the better of me. One of the friends I made on the *Dolittle* tour was Simon Schofield – no relation, and a much better singer than me. Simon is also now among my closest friends. He now has his own production company and recently over a few beers he pitched the *Knights of Music* concept to me. A group of West End singers and dancers would perform songs made famous by either Sirs, Lords or Dames. There was a wealth of material to choose from. I would narrate the show. It sounded fun. Over a couple more pints, he persuaded me to sing both 'Close Every Door' and 'Any Dream Will Do'. I agreed, but I was too scared to sing on my own so I insisted we duetted. I also agreed to wear 'the Coat'. We did ten shows, which were beautifully put together. Simon's lovely fiancée, Beth, was in charge of wardrobe, and the whole production had a happy, family feel to it.

In the finale, when I appeared in 'the Coat', the reaction was incredible. My voice had mellowed and improved and I sang those songs better than ever. At the end of each show, I felt like a pop star. However, every day before the show, I was crippled with nerves. What if I made a mistake on one of

Back on stage with Simon Schofield.

the songs and it ended up on YouTube? It was irrational. Though every performance had gone perfectly, I had to tell Simon that nerves prevented me from doing any more. To give him his due, he has bought me a few pints and tried to wear me down, but all to no avail, so far.

The last time I sang in public was for Ant and Dec's 'end of the show show' on *Saturday Night Takeaway* in March 2018. In a seventieth-birthday tribute to Lord Lloyd Webber and all dressed in Dreamcoats, they sang 'Any Dream Will Do' along with James Corden and Joe McElderry. I was the surprise finale. Only they could persuade me to sing in front of 8 million people. I didn't tell anyone I was doing it other than Steph and the girls. They were with me in the dressing room, holding me together. I even kept it a secret from Holly, who over the years had become one of my closest friends and confidantes.

She texted me immediately after the show came off air and said that she was watching it with her husband, Dan, and she had said to him, 'Phil should be doing this,' and then I walked out! Again, it was an incredible experience. I'll never forget the roar as I walked out. But the nerves nearly killed me. So either Britain's most famous TV phobia experts, the Speakmans, will have to rid me of my fear, or my singing days are now behind me.

In 2001, after I returned home from the tour, the gang came over to the house for a celebration. Russ Lindsay took me to one side.

'Mate, we may have a problem,' he said.

'Why, what's the matter?'

'I was in a cab a couple of days ago and the driver asked what I did. I told him I was a manager and he asked who I managed and when I got to your name he said, "Whatever happened to him?"'

'Why is that a problem?'

'You've been doing theatre too long. People have forgotten about you.'

It was true. I may have been having a blast every night on the stage but, for a television audience, I had disappeared. Celador had once again looked after me with the National Lottery's *Winning Lines*, but the beginning of 2002 was terrifying. I can clearly remember having a bit of a cry at the kitchen table as I said to Steph that I'd messed up. Flicking through the start of that 2002 diary still makes me anxious. It is a vivid reminder of just how tenuous a job in TV is. It is very easy to be forgotten – no one is irreplaceable. It can all be over in the snap of a finger. You are there only because people want you to be there. When they don't, you can be absolutely assured, you're yesterday's toast. TV executives also move on; they have their favourites. For a while, I wasn't one of them. I couldn't get arrested on ITV.

The team at James Grant were working hard to find something for me to do, but pickings were slim.

I presented a *Design Challenge* show for a satellite channel and a series of interviews with people of note who lived in the West Country for TSW (which used to be Westward TV). I really enjoyed that one. I got to work with David Rodgers again, who I'd first met at Hospital Radio Plymouth. I also got to meet some fascinating people: Joss Ackland (best speaking voice *ever*), Jean Shrimpton, Jenny Agutter and, best of all, Hugh Scully. Hugh had been a friend for some time. David Rodgers, Steph, Hugh and I would meet up for lunch, usually at Rick Stein's in Padstow. We would eat lunch, drink wine, talk and laugh, drink more wine and then be in the perfect place for dinner, so just carry on.

Hugh was one of my favourite raconteurs. He was brilliantly funny, with the best stories, and also incredibly intelligent and utterly charming. Funnily enough, working for Westward was another tick on my fantasy broadcasting list. It was the channel I grew up with in Newquay. I fondly remember watching David Rodgers present *Treasure Hunt*, marvelling at how Roger Shaw said, 'temp er a TURE' and listening to Ian Stirling try to sort out a link when he had endearingly arsed it up. Judi Spiers was also a big star on the channel. As a kid, I stayed awake to hear her do the close-down. She always messed around and was quite obviously breaking the rules. At about fifteen, I answered an advert placed by Judi in the *Cornish Guardian*. They wanted a young presenter for a show called *Down the Line*. I have relentlessly reminded her that when she phoned to personally tell me I hadn't got it, she broke my heart during my brother's birthday party. Sadly, although I met all of them and even became a friend to many, I never met Gus Honeybun.

Come to think of it, it was in David Rodgers' sitting room that I first met Ruth Langsford. She was on her hands, dragging her bum across the sitting-room carpet, pretending to be a dog with worms. (Sorry, Ruth, hehe.)

It wasn't until April 2002 that the BBC rode in to the rescue. Would I co-host a new show that would be big, live and test the IQ of the audience? My saviour was *Test the Nation* and my co-host was Anne Robinson. I make it a point to get on with everyone I work with. I love the job so much I want it to be enjoyable. I have worked with a lot of amazing female presenters – Fern Britton, Sarah Greene, Emma Forbes, Claudia Winkleman, Emma Willis, Amanda Holden, Ruth Langsford, Fearne Cotton, Carol Vorderman, Davina McCall, Clare Balding, Myleene Klass, Suzi Perry, Lorraine Kelly, Caron Keating, Alison Hammond, Christine Bleakley, Holly Willoughby, Rochelle Humes, Julie Etchingham. It is a very long list and they're all amazing . . .

Anne Robinson was . . . unique. I liked Anne very much, she was fascinating. Her success on *The Weakest Link* had been global and, in her own words, her husband had only gone to America to carry the cash back, in real life, in the studio, she was as tough as her TV persona. As we sat in make-up, side by side, I told her we'd just bought a little house in Portugal.

'How much was it?' she asked.

'Not expensive. It's not grand, just a little farmhouse type of thing.'

'How many staff?'

'Staff?' I laughed. 'No staff, just us.'

'Who cleans?'

'We do.'

'Who cooks?'

'Er, we do.'

'How quaint,' she sniffed, and having lost interest, she turned back to the mirror.

She was fascinated by money. At the end of each show she wanted to know what I was going to buy with what I'd just earned. I was intrigued by the guy who was employed to put her earpiece in for her. When she was ready, she would tilt her head to one side and impatiently cough until he had spotted his cue and stuck it in her ear. When Anne rehearsed, there was silence; when I rehearsed, she looked at me and made a 'papapapapa, tch tch tch shhhhh' sound and clicked her fingers at me. I had to rehearse without actually speaking. I reiterate: I liked Anne, she was interesting to observe and unlike anyone else I've worked with, not brilliant technically, but quick and acid-tongued. A bit like a fairground curiosity.

Test the Nation did, however, give me the chance to forgive Piers Morgan. After the glowing review he had given me in

Joseph, Piers and James Grant had a friendly relationship. Obviously, he still took no prisoners, but he was a bit of a fan so I got off lightly.

I was told by the office that Piers wanted to write a series of articles about me for the paper and he would love to have my cooperation. I said I was flattered and of course I'd do it; what did he need? Did I have any memorabilia he could use? Photos? An old BBC pass? A student railcard? As I think I've said, I save everything, so interesting bits and pieces were hunted down then sent to Piers. Nothing appeared in the paper. I was worried he may have lost all my mementos. We asked for them back. Nothing. Eventually, unannounced, they arrived safely back at the office.

A few weeks later, the unofficial biography he'd written about me, including all the stuff I'd sent him, appeared on the bookshelves. I was furious. Not so much that he had written the book, but that he had deceived me. We didn't speak for a long time. There were awkward moments: once, the two us were in a lift for what felt like an endless descent. At a James Grant Christmas party, a heavily disguised Santa was hired. We all laughed as we sat on his knee and told him what we wanted. It turned out it was Piers. I was not amused.

Piers appeared a couple of times on *Test the Nation*, and one day I realized how stupid this feud was. I was angry, and he'd actually been flattering and kind in the biography (although utterly deceitful). It was time to make up. He was nervous when I walked over.

'Enough,' I said, and I shook his hand. We've been fine ever since. Lunch with Piers is always riddled with gossip. The book he wrote was called *To Dream a Dream*. It's actually not a bad read, and mostly accurate.

Wow! Look where we are!

This Morning had been on my radar from the moment I watched the first-ever show from the *Going Live* office on the twelfth floor of the East Tower in 1988.

I always enjoyed travelling up to Liverpool to appear on it. There was a brilliant 'organized chaos' feel to the Albert Dock studios. I learned very quickly, through the experience of others, not to go on the show if I was one of the last guests of the day. Brilliant as Richard and Judy are, they were shocking at keeping to time. By the time they got to the end of the show they would be over-running so much that the last guest would regularly be dropped. That meant whoever it happened to be had invariably travelled from London the night before, stayed overnight in Liverpool, got up way too early and sat in the studio until twelve thirty, only to be told, 'Sorry, couldn't fit you in.' Nope, I wasn't having any of that. If I was expected to be on after midday, I wasn't going. I'd been on the show to promote *Joseph*, *Dolittle* and a host of TV shows, and it was always great fun to do, because no one knew where Richard's head would go.

When the show moved to London I was a guest on one of the first shows from the ITV Southbank studios. I accidentally made Judy cry. I knew that it had been a wrench for them to move from the North-west and at the end of the interview I asked how they were settling in to their new studio. Judy burst into tears. Slightly awkward.

I actually presented the show for a week with Caron Keating in 1998 and *loved* it. It was like *Going Live*, but for adults.

But going back through my diaries, it looks like it wasn't until the week commencing Monday, 2 September 2002 that I had a meeting which may very well have been pivotal in almost every aspect of my life.

Fern Britton was presenting *This Morning* with John Leslie. The show was getting back on its feet. After Richard and Judy had left, it had had a rocky time with presenter chemistry. Colleen Nolan and Twiggy are both totally delightful ladies and, individually, they are very talented, but together as *This Morning* presenters they didn't work so well. At the end of it, it wasn't glory that everyone was covered in.

Fern and John had steadied the ship; their relationship on air was great. John floated the idea that he would like to take Fridays off. So, if that were to happen, who would do Fridays with Fern?

I wasn't sure why ITV had asked if I would go in for a meeting. When I got there, I met the assistant head of Daytime TV. There was an opening on the show for a Friday presenter. Would I be interested? I said I would. I was told that a presenter on the show had to have certain qualities. To be versatile, trustworthy, happy to talk about family life, able to work with a team and interested in doing a wide variety of interviews. I said I was very happy with all that. 'Then we are happy to have you on board.'

I saw it very much as a temporary job. I was pretty sure that John Leslie would eventually want his Fridays back, but after working with Caron on the show I knew it was great fun. There is something about live television – people stand a little taller, are more alert, think faster. *This Morning* was and is the best kind of live TV. Sometimes deadly serious, sometimes frivolous, sometimes happy, sometimes sad,

David O'Brien and Lyn Evans, part of my 'glam squad'.

occasionally inappropriate, and often ruder than you would think the time slot would allow.

Fern was warm and welcoming and introduced me to the team, some of whom are still working on the show. David O'Brien was Head of Wardrobe then and still is now. He has also, since the day I met him, designed everything I've worn on pretty much every show I've presented ever since. Lyn Evans was Fern's make-up artist and would also be mine. Mel Wiffen on autocue had started with Richard and Judy. She's freelance these days but it's still a delight when she pops in occasionally and says 'hi' and that she's back for a couple of shows. We call Mel 'the Predictor' because she can change words in the script before you even suggest it. She can also read minds and can spot an issue long before it occurs. Floor manager Tim Carr had also started with Richard and Judy and still occasionally works on the show.

My time on *This Morning* was shaped by the intelligent, talented women who steered the ship. Shu Richmond, the editor; Debra Davidson, her deputy; the boss Dianne Nelmes and later Fiona Keenahan, Anya Francis and Helen Gibson were all totally switched on to the pulse of the show and the viewers and they were all so welcoming to me.

I think it's safe to say that pretty much everyone who has worked on the show has a deep fondness for and pride in it. Many of the names you see on the list of credits after a programme finishes will have cut their teeth on *This Morning*. Invariably, someone will start out as a researcher, leave to get experience elsewhere and come back as a producer. Pete Ogden, who went on to become executive producer on *Saturday Night Takeaway*, started as a researcher at roughly the same time as I started, became a producer, left for a while and then came back as editor! We always joke that *This Morning* is like the Eagles' 'Hotel California'. You can check out any time you like, but you can never leave.

I loved my Fridays on the show. *This Morning* has its own broadcast language, which takes a few days to learn but, obviously, I revelled in that. Fern was a joy to work with, the team was fun, but I knew I was the stand-in – until one day in October 2002 when I wasn't, because John Leslie had to leave suddenly.

The show must go on, but I knew how fond of John Fern was. These were definitely not the circumstances I wanted to take any job under. I was asked if I would step in from the following Monday and present the show. I agreed. I knew Fern and the team and so I knew I could be sensitive.

Fern and I presented *This Morning* together on the Monday.

After every show there is always a meeting to discuss what happened during the show. What could we do better? What would be on tomorrow's show? After the Monday meeting Fern said to me:

'Are you in a rush?'

'Not at all.'

'Hang on here. I'll be back in a minute.'

She rushed out of the meeting room. A minute later she was back, bringing with her a bottle of Scotch she had been given and two paper cups.

'If we are going to work together, I think we'd better get to know each other,' she said.

We drank most of the bottle. We were honest and open and it was both emotional and extremely funny. And no, I didn't discuss 'that' with Fern because, in 2002, I was a very long way from even knowing 'that' existed. We talked about families, our ups and downs, our heads, what made us tick. I'm pretty sure I mentioned over that bottle that I didn't just love my job, I was obsessed by TV, I always had been. I'm pretty sure I told her that I liked to look at all the aspects of a show I was presenting; it meant I spotted issues that might have been missed.

I'm pretty sure I mentioned all that.

If I didn't, then I wish I had, because years down the line the fact that I had an eye on most things really pissed her off.

As we quickly got to know each other, it was clear that we had exactly the same sense of humour. It worked at the same speed for both of us, we were hopeless gigglers and we were both filthy. In all my TV career, those planets have only been perfectly aligned twice: with Fern and with Holly.

If you are really lucky, you achieve that holy grail of TV: chemistry. Chemistry is when you don't have to try, when it's natural and just 'is'. Fern and I never discussed how we were going to present an item, or even who would go first in an interview; it just happened. We would always know where the other was going with something, always had the same questioning lines and ideas. It was delightful synchronicity.

It's safe to say that with most professional people there is an 'edit' switch, or at least a reasonably effective control button to prevent whatever you are doing from descending into chaos. I've wondered if our giggling fits would have been as bad if we were working together but in another career. If that were true, thank goodness that, in an alternative universe, we weren't standing next to each other in an operating theatre.

Occasionally, we were surprisingly unprofessional! We definitely laughed at the wrong times. We laughed at Mr Song Dong who came in with a city of biscuits because he had such a fantastic name. We laughed when we were told we would meet a guest who was allergic to light and so her mother had written to NASA to get some of the material they used to protect astronauts from dangerous light radiation. We imagined a woman arriving in a discreet catsuit that could be worn under clothing. When our guest arrived, she sat down to do the interview in what resembled a full beekeeper outfit with huge protective headgear. Gradually, over the course of the interview the visor steamed up and we lost sight of the guest inside. That wasn't our finest hour.

One morning I happened to say that I hated dunking biscuits. Later in the show when we both had a slice of roast beef and a pot of horseradish in front of us, Fern innocently said, 'There, you see. You don't mind dunking a bit of beef, do you?' There was a second's beat where we both got there in our heads at the same time, and then the show fell apart.

We laughed when she said she had dropped a pot of mint sauce on her kitchen floor at home and it had splashed up the inside of her nighty. In make-up I called her 'Minty minge'. On the telly, just calling her 'Minty' had the desired effect.

She made me roar when she said that once, she was closing a sash window whilst naked. She suddenly realized the next-door neighbour was looking up at her and immediately repeated the pose in front of the bedroom mirror to see how she looked! She thought she must have looked like the three of spades!

I had been presenting the show for a few weeks when Dianne Nelmes, the then Director of Daytime, asked to see me. It was a meeting that had been set up by Darren in the James Grant office. Dianne and I met after the show in one of the empty dressing rooms. It went disastrously wrong.

Dianne had been the editor on the show when it launched in Liverpool and it was she who brought Jeremy Kyle from radio to TV. We'd been getting on pretty well, I thought.

'How are you enjoying the show?' she asked.

'I'm absolutely loving it,' I gushed.

'You have a great relationship with Fern, and the team love you.'

'Well, that's great to hear. I'm having so much fun with Fern and the team are fantastic.'

'So we thought we'd better put you on tape – make it official, sort of thing,' she said.

'Oh!' I laughed. 'I thought it sort of was. I'm sorry. I think I've misunderstood.'

'Not at all, but we'd like to offer it to you permanently, so we'll need to set up an afternoon for an audition.'

'Pardon?'

'We would need to get an official audition down on tape.'

'Er, well, I've sort of been presenting the show for weeks full time, and before that every Friday for months. Doesn't that count as a successful audition?'

'Well, no, not really.'

'Well, this is a tricky one,' I said. 'Because I don't think I'm prepared to audition for a show I'm already doing, and which, I should add, seems to be going pretty well.'

'Well, I'm sorry, Phillip, but I must insist.'

'With the greatest respect, Dianne, I'm going to have to decline the offer.'

'Well, that's such a shame, but thank you for everything.'

'Okay. Well, thank you very much. I've had a great time.'

'No, thank you.'

I left the dressing room and walked around the corner to my dressing room, opened the door and just stood there. What the hell had just happened? I called Daz in the office.

'Hi, mate, it's me.'

'Hi, Phil. How did the meeting with Dianne go?'

'Well, she fired me, or I might have resigned. I'm not totally sure.'

'*She what?* What happened? What did you do?'

I explained. He said he had to go and make some calls.

At the same time, Dianne Nelmes was calling David Liddiment, the Director of Programmes.

'David, it's Dianne. I have a bit of a problem.'

'What's the matter?'

'I just accidentally fired Phillip Schofield.'

'*You what?*'

That afternoon there were numerous calls back and forth between James Grant and ITV. It was soon sorted out. It was just an unfortunate accident, a conversation that took a wrong turn. No damage done? Absolutely none.

Every time I see Dianne we laugh about that conversation and wonder how the hell it had gone so wrong. The following Monday, I was back on the TV as if nothing had ever happened. I'm still waiting for the audition idea to be formally abandoned. Maybe, after eighteen years, I've convinced them that I can do it. Dianne was, incidentally, a lovely boss.

The talented all-women powerhouse that drove *This Morning*.

I have an alarm bell that rings in my head in times of potential trouble on TV. It can ring way off in the distance, maybe get louder, maybe fade away as the potential danger passes. It can start to ring if I meet a guest and can tell that something is wrong. Sometimes, when I'm told something, it can be deafening from the start. In the meeting for one *This Morning* it rang very loudly.

'We're going to try to break a knife-throwing record.'

'Live?!' I asked. The alarm bells in my head started ringing.

'Yes, definitely live.'

'Shouldn't we record it, just in case there's an issue?'

'No need for that. This couple have been in circuses for years. This is what they do.'

'I'm not sure it's a good idea.'

'It'll be fine. Don't worry.'

If the alarm was loud in the meeting, it was deafening on the studio floor the next day. It was a young couple, and he would throw; she wouldn't blink. She seemed a bit timid to me. Had it ever gone wrong? Apparently, nothing 'serious' had ever happened.

I whispered my concerns into my mic to the gallery. Were we *sure* this was okay?

We came out of the commercial break and explained what was about to happen. A record would be broken for the most knives thrown in a minute.

'Everyone, take your positions.'

Fern and I stood to the side. The minute began.

The knives were thrown at lightning speed, all accurate . . . until.

One of the knives glanced off the woman's head. She winced and immediately a trickle of blood ran from her hairline. Fern and I took different approaches. I ran and stood in front of the camera to hide the woman from shot and then, ludicrously, asked if the record had been broken. Fern, on the other hand, cried out, 'Oh, there's blood! There's blood!' thereby somewhat giving the game away. The couple seemed fairly non-plussed. A few moments later, sitting on the sofa and a bit shaken, Fern and I looked across the studio. One of the crew was mopping up the blood so they could set the fashion item. The show always goes on.

The fun wasn't confined to the studio. Getting ready in the mornings was also great fun (it still is). Fern and I would sit in the make-up room with David and Lyn as we got ready. We gossiped, told stories and laughed. I can remember saying, if laughter makes you live longer, we would all make it to a hundred and fifty.

It was in that make-up room that Fern persuaded me to

stop colouring my hair. As you know, I had already, teasingly, showed my true colours when I first moved to ITV, but they didn't like it at all.

'Just let it grow out,' said Fern. 'The great thing about being on TV every day is that it will happen gradually.'

She was right, and it was such a pain in the arse to keep colouring it. Every five weeks from the age of nineteen I had sat in the hairdresser's chair as they hid the grey. Not only was it unbelievably boring, it was also bloody expensive. 'Right, then,' I said. 'That's it. I'm not colouring it again.'

So that I didn't have a hard root line, my very talented long-standing hair stylist and friend, Lino Carbosiero, used a skilful camouflage of highlights and lowlights to ease the transition. Bit by bit, it was revealed. I, like everyone else, had no idea what it was going to look like or what colour it would be. I actually love my hair colour, I love that it's so distinctive. I'm happy with the 'silver fox' label. I'm less happy that it's such a beacon! It's useful for Steph to find me in a supermarket, but anywhere else it just screams, *'I'm over here!'* People constantly say that they recognize me because of my hair. If I put a baseball cap on, the noise from my hair is instantly quietened, sadly at the expense of looking like a dick, because I don't suit hats of any kind.

Fern decided that she, David, Lyn and I should go on outings. We went to the War Rooms and to Westminster Abbey but our most successful visit was to Kensington Palace. We had principally gone to look at a collection of Princess Diana's dresses and gowns – not really my thing, but I love a good palace. When we arrived, we discovered that the exhibition had, unfortunately, been delayed. Fern's disappointment must have been obvious because one of the senior staff came over to apologize. We all said it was perfectly okay and that we would come back another time. The palace official said he would make it up to us and show us a part of the palace that was usually closed to visitors.

Now this kind of thing is right up my street. If there is a door marked 'No Entry' or 'Private', *that* is the door I want to go through. If there is a roped-off area, I want to step over the rope. I actually came up with a TV format years ago called *Behind the Rope*, which took me to 'forbidden' places. Sadly, I still couldn't get behind the particular ropes that I had my eye on. If you're a TV exec reading this, I'm only interested if you start at that windowless ivy-covered building by Horseguards. Oh, and what's behind that metal door at the bottom of the steps that we were warned away from on *Schofield's Quest*?

We were led through a door or two and were shown into Apartment 1A, the spacious and empty rooms where Princess Margaret used to live. It was an extraordinary step back in time. The kitchen is said to have been designed by Antony Armstrong-Jones, and there was a jacuzzi bath that still had the instructions beside it. We all agreed that it was a home that had seen a lot of parties. It would later become the home to the Duke and Duchess of Cambridge.

Dressing-room space was limited in the old *This Morning* studios on the Southbank. We only had two guest dressing rooms and, tucked around the corner, hidden away near make-up and wardrobe, were the two 'presenter dressing rooms' that were used by Fern and me. Fern had had other signs made up for our doors: on hers was 'The Spa'; on mine 'The Club.' Occasionally, if a big star came on the show, we would be asked if they could use our dressing rooms because they were nicer and had their own bathroom. We would pack our stuff into a bag and stick it in the wardrobe. I let Robert Downey Jr use mine and, allegedly, when a producer went to brief him, only his manager could be seen. Where was Mr

Downey Jr? 'He's hiding,' said the manager. The producer was a little unnerved. Hiding? Was she supposed to look for him? She found him fully clothed, standing in a dry shower. Apparently, he thought it was hilarious.

Michael Winner also used my dressing room. I had read before he arrived that he had enjoyed a spectacular lunch and had drunk some *very* good wine. I was fascinated so I knocked on my door. I said we were looking forward to having him on the show, but I was interested in the wines he had drunk at that lunch. Bearing in mind the wine company I was now keeping, the places I had visited, the stellar wines I had tasted and the fact that I now owned five thousand bottles, his answer was dismissive in the extreme. He simply said, 'You wouldn't understand.' I told Fern, and the seven-minute interview he was due to have inexplicably finished three minutes early.

Fern was asked if Lauren Bacall could use her dressing room. 'Of course,' came the answer.

She had just been given a very expensive candle and decided to light it for Mis Bacall to add a touch of atmosphere. The Hollywood legend was everything we hoped she would be, charismatic, fascinating and elegant. Fern and I went to the corridor after the interview to bid her farewell. Ms Bacall walked out of Fern's dressing room, gave us a sultry smile and huskily thanked us for a lovely chat. As she walked past we noticed something smoking in her hand.

'Fuck me,' said Fern. 'She's lifted my candle.'

We were an amazing on-screen team, and others liked the dynamic, too. Paul Smith's Celador had once again had a great idea for Fern and me: would we like to resurrect *Mr & Mrs* for ITV prime time? It was such a fun show to do. The intimacies the couples admitted to on that show were things they would never have discussed on the *This Morning* sofa.

Presenting the Soap Awards with Fern.

It was going well. David O'Brien and Lyn Evans made up our usual foursome, and we were a happy team.

I honestly have literally no idea why it went so badly wrong.

In the copy of Fern's autobiography that she gave me is the handwritten note:

To Dearest Phillip

What fun we've had for a couple of twats.

Love you
Fern

I know that the publication of the fact that she had had a gastric-band operation hurt her deeply. Fern was always extremely private about those kinds of personal details, as most people would be. In her mind, it was no one's business. She had also been involved with Ryvita but had been very careful never to connect her weight loss with the brand. I watched the crash happening beside me, knowing that my friend was being deeply wounded. It was the first time I realized and witnessed the fact that, when it comes to criticizing women, the worst and cruellest culprits are other women. She was relentlessly followed; she believed she was spied on, bugged and tapped. Long lenses intruded upon her and her family and it was causing immense heartache.

I always believed I was being a true friend. I always believed that I had properly got her back. If I made an error, to this day, I don't know what it was. There was intense speculation that the difference in our pay was a male/female imbalance and a source of friction. We both knew that wasn't the case. We never discussed money. I was on an exclusive contract with ITV and wasn't allowed to work for anyone else, so my salary was higher. Fern was offered something similar, but didn't accept. She didn't want the restriction and wanted to be free to work wherever she pleased.

No matter what I did, I couldn't seem to make it right. I have mentioned before that I want to be involved in all aspects of a show, not in an interfering way, it's just that I have many years' of experience and I've presented through problems that could've been avoided. Sometimes a team can work on a show late into the night, and in the light of morning a fresh set of eyes can spot something that has been missed. *This Morning* is not the kind of programme that benefits from presenters without opinions or input. We are all deeply proud of what we do and the environment is one of friendly discussion, consensus and ideas.

By the start of 2009, the atmosphere in our make-up room was not as happy as it had been. We were all concerned about our friend. A producer walked in to run through that morning's show and as we got to the end of the meeting I looked at the timings for a fashion item. I noticed there were six minutes before a break and seven minutes after. I looked at the daily briefs to see how much fashion content there was to fill the time: to my mind, not enough by far. I asked the producer if he was sure he had enough content to fill thirteen minutes.

As he looked back at the script, Fern said to me, 'Why don't you just stop meddling and let him do the show?'

I replied, 'Because if we don't have enough content, it'll be us that has to fill the time.'

'Just leave it alone!' Fern answered.

'You're right,' said the producer to me. 'There's too much time. I'll change things around.'

I left the room and stood in my dressing room, staring out of the window. I knew the intense pressure she was under but I was stunned that she would lash out at me. I walked back into the make-up room and calmly said, 'Please don't do that to me again.'

I think, for whatever reason, that was the point Fern decided she didn't want to do *This Morning* any more. She had been gradually reducing her days, but I think, at that moment, she'd had enough. When she announced that she was leaving I was heartbroken. Heartbroken that our friendship had inexplicably gone so sour, and heartbroken because I'd never had a presenting partnership like that before.

I have tried over the years to make it right, but Fern has moved on, and I understand that. I still miss her deeply though, and in recent times would have valued her counsel. When I came out, she didn't text me. She did text Steph though, which was really kind.

When Fern left, there was only one person I wanted to present *This Morning* with. I'd been co-hosting *Dancing on Ice* with Holly Willoughby for three years and she was perfect for the job. Looking at where we are now, it was a surprisingly difficult idea to sell.

The first time I met Holly was at a production meeting for *Dancing on Ice* (*DOI* from now on, because it's quite long to type!). Holly was another graduate from the school of Saturday-morning TV. It's really quite incredible how many of us started in children's telly. Holly had a brilliant onscreen chemistry with Stephen Mulhern. Very early in his career, Stephen, who is also a talented magician, had come to our house to perform at Molly's birthday party. I love how all our paths have criss-crossed over the years.

DOI was a risk – in fact, there was no real belief that it would be a hit. Could ice skating be made sexy? Would it interest an evening audience? Even with ice-skating legends Torvill and Dean on board, expectations were not high. As we got closer to transmission Holly and I shared our nerves together. I'm always the same: usually very nervous for show one, and then fine afterwards. For Holly, this was her first big prime-time show and she was terrified. Our opening-night cards to each other both featured similar 'shitting ourselves' messages. The show was looking incredible, but there was still no great excitement from anyone at ITV. It was, however, a surprise hit and went on to be the third-highest-rated show in 2006: the final got 13 million viewers.

When the figures came in the next morning, we were all stunned. ITV were ecstatic, and Holly and I were deeply relieved. I was also pleased because I'd been in to Mappin and Webb on Regent Street and had bought the principals of the team a diamond that they could have mounted however they liked. Maybe that 'ice' was lucky for us.

The reaction from the public was huge! They loved the show. That was principally proved by the huge uptake of excited families rushing out to their local rink. We constantly heard stories of skate shops running out of supplies because of the influx of new skaters. I still had the occasional cigarette, and the *DOI* smoking club was one of the best. If you stood outside in the cold with everyone, there was a unique camaraderie. It was outside in those five minutes that we got the best gossip. 'She hates him.' 'He's a total arsehole.' 'What a bitch.' It was never quite the same when I moved on to vapes.

Over the years, it has been such a happy ship. While the scandals, affairs and meltdowns have happened on the ice, the production team, led in the early days by Katie Rawcliffe, loved every trauma. The gossip at the Sunday-morning script read through is always sensational.

'She did *what*?'

'You'll never believe who shagged who last night.'

Our end-of-series 'blooper reels' are legendary.

Holly left the show for a couple of years to present *The Voice UK* and Christine Bleakley stepped in. At the time, Christine was getting a battering by the press, mostly the same kind of female columnists who had been so cruel to Fern. It was horrid to see her go through it, especially because Christine is one of the most thoughtful, kind and genuine people in the entire business. It was during Christine's tenure that I was finally persuaded to learn a routine on ice.

Even to be asked was a turn-up because on my first-ever

day at the *DOI* rink, on the morning before the show, I had asked if I could have a skate. Boots were found and I was taken around the ice by Chris Dean and, I think, Matt Evers. I was loving it. When I looked over to the stage area there were four 'suits' with stern faces and folded arms. I was told I wasn't insured. During the following week, I figured that as long as I accepted full responsibility they'd be happy.

The next Sunday, I was back on the ice. No one said anything: It must be okay. On the Monday morning I got a call from Paul in the office. Even though he's one of my best friends, if Paul calls unannounced my heart usually sinks. It means there's some kind of trouble.

'Hi, mate, it's Paul. We've got a bit of a problem.'

'Oh God. Okay. What's happened?'

'It's about your skating.'

'Huh?'

'Apparently, last week you were told you weren't allowed to skate and this week you went on the ice again. The shit has hit the fan.'

'But . . . but I said I'd take full responsibility, I'd sign something to accept liability.'

'Nope, you're forbidden.'

'Forbidden?! What will they do to me if I ignore it and go on?'

'They've said that YOU won't get into trouble but everyone else who's involved in allowing you on to the ice WILL be in trouble.'

That was the end of that. There was no way I'd get anyone into trouble, so my dream of weekly skating lessons with Torvill and Dean had quickly melted. They did give me an amazing pair of signed skates, though. Unfortunately, I'm too scared to put them on in case the wet ice rubs off the signatures.

So, after all that, six years later, I was now being *asked* to skate on the ice. After agreeing, I grumbled, 'Think how bloody good I would have been if you'd let me have six years of lessons.'

Christine and I had lessons for three weeks with Karen Barber and the team and I was happy with how I was getting on. On show day, I was nervous, but pleased with the way our little routine was going. It felt fast! When I watched it back, I was horrified, I was like a tortoise on ice. It may have *felt* fast, but it certainly was *not* fast. I would definitely have been faster if I'd had all those lost lessons.

Dancing on Ice has always been a firm favourite of all our family and friends. One of Steph's most tiresome jobs of the year is sorting out the tickets for those who want to come. There's a waiting list! I get a small allocation for each show and, even though the show doesn't start until January, they've usually all gone by the end of October. There's no question that it is a great show to watch. My mum and dad loved being in the audience, but my dad was getting poorly.

I've been dreading getting to this part of my life. It's one of the reasons I won't do *Piers Morgan's Life Stories*. I can't tell this story out loud, and I know he'd make me. Oh! I've just realized, I'm going to have to for the audio book! That won't be easy.

My dad was my hero – I hope you've got a sense of that by now. Having devoted parents has meant I've been truly blessed. When you're young, you always think they're invincible. New Zealand had proven that Brian Schofield wasn't. I mentioned that the events of that horrific night in New Zealand had given him another twenty-five years. Those twenty-five years were nearly up.

Though my mum never fell out of love with Cornwall (she's in lockdown there now), my dad did. Our girls have been lucky to have four incredible grandparents. Steph's mum

Dad with Molly. I love this picture, I've always
thought Molly looks like a baby seal.

and dad, John and Gill, live closer to us. My folks always had
to either come up to see us from Newquay or wait for us to
drive down to them. My dad always cried when he had to say
goodbye to the girls. On one of their visits up to us he floated
an idea. We had an old stable block in the garden. What would
we think if they sold up in Cornwall, converted the stable and
he made it into a cottage? His health was beginning to falter.
I had no problem having them closer.

By the side of their cottage is a garage which I said was his
to keep. My dad always had to have a workshop. Every day
when I came home from work, the door to the garage would
be open. When he heard the car, he would pop his head out
and wave. Tony, my brilliant and devoted driver who has been
with me for sixteen years, always said, 'There's the smiler.'

Tony has become a friend of the family over the years.
He's seen both me and Steph at our most drunk and has

discreetly scraped us up and got us home. He knows all my friends and knows which of them will lead me astray. I've set off for a night out, got lost, turned to look up the road, and there was Tony, following behind at a crawl to make sure I was okay. He has a remarkable ability to be parked exactly where you look for the car after a big event and, because he makes friends with the police, he's always the first to arrive to pick me up. One year, I was hosting the Royal Variety performance. When it was over, no one could leave the theatre until the Queen had left. My dressing-room window overlooked the stage door. I watched out of the window to see Her Majesty walk out beneath me to her waiting car. Her motorcade pulled away and, as the last flashing blue light left, Tony pulled in behind. It was at that Royal Variety performance that I ended up standing in the wings with Joan Rivers and Robin Williams, just the three of us, for about fifteen minutes. I have never seen such comedy genius in my life as they sparred off each other. It was better than anything that was going to be on the show. I felt incredibly privileged to have been a part of that moment, and they loved me because I was an extremely willing audience.

Tony's finest hour, though, was one day on the way home from *This Morning* as we drove through Parliament Square and we accidentally got caught up in the motorcade of the Australian Prime Minister. We were with them from central London until they peeled off the M4 to go to Heathrow. It was the fastest we've ever got out of London, and neither of us can understand how it happened or how we weren't arrested.

It's hard to know when the first indications of decline in my dad began to show. After his heart attack in New Zealand he completely changed his diet. As he lay recovering in hospital, he had turned on the radio. The first words he heard were, as if by divine intervention: 'No one needs to die of a heart attack.'

Quite obviously, my dad sat up (figuratively) and listened. The words were being spoken by an ex-Qantas pilot called Ross Horne. Ross Horne had written a book called *The New Health Revolution*. In short, wellness, being in touch with ourselves and, principally, diet are the key to a long life. This was a very new concept in 1984 and some would suggest back then that it was all a bit 'hippy shit'. Now, of course, millions of words have been written on the subject and 'diet', 'fitness' and 'wellness' are buzzwords in our everyday lives. They're also the source of many interviews on *This Morning*. My dad asked me to get the book for him. When he had read it, he entirely changed his diet. He was slim, appeared fit, yet his heart had nearly finished him off at forty-seven. From that day on, he maintained a strict low-fat, low-salt, low-sugar diet. In the end, it wasn't enough.

He and Mum had been to Italy and they had had to run for a bus. He struggled. The girls always wanted to drive with 'Bo and Bri', as they call them, whenever they could. On one holiday in Portugal we had gone out to dinner. The girls had travelled with my folks, Steph and I had gone on ahead. When we met up, my mum quietly said to us that it was the last time the girls could travel in their car because she was worried about Dad's driving. And then, one morning, she called us from their cottage, panic stricken. He was very unwell. He had been under the care of doctors at the Royal Brompton Hospital, so we immediately drove him there. He was quickly admitted and seemed gravely ill. We took it in turns over the next few nights to sleep on a camp bed in his room. Then, one morning, he perked up, had toast, he was being his usual funny self. Tim and I spoke to the nurse. It was explained to us that his heart was greatly enlarged and failing him, that he may temporarily perk up, but that we should all enjoy what time we had left together. It was like a punch to my stomach. What I had feared was actually happening. I don't think Tim and Mum would mind if I said that they just wouldn't believe that it could be true and both went into denial. Mum said to me only a handful of days ago that, right to the end, she refused to believe he was going. I knew he was. How ironic that he should die from a big heart.

When he came home to the cottage in our garden he was more or less back to his usual self but looking frailer by the day. We had that wonderful family day where he was fly fishing in the garden, tapping the fly on to a side plate thirty feet away with incredible accuracy. One night I went over to see him. He was reading a fly-fishing book in bed, his glasses halfway down his nose. I hugged him and told him I loved him. He said, 'I know, I love you too.' He hadn't closed the curtains, and when I left I stood in the dark on the wall outside his room, unseen, watching him read.

He was first confined to a chair, then to bed. All I hoped was that this incredible, kind, wonderful, gentle, funny man would be allowed to pass from his life without pain and at peace. He was cruelly denied that. As his heart failed him, he slowly closed down in front of us. The girls were brought in to say hello; we knew it was goodbye. His eyes filled with tears. Cruellest of all was that we couldn't hug him. His whole body hurt if he was moved. Even when he became unresponsive he still winced in pain if he was touched.

When I was fourteen we bought our first stereo record player. Dad and I marvelled at the sound and made sure the speakers were in the perfect position. I held the stepladder for him as he mounted them on the wall. One of the first records he bought was an album called *Nights are Forever* by England Dan and John Ford Coley. His favourite track from the album was 'I'd Really Love to See You Tonight'. In his final days, I lay on the bed beside him singing it to him, hoping he could hear. I can't listen to that song now.

Mum, Dad and Tim.

Mum, Tim, Steph and I took it in turns to continue an unbroken vigil by his bed, but when the time came, he still tried to slip away unnoticed. On 1 May 2008 at 5.50 p.m. I was sitting by the bed and Mum and Tim were in the kitchen. Steph had just arrived back at the house with the girls. I stuck my head out of the door for thirty seconds to say 'hi' and when I went back into his room, his breathing had changed. I yelled to everyone to come quickly. We were all with him, moments later, when he went. As he died, a huge tear rolled from his eye and smashed our hearts into a million pieces. We all hugged him close, because it didn't hurt him any more. I always make sure I'm on the phone to my mum at ten to six on 1 May.

Two days after Dad died, I was booked to host the British Soap Awards. I was gently told that I didn't have to do it; everyone would understand. Absolutely not. My dad would be mortified if he thought I had missed a show or let people down because of him. The show must go on. It was a very tough show to host, but it was in TC1 at Television Centre that year and I felt strangely comforted by that.

The *Soap Awards* are great fun to host, especially now that they are live. I always have a huge respect for the stars in the audience – their workload is immense. Considering the amount of episodes and the turnaround, the quality of our soaps constantly amazes me. The phrase 'continuing drama' is often used, and I think that's much more appropriate. Standing onstage and saying hello to everyone is always totally surreal. Looking into the audience and having the whole of Soapland looking back at you is always disconcerting. When the show was recorded, I think they all appreciated that I tried to get them into the bar as fast as possible. This is a group of people who know how to party.

I have a tradition around the *Soap Awards* that involves 'red 19'. The night before the show Simon Schofield (who plies me with pints to get me onstage!) and I try to meet up and take our chances on the roulette tables. It started when we were in theatre and all went out as a group. It has continued as an occasional treat ever since. Nineteen has always been my lucky number. There's a casino in Manchester that is frequented by footballers, and the money they throw at the table totally eclipses the piddling amounts we play with, but the thrill of a win is always great, regardless of the size of the bet. Simon and I have a rule: only take in the cash that you want to play with. That means we don't take our debit cards, and don't go to the cash machine if we lose our money early doors. It's a rule that isn't always adhered to.

As we work our way through lockdown, have you thought back to the last 'normal' night out you had? The night before the wheels fell off the bloody world?

I had only been 'out' for a month or so. Simon was one of the close group of friends I had confided in. He had been suggesting we go for a pint. I was nervous about going out. What would the reaction be? I warned him that although he was deeply heterosexual, if he went to the pub with me he'd almost certainly be labelled my 'new lover'. He burst out laughing and said he didn't give a shit what people or the papers said, he'd be proud to be my imaginary lover. As it happens, we had the best night out. Everyone was so kind. I was stunned when we walked upstairs in a pub on Bruton Street and an entire table stood and applauded me. I thanked them with very teary eyes. Sadly, by the time we got to the Ritz casino to take our chances on the roulette tables, we were too pissed to play. We stumbled out on to Piccadilly, thankfully unnoticed.

The best-ever 'red 19' night was with Steph. We were in Antigua on holiday and decided to try the resort's casino. We'd both had a good night. The wheel had been kind and I had been squirrelling away the bigger chips we had won in my pocket. By the end of the evening, we were the only two players in the entire casino. I said I was ready for bed, 'Let's call it a day.' We both got up from the table and I took all the winnings from my pocket and put them all on nineteen. Steph said:

'What the hell are you doing?'

'Dunno, crazy impulse.'

'Well, that's just bloody stupid.'

We walked away. The only chips on the table in the empty casino was our tower on nineteen. As we walked past the croupier and the supervisor, I heard the ball drop and saw the bored expression change on their faces. We turned to look at the table. Spinning slowly was the roulette wheel, with the ball snuggling in nineteen. That impulse was nearly enough to pay for the holiday.

'I think Holly would be perfect for *This Morning*,' I said to the Head of Daytime.

'I'm not sure about that,' she replied. 'She lacks gravitas.'

'Gravitas?! *I lack gravitas.*'

'I just don't see it working. I'm sorry.'

'It has to work. She's my only choice.'

I had to make it clear that, if I was to continue on the show, Holly was the only person I wanted to work with. I've always tried really hard to pick my battles in my job, and this was a battle worth fighting and a battle I intended to win. Thankfully, in the end, I got my way.

On 14 September 2009 Holly stood beside me for the first time in the *This Morning* studio. She was extremely nervous. In the opening link, I pretended to walk off and she grabbed my arm and pulled me back. In the eighteen years I've been on *This Morning*, because of holidays or sickness or babies, I've presented with lots of co-hosts. I would hope that all of them felt safe beside me, that they knew I'd be there immediately if they needed me, that I had their back. Holly knew I was there, like a big safety net. She didn't need me, and I knew that would be the case. Yes, she asked for advice; yes, we talked things through. But as a broadcaster she was instantly across it all. I smiled internally and externally. This was going to be fun.

I hope Melinda Messenger doesn't mind me telling this story. I only do so out of affection – Melinda is absolutely delightful. Before Holly arrived I needed a co-host for the show and Melinda agreed to come and play. She listened attentively in the meetings, asked important questions, made sure she was fully briefed and across the show. At ten thirty we stood beside each other waiting to start. As the familiar opening titles started to play, Melinda said:

'This is so exciting. When does the show go out?'

'Huh?'

'When does it go out?'

'It's live! It goes out *now*. This is it. We're on!'

'So, what we say now goes straight out on TV?'

'*Yes!*'

'Oh, I see!'

'Good morning . . .' I said to Britain, with a look of wide-eyed fear in my eyes.

For the rest of the show, Melinda was flawless.

We all watched Holly grow in confidence and laughed when she had to say 'vagina' for the first time on TV. I told her she would say worse. The teams instantly fell in love with her, as did the crew and the viewers. Filling Fern's shoes was no easy task. The viewers were suspicious at first: they were, quite rightly, very loyal to Fern. In her unforced, easy way, Holly charmed everyone, both viewers and crew. The funny, outrageous, naughty atmosphere in make-up was back. We started a quote book for all the things that we said in there. Holly wears her heart on her sleeve and just says it as it is. Ninety-nine point nine of our quotes are absolutely not repeatable, but here are four of Holly's from our quote board:

'Miss Piggy was there, so I went and had a chat with her. She was the only one I knew.'

'I can't turn right on a bike.'

'Oh my God, Prince Charming smokes Marlboro Reds.'

'I think I used to be Nefertiti.'

In the studio, she was completely endearing with her honesty. The camera that is on air has red lights around it; the ones not on air have green lights. Holly said it was confusing her because red was for danger and green was for go, which was why she was looking at the wrong camera. She is also dyslexic and doesn't like being surprised by names, so she takes care to check everything out beforehand. If she sees one she doesn't know, she'll ask me for help. It sounds mean, but we've both laughed as I've given her three wrong pronunciations, saving the correct one until just before she needs it. There have been a few commercial breaks we've come out of where she's just said, 'You are such a shit.'

On her own cognisance, she ended the show with, 'And on tomorrow's show, we have Anal Kapoor . . .' Another morning, she said that Burke Bacharach would be on the show.

She also inserted an unfortunate pause in 'Shit . . . akee' mushrooms, and I think it's best not to mention the Country Casuals moment.

From very early on, I have regarded Holly as the sister I never had. We can tease each other, totally confide in each other, say anything to each other. And like most big brothers would do to their younger sister, I take great delight in making her jump. Holly is scared of everything – literally everything – from a fly, to a ghost story, to a pickled walnut. There have been so many moments I've made her jump so hard she has nearly sworn. She's said on numerous occasions, 'If you make me say fuck on air, I'm taking you down with me.'

I could never have imagined that the laughter we had all enjoyed with Fern would come so quickly with Holly. My wheezy laugh made her laugh even harder, which made her drop to the floor so she didn't pee herself, which in turn made me laugh harder. It was, and remains, a very dangerous dynamic.

Holly definitely makes having to get up at 5.30 a.m. better. In all the eighteen years that I have been doing the show there has never been a single day when I've been happy to hear the alarm. I can get up, get showered, shaved, dressed and ready without even opening my eyes. Tony is sitting outside at 6.30 a.m. and has the script and briefing notes all ready for me. That's when I wake up. It takes about two hours to get from home to work and, in that time, I'll have studied the show, come up with any ideas to run past the team and written about six interviews.

Before lockdown, I'd arrive at work and make-up would be the centre of our world. My team of David and Suzie Narden (who took over when Lyn retired), alongside Holly's make-up artist Patsy and the various nail and hair experts that are in that day. Sometimes the team around Holly can look like a Ferrari pitstop. We laugh, gossip and recommend TV shows to each other. At eight fifteen the production team for the day, along with our editor, Martin Frizell, come into make-up for the morning meeting and to chat through ideas that the pair of us may have had.

I have always loved the inclusive nature of *This Morning*. Everyone's input is essential. We can have ideas in that meeting that change the structure of the entire show, we can recommend guests, items, jokes and props, and the team are so nimble and fast that it's usually all ready to go just before the show starts at ten. Sometimes it's still evolving as the opening titles play. No one can 'just' be a presenter on the show, we are all part of the production team, and occasionally when a guest goes rogue we end up as part of the legal team, too, always ready to offer a legal voice to those who aren't there to defend themselves. That's what I love about the show: there's nothing like it anywhere on TV. As a presenter, it's deeply satisfying and constantly stimulating.

No matter what Holly and I are doing, it turns into a competition. I've asked my daughters Molly and Ruby if they think I'm competitive. They both agreed I'm not, but when I'm on air with Holly it all changes. Make a cocktail – whose is better? Get on a scooter – who goes faster? Plant a terrarium – whose is prettier? We do it with everything. Last year, for pancake day the team built an assault course for us outside to run around while we tossed our pancakes. I was slightly in front but the wind caught my flying pancake mid-toss and blew it on to the floor. I completely forgot I was on TV. I was in a competition with Holly and that was all I could concentrate on. As the pancake hit the deck, I shouted, '*Shite!*' at the top of my voice. After the race, while I was having to apologize to the viewers for my language, I thought Holly would definitely pee her pants.

I have never seen anyone run as fast as Holly can run in high heels. It's astonishing to behold. There is one link on *Dancing on Ice* where we have to run from the audience, right around the back of the set, to emerge by the judges. It's a hell of a distance and has to be done very quickly. To see her hitch up a stunning ballgown and run at full pelt in ridiculously high heels is a truly Olympic sight.

On the subject of heels, there are moments when it takes one of your best mates to burst an awkward bubble.

Holly and I were presenting *Text Santa* together, ITV's Christmas charity extravaganza. At the end of the show, the gag was that, in a commercial break, Holly and I would have completely swapped looks: hair, clothes, shoes. It was a very rapid change – we had about four minutes. We ran to a room just off the studio and swapped clothes and both put on wigs. I had blonde, flowing locks, and Holly crammed her hair into a wig that was quickly sprayed silver. Both us and our teams nearly passed out from inhaling hairspray and silver paint. We made it back into the studio with seconds to spare, completely transformed into each other. We closed the show and came off air.

I was in a red dress, tights and high heels when a runner from ITV2 ran up to us both. Could we please come as quickly as possible to Studio 2 next door to do an interview? I won't lie. I was not happy.

'Hang on,' I said, 'You want me to go on ITV2 dressed like *this*?'

'Yes, but we have to be quick,' said the runner.

'Hang on a minute. I'm wearing all this for a joke on a show that understood why I was doing it! On ITV2 it'll just look like I'm in fucking drag!'

'It'll be funny,' said the runner, and set off.

'It'll be fine,' said Holly. 'It's clear what we've done. I've got silver hair.'

We walked off to the studio. Well, I didn't walk, I stomped. A very angry man in high heels, a red dress and flowing blonde hair. It was a very inelegant walk. Holly and both our teams were silent. They knew I was cross.

As we neared the studio, my limited skills walking in high heels finally failed me. I fell. I didn't just fall, I went down like a factory chimney when the detonator button has been pressed. I hit the deck, a crumpled, dishevelled wreck, wig lopsided, and having lost a shoe.

There was silence in the corridor – utter stunned silence. Nobody could breathe. The runner was mortified.

Then Holly snorted. She burst the bubble. Her snort became a laugh and I started to laugh too. Everyone around us started to laugh. Holly dropped to the floor, trying not to wet her pants. Our entire group were screaming with laughter in the corridor. I was helplessly rolling on the floor, with tears flooding down my cheeks. We began to calm down until, still lying on the floor, I said, 'Oh, bollocks, I've laddered my tights.'

We asked everyone around us if they had captured the moment on their phones, but no one had. We scoured the area to see if there were CCTV cameras, but there weren't. Sadly, nothing exists of the moment. Except my continued admiration that Holly can sprint in heels.

I developed the skill of ballgown social distancing on *DOI* long before social distancing became a thing. I have had to walk at varying distances behind Holly, depending on the stunning creation she is wearing and the length of its attendant train. Sometimes I can walk right behind, sometimes I'm six feet behind her. We've both pictured the scene as we run around the rink: I step on the train by accident and the entire dress is ripped off her!

Holly is a very spiritual person, open to all influences from the universe, interested and inquisitive. I like to think that I'm open to all of the influences the universe can exert upon us, too, but I think my time at *This Morning* might have made me a little sceptical.

The lady who can read asparagus. The man who told me that in his hotel room before coming on the show he turned on the tap in the bathroom and a voice came out of the water; someone called Stan wanted to say 'hi'. But I didn't know a Stan. 'Ah,' he said. 'What about Frank?'

I've interviewed a man who contacted the dead through the noise of his lawnmower and the woman who left her fiancée for a ghost. Sadly, it didn't work out, though apparently the spirit sex was amazing. At the end of most of those interviews, I will look at Holly and say, 'What a load of bollocks,' and she will invariably say, 'You never know.' However, we did smile at the man who had sex with his car, and the woman who fell in love with a five-bar gate. As Fern used to say, 'Every pot has a lid.'

If there was one seal of approval we all sought when we joined *This Morning* it was that of Denise Robertson, the stalwart of the show. She was an original member of the team, along with Dr Chris, and you couldn't help but want them both to like you. Denise would sail into the studio, a galleon full of sound, sensible advice. You knew you had won her approval when she said, 'You're absolutely right,' during an item. When it happened, separately, to me and Holly, we both swelled with pride. Denise was exactly the same off air as she was on. Our kindly no-nonsense telly mum. We were all heartbroken when she died and were proud to be invited to her funeral to say goodbye to such a wonderful woman.

One challenge that played directly into everything I love about my job was my *Text Santa* twenty-four-hour non-stop broadcast marathon. As soon as it was pitched to me I was hooked. Something on this size and scale had never been done on British TV before. I broadcast over three channels: ITV 1 2 and 3. Starting the moment I came off air on *This Morning* with Amanda Holden and leaving the studio to begin the challenge was both daunting and exciting in equal parts. I became a continuity announcer, I presented the weather, Ben Hanlin taught me how to walk on broken glass, I had a party on the roof of the ITV tower with Davina McCall and travelled across London, broadcasting all the way to, and then inside, Number Ten. Steph and the girls took part and pretty much all my TV friends came to play in one way or another.

There was no time for me to check my social media at the time, but when it was all over the response had been incredible. It had been an amazing insight into the behind-the-scenes action in TV and had gone down very well. I know, as a kid, I'd have been totally glued as we showed literally everything. What it proved without question was what can be achieved logistically and technically if everyone pulls together. As a company, ITV was extraordinary. Nobody said 'no', no matter how mad the idea.

It was one of those incredible moments when an entire company comes together to do something unique. As I abseiled down the side of the building and past the office of my boss, Kevin Lygo, he at his desk, me dangling outside, we both laughed through the glass and shrugged in a 'look what we're doing' kind of way.

The next year, I agreed to the challenge of appearing in every single ITV programme during the *Text Santa* day. It took weeks to travel up and down the country, fitting in with all the schedules of each of the pre-recorded shows, wearing a different and extravagant Christmas jumper each time.

On the big day itself, with all the recorded shows ready to be aired, I had to complete the challenge by appearing in all the live shows. The day started with me standing behind a *Good Morning Britain* reporter on the doorstep of Number Ten, and then I would appear on every show from *Judge Rinder* and *The Jeremy Kyle Show* to *Tipping Point* and *1,000 Heartbeats*. The best one, though, was appearing in the back of shot in David's shop in *Emmerdale* buying an Ordnance Survey map.

On TV, it was a great day. In reality, it was dreadful. Two days before, on 28 November 2015, Steph, the girls and I were all watching *I'm a Celebrity* . . . when the phone rang. It was my brother Tim's wife, Petra, to tell us that Tim had had a serious heart attack and was in intensive care in Bristol. We had all had a glass of wine so we couldn't drive. We called a local taxi and then set about trying to find Mum. She was somewhere in Birmingham at a Christmas fayre. As we were racing down the M4 she was located and also jumped into a cab.

We all arrived at the Bristol Royal Infirmary at more or less the same time. Petra was waiting for us. God, I hate those 'family rooms'. Not that the BRI's wasn't lovely and caring, it's just all the sitting and waiting. Details were sketchy, but we pieced together what had happened as we waited for news of Tim's condition. As it turned out, Tim had about three lifetimes of luck on that day. He had felt unwell, pulled over in a lay-by at the top of a remote hill near Bath and called 999. The operator was incredible, trying to keep him calm as she dispatched the emergency services. We know just how kind and caring she was because Tim later got access to his 999 call. He had no recollection of what had happened.

Within minutes, a paramedic arrived, at the precise moment Tim went into full cardiac arrest. The paramedic dragged him out of the car and performed CPR on the car-park gravel until the ambulance arrived. The two-ambulance crew *should* have been in an air-ambulance helicopter, but it was out of service that day, so they had decided to work, but in a road ambulance. The helicopter had a CPR machine on board that is not generally available in a road ambulance. It could keep giving CPR long after a human would tire. Fortunately, they had made the decision to take that equipment with them.

They arrived and took over. Tim was 'zapped' by the ambulance crew and stabilized enough to be taken by road. The next decision was critical. Should they take him to the local hospital, which was much closer, or to Bristol, which had better facilities? They decided to go to Bristol. On the way he arrested again; only the helicopter kit could have kept him alive for such a long period of time. They stabilized him once more. As he arrived at the hospital he arrested again.

They got him back and he was rushed to theatre, where it just so happened that one of the best stent surgeons in the country was on duty. Tim was immediately operated on.

We were allowed to see him in the ICU. We had been warned that he would be very cold if we touched him; his body had been chilled to help in his recovery. He was in a coma, and he would remain so for nearly three weeks. The prognosis was dark. We all listened, ashen-faced, as we were told that although his heart was now performing well, there was no way of knowing how successful his recovery would be. There were grave pneumonia concerns and because he had 'died' so many times, there was also no way of knowing how damaged his brain would be or how much of him we would get back when he came out of the coma. All we could do was to take it in turns to sit round his bed and marvel at the astonishing mass of machinery that was keeping him stable, and stare admiringly and in awe at the staff. We were in the company of angels.

In two days' time, it was *Text Santa*. My challenge to appear on every show that day had been launched. Christmas jumpers were being sold in my name to support the day and the charities. I had already appeared in all the recorded shows, so they were all 'in the can' and waiting to go out. I still had to do the live shows on the day and the main *Text Santa* show that evening. But here I was, sitting beside my gravely ill brother. The decision was agonizing. I would have to leave him for the day. Too much work had already been done. Overnight, on 1 December, I headed back to London.

As I stood in the back of shot on *Good Morning Britain*, outside the door of Number Ten, Downing Street in the cold, an extravagant Christmas jumper, I remember thinking, 'This is a bloody bizarre job.' I've said it before but I'll say it again, the show must go on, eh.

The happy ending to this particular story is that I have just been WhatsApping my wonderful brother to tell him what I'm up to. His recovery was slow but steady. I lived in a Bristol hotel room for a while so I could be by his side. Now, five years later, he's mostly okay. He just has a good excuse for a pretty shit memory.

Telling this story enables me to reiterate what Tim and I said together on *This Morning* and in the newspapers when he had recovered. We could publicly, proudly and loudly sing the praises of the NHS. Not only had they fixed him, they were also incredible with us as a family and held us together. During lockdown, we all clapped at 8 p.m. on Thursdays to acknowledge how unbelievably lucky we are to have the angels and heroes of the NHS. Not just now, but always.

13

I like to think that when I'm sent a new format or idea I'm pretty good at spotting one that will work for me. I've presented lots of shows over the years – some have worked, some have not – but sitting here right now, I don't think there are any I wish I hadn't done. TV is all about trying new things out. If it sticks, great; if it doesn't, you dust yourself off and try again. There have also been shows that I was sure would work but, for whatever reason, the stars weren't aligned.

It's Now or Never was a superb format; essentially, it was a flashmob before they were invented. We shot two pilot episodes, and after both of them, we were all sure we had a hit on our hands. The premise was simple: someone wanted to say something special to someone else, and they did it with a surprise song-and-dance performance, in public. We booked the whole of Camden Market for a guy who wanted to propose to his girlfriend. We had recorded him rehearsing and telling us why he loved her, and then came the big day.

Hidden cameras were everywhere. They were sitting in a busy boat on the canal, just chatting, then he started to sing. Her face was a picture – she was mortified. The bloke next to her boyfriend started to sing, and her head snapped round, then a couple behind, then the whole boat and then the whole market. An entire, full-on sudden song-and-dance routine. It was spectacular. In the second show a lady wanted to thank her friend for getting her through her cancer treatment. We booked out London City Airport. At the check-in desk the friend started to sing 'Thank You for being a Friend'; next the check-in staff joined in and then the entire airport. It was a guaranteed hit.

However, because of a very sunny weekend (few of us stay in and watch TV when the sun is shining), and a tentative senior executive, it all went tits up. One show went out with poor figures; the next, scheduled to go out the next night was pulled. I begged the boss to let it play. If it didn't perform well, we could rethink, but if he pulled it the idea would be totally dead. He pulled it. The flashmob would have to be invented by someone else.

I had just signed a new contract with ITV at the time. The headlines read: 'Phillip Schofield signs new ITV deal and has series pulled.'

That stung (we'd only made the two pilots!). Piers Morgan saw the headline and texted me with what is now in his Twitter profile and is in fact a quote by Margot Barber: 'One day you're cock of the walk, the next a feather duster.'

How very true.

I'm not naïve or precious enough to expect that every show I do should be a success – over the length of my career, some have definitely been better than others – but the failure of *It's Now or Never* really hurt, simply because I knew it could have been a bloody good show.

When I was sent the treatment for *The Cube* and *5 Gold Rings* I had the same excitement, only this time, thankfully, they were both hits. *The Cube* was such an inspired idea. The creators at Objective Productions had written out the whole game-play as a storyboard on a large sheet of paper (eventually they cut it up and gave us all a piece). Right from the word go, it looked gripping. We rehearsed it in Objective's offices, and I played some of the games. They were impressed that I completed 'Stack', putting ten Perspex cylinders on top of each other, while everyone around me fled the building as the fire-alarm bells rang.

Fountain Studios (dropbox, chipped floor) was the only one high enough to house the crane that held the overhead camera that was so important to the viewers. That was the shot that made the games look easier, so everyone watching would be screaming, 'How can you not *do this!*' at their tellies. Colin McFarlane (from the Batman movies) was the Voice of the Cube, and though I'm not allowed to tell you the name of the Body, I can tell you she was very funny, especially when she was recording 'how to play a game perfectly', and continually arsed it up.

Trouble was, we had created a game that only one person ever won. We had a full gold lighting change ready for anyone who 'beat the Cube'. To add to the drama, the only time I was ever seen on TV inside the Cube was when someone actually beat it. Both the golden lights and my trip inside the Cube only happened once, when Mo Farah became the only person to beat it and he won £250k. It never happened again. No one else beat the Cube. Never say never, though: it's always possible.

5 Gold Rings was another format that leapt off the page. I was sent a few mock-up games and we played them on a laptop at home in the kitchen. As I stood back and watched Steph and the girls putting their fingers on the screen, trying to guess where an anteater's eye was, I knew we had a hit on our hands. One of the greatest joys of presenting *5GR* is asking anyone playing it to post pictures on Twitter. I love seeing families coming together to play. It's one of the few reasons I still have Twitter!

I like being taken out of my natural habitat and I love a challenge, but nothing galvanizes me more than a massive outside broadcast, especially one with a department I've never worked with before, or indeed that I had ever expected to work with.

'ITV News have been on the phone,' said my manager Emily. 'Would you be interested in presenting William and Kate's Royal Wedding with Julie Etchingham outside Buckingham Palace?'

News! 'Bloody hell. Okay.'

When it came to the Royal Family, I'd had a moment with Prince Edward at an awards ceremony years before. He turned to me and said, 'Ah, hello. You've just been on a programme with my mother.'

Quite obviously, I racked my brains to think when I might have co-hosted something with the Queen. I was pretty sure I wouldn't have forgotten! It turned out that the programme HRH was referring to was *A Party in the Park* for the BBC. Her Majesty had been at one end of Hyde Park in a carriage, and I was at the other end with a giant sausage sizzle, a sort of huge barbecue, grilling a sausage big enough to feed hundreds of people. It was my most remote co-hosting duty ever.

Walking into the News HQ on Gray's Inn Road was something I'd only done once before – I'd stood beside Tom Bradby at the end of *News at Ten* on my *Text Santa* challenge. I was really, *really* nervous walking in this time. What would it be like, working with a news team? Of all the career considerations I had ever had, news wasn't one of them. I thought they would be serious and severe but, although incredibly sharp and professional, they were the opposite and absolutely delightful. Julie Etchingham is a dream to be around. I'm sure she won't mind me saying that she's like a head girl. She absorbed all information, had read every book, knew every fact, detail and person. Me, Steph and the girls had all been on holiday to the Maldives just before the wedding.

They had had a ball in the sun while I spent my days inside doing my 'wedding homework'.

I still didn't know as much as Julie, though. Our coverage was a mix of interviews, films and live commentary, and I absolutely loved the size and scale of the news resources. If something happened, we instantly knew about it. It was a big undertaking for ITV and I deeply appreciated being trusted to be part of their team. The programme was very well received and everyone was very happy with the chemistry between me and Julie. It was also incredibly long! Unbroken by the usual commercial breaks, neither of us could have anything to drink because we wouldn't be able to go for a wee for six hours! We both said that our bladders were like the Sahara. My favourite part of the day was after we had come off air. Julie and I walked past a spit roast. We were famished by that stage.

'Fancy a sarnie?' I said.

'Damn right,' said Julie.

Watching the sheer delight on the face of this senior ITV journalist as she stuffed a pork sarnie into her mouth and wiped the juices from her chin was sublime.

David O'Brien had, as always, sorted out my suit and made sure I remained uncreased. As I parted from the team, very happy after a job well done, he and I walked across Green Park, found a hotel bar and drank enough Jack Daniels to anaesthetize a rhino.

I've worked with the news teams a number of times since then. The last time was in Windsor Great Park on a stunning day for the wedding of Harry and Meghan. As their carriage drove past our commentary position, all dignity left Julie and I and we got up from the sofa and turned to wave. Harry smiled at us both as he waved back. We both squealed with delight. Job done.

My connection to the Royal Family doesn't stop there. I'm

very proud to be one of the longest-serving ambassadors for the Prince's Trust. The day I knew I wanted to be involved was the day I introduced Prince Charles to give a speech. He was expecting a group of suited businessmen and as he took his speech from his inside pocket, he looked up and saw a room full of wide-eyed teenagers. He slid the speech back into his pocket and abandoned it. The next twenty minutes were among the most inspiring I've heard, and it was all performed completely off the cuff. I immediately thought, 'I want to be in your gang.'

His father, though, takes no prisoners. When I was asked to make a documentary with the Duke of Edinburgh to celebrate sixty years of the awards named after him, the first question I asked was 'Does he want to do it?' I didn't want to be badgering him if he was reluctant because I knew he'd bite my head off and he's preceded by a mighty reputation. They assured me he did, but I remain unconvinced. He definitely wanted to celebrate the awards, but I was told (and could tell) that he hates being on TV.

'Oh, bloody hell, you again,' was his usual greeting.

As part of the documentary, I spent two days at Buckingham Palace with him. He was extraordinary – his memory is absurd. He can not only remember all dates and details, but what the weather was like sixty years ago on a given day. He walked and walked and walked around the palace gardens, shaking hands by the thousand. By the end of the day, my feet were killing me, but the Duke was still bounding around. Part of the Duke of Edinburgh celebrations involved individuals taking on a challenge. It could be anything – learning a language, climbing a mountain. I was asked if I would do something. My time was limited so I couldn't learn to play the cello or hike in the Cairngorms, so I suggested a wing-walk. The team was delighted, and it would only take a day to film. At the start of filming for the programme, I was expressly told not to interview the Duke, or to ask him questions about himself. That makes the structure of a conversation for TV rather tricky. It turned out he had more fun teasing me. The producer asked me to explain my challenge to him.

'Oh, bloody hell, you again.'

'Good morning, sir.'

'What are we talking about today?'

'I'm doing a Diamond Challenge. I'm going to do a wing-walk.'

'What the hell is that?'

'I stand on the wing of a plane as it does aerobatics.'

'Why?'

'For the Diamond Challenge.'

'Well, you're mad.'

After the chat he wandered off. It had gone okay. A couple of minutes later, one of our team said, 'Phil! He wants you.' I looked over to where he was in conversation with a small group of people and he was beckoning me over.

Showing the Duke my wing-walk.

'I want you to meet this man,' he said, pointing to a gentleman in the group.

'Of course, sir.'

'He's going to jump out of a plane,' said the Duke. 'I thought I'd put two bloody idiots together, make sure you don't die.'

The last time I had wing-walked had been that fateful day in Southend when I was wearing purple leathers. My challenge this time was a wholly different experience. It was a sunny day in Oxfordshire and the aircraft was a bright yellow biplane. 'Do you want the full works?' said the pilot. 'Damn right,' I said.

It was exhilarating in the extreme. The plane performed similar manoeuvres to the ones the Red Arrows did, except this time I was outside, strapped to the wing. As we flew directly down towards a lush, green field, I thought, 'If he doesn't pull out of this, they'll be a week digging me out of the hole, but at least it'll be a quick end!' It was profoundly exciting in a 'you're very close to death' kind of way. I don't seem to get scared in moments like this, just exhilarated. The only time I've felt deep, undiluted fear was when I climbed to the absolute top of the Shard for another *Text Santa* stunt. The programme had hired a helicopter to get aerial shots of me at the pinnacle, and as I stood on a tiny girder 1,016 feet in the air, I knew that the best shot would be of me letting go and holding both arms above my head. Even though I was safely tethered and couldn't fall, and I'm not scared of heights, every atom within me was screaming, 'Do *not* let go!' When I did, I can only describe the fear as . . . primal. But it was a hell of a buzz.

When the Duke of Edinburgh documentary was broadcast, my mum was watching. Now, my mother is not an adventurous woman, but her words left my mouth open.

'Oh, Phillip, of all the things you've done in your whole career, that's the only thing I'm envious of. I'd so love to do that.'

Possibly the most senior loop de looper in the world! My 80-year-old mum loving life.

Defying gravity!

'*What?*'

'Yes, it's a dream. Your dad would have never let me do it.'

'Mum, are you saying you want to do a wing-walk?'

'Yes, just like you did, the whole thing, the loops and the twists.'

'Er . . . okay.'

A few months later the whole family were back at the airfield. I watched as my mother got on to the wing and was secured. The girls laughed at the absurdity of their grandmother thundering down a runway while standing on top of a plane. She was spectacular and absolutely loved it. It's disconcerting to watch your eighty-year-old mother, a tiny speck on top of a plane, as it loops high in the sky. A few weeks later she received her DofE Diamond pin. We believe she is one of, if not *the* oldest woman to have looped the loop! My dad would have been going bloody spare.

Discussions were being had about a possible move for ITV. The famous Southbank studios were on prime real-estate land. There were grand schemes of a temporary move while they built a new residential and studio complex, similar to TV Centre. If we did move, where would we go? Where would our new home be?

The London Studios, or TLS, were a strange, higgledy-piggledy affair. They had the slowest lifts in the world and it was very easy to get lost. The three main studios were on the ground floor, the dressing rooms on the first. Most presenters took the stairs from their dressing rooms to the studio, not because it was only one flight, but because the light in the studio lift was so unflattering it made you feel like you were ready to retire from the business, even if you were twenty!

For newbies, getting from the main building to Studio 8, the home of *This Morning*, required the homing instincts of a swallow. If you found yourself on the bridge, you were on the right track.

Our little complex was perfect, neat and tucked away and all self-contained. My favourite thing about it, though, by far, was the view. The river behind, constantly changing, was very calming. I always found that in the commercial break after a particularly harrowing interview on the sofa, if I stood looking out of the window for the four minutes I had before we were back on air, it would re-set my head. I enjoyed watching the world go by. People going about their business was a great distraction. The windows had a one-way filter on them. We could see out, but it was very hard to see in. If you looked up, you could see the darkened studio lights and maybe a silhouette, but you wouldn't know that Holly and I were standing there. We'd stand together side by side, taking in the same view, but as I focused my view on a new boat,

Holly would be admiring the sartorial choices of someone walking by. 'Ooooh, I like her shoes.'

We used the outside a lot in the summer. There was a set of stairs beside the studio that led to a secret door on the Southbank. Holly and I would zip in and out for various items. On one occasion, we had used the door to get to an army inflatable which would take us up the river. As it happened, the boat broke down and, live on air, Holly and I ended up drifting helplessly towards Southend. We used the door to get to cooking items, fashion slots and musical performances. The door always had a security guard on it ... except when it didn't. One day we all ran back up the stairs and to the studio after an item, and as we carried on with the show we noticed two people we didn't recognize behind the cameras. They had big smiles on their faces, were looking very interested and loving life. They were politely asked who they were.

'We're tourists from Canada and we're thrilled we managed to get on to this studio tour. We were just passing.'

They'd seen us all re-entering the building and tagged along! Fair play. Holly and I had our picture taken with them and they went happily on their way.

On one of the days that door was open, it let in the studio fly. I'm convinced it was always the same one; it loved being on the telly. Year after year it found ways to appear. It was like a B52 bomber. No one could ever catch it, though I did successfully flick it once.

Richard and Judy were back on the show for a chat and the fly landed on Holly's leg, so I flicked it. Unfortunately, I flicked it on to Judy and there was pandemonium. It was also the studio fly that sat on Barbara Taylor Bradford's chest for so long that it was mistaken for a brooch, and the one that got caught in Denise Robertson's hair and none of us could get it out.

We had a lot of very happy times in that studio, but the

decision had been made. We would move out of the South-bank studios and the temporary new home for *This Morning* would be . . . Television Centre! I couldn't believe what I was hearing. Very few people (now including you) could know the significance of that decision.

Our last show from Studio 8 was on 29 March 2018. Holly and I posted a black-and-white Instagram pic of us both looking through the window for the final time. It was also my and Steph's twenty-fifth wedding anniversary, so I'm glad she was there to share the moment with me.

I lingered for a long time after that last show. There were so many incredible memories, mostly good, some bad, one that was physically painful! There had been a huge internet craze called 'The One Chip Challenge', in which a tortilla chip covered in Carolina Reaper dust (in 2013, it was declared the hottest chilli in the world by the *Guinness Book of World Records*) had to be eaten. The person eating the 'chip' was then up against the clock to see how long they could stand the intense heat without water, milk . . . or throwing up. It was in that studio that I decided to take on the world and beat the times set (I unofficially did). As Holly watched and Alison Hammond sat beside me eating ice-cream, I ate the fiery tortilla. It set fire to my mouth, then my throat, then the lining of my stomach. Holly and Alison watched with interest, initially laughing and then with growing concern. As I finally gave in to the pain and sickness and ran from the studio, Holly shouted after me, 'Shall I hold your hair back?'

This was the studio that Holly and I had stumbled into the morning after the National Television Awards. We were so happy to have won and to have picked up the award for our amazing team, but the wheels came off quite quickly. After the show, we went up to the ITV box to see everyone. Steph and

Holly's husband, Dan, were there to congratulate us and the champagne was flowing. It was a raucous evening. We ended up in McDonald's, pissed and brandishing the award in front of the confused staff. At that point, we split up. I had, apparently, decided to go home. I'm not sure I remember! I know I got a call from Holly, who had turned into Martin Luther King.

'Where are you?' she said.

'On the way home.'

'Don't be that man!'

'What?'

'Don't be that man. Don't be the man who lets the moment pass. Don't be the man who doesn't celebrate success. Don't be the man who goes home. Don't be the man who is a disappointment. Don't be that man.'

'Okay. Where are you going?'

'We'll meet you at Ant's.'

The party continued at Ant McPartlin's house. Out came the 'Pie Face' game. Rather than whipped cream, we put

The wonderful NTA-winning Emma Gormley and Martin Frizell.

In a lift at the NTAs.

piccalilli in the scoop and then sweet chilli sauce. I think mustard followed! The stakes were very high. At the end of the game, Holly's beautiful cream National Television Awards dress was covered with yellow stains from the piccalilli. This was desperately risky behaviour – we were due to be live on TV at ten thirty. I don't actually know how either of us found our way in. I remember slumping in the doorway of the make-up room, before and after the show, head in hands. My head was spinning, my words were slurred. Holly and I just kept looking at each other and saying, 'Oh no. Oh, no no no.'

I was still in my clothes from the night before, and make-up wasn't going to help my red eyes. Holly, of course, looked magnificent. I have never seen her looking anything other than beautiful. First thing in the morning, she is gorgeous; drunk off her face, the same. Last summer in Portugal we all had a party and Holly fell asleep. Steph said, 'Only Holly can look like Sleeping Beauty when she's pissed and asleep.'

Today, the morning after the National Television Awards, she looked like a fifties Hollywood star, a piccalilli-stained Marilyn Monroe. We staggered into the studio. The crew were in hysterics. The head of Daytime came down and said, 'My God, you both smell like old bar mats.' Just before we went on air we both started to laugh, hysterical laughter at the fact that this was about to happen. Holly seemed to be getting more pissed.

As the titles rolled, the gallery was laughing. Our editor, Martin Frizell, shouted, 'Get them another drink!'

Some people tweeted that it was shocking that we had been allowed on air in such a condition – the 'professionally outraged' were not happy. The rest of the country, with a sense of humour, enjoyed the fun. The truth of the matter is,

The morning after the night before. Should we be allowed on air like this?!

We're about to present a show . . . !

yes, we were in a state, yes, we were still mildly inebriated, but everyone knew, including us, that it would be okay, that we were on the right side of the line. If that hadn't been the case, we would never have been allowed on air . . . I don't think.

We stumbled and giggled our way through the first part of the show. Holly was beginning to feel sick. In a commercial break, we looked at each other and agreed that we had to get our shit together. It was funny up to a point, but there's a fine line. We both straightened up and tried a lot harder to be professional . . . ish.

When we won again the next year we tried to get matching tattoos, but no one would come out to us because we were too drunk to be responsible. The actor James Nesbitt volunteered to do it for us, but we couldn't find ink or a needle . . . thankfully!

Holly can be a dangerous friend to have. In my old school reports, some of the teachers would write that I was 'easily led'. In my adult life there are a very few friends that I trust to lead me into mischief, but Holly is at the top of that group. We have enjoyed wonderful and outrageously drunken lunches, when, just occasionally, we had the time to let our hair down and reflect on life. Once, after a particularly 'long' lunch in Nobu, we parted and staggered off to our respective homes. The next day, I phoned Holly because I couldn't remember paying the restaurant bill. Holly said, 'Check your coat for the receipt.' When I put my hand in my coat pocket I found a full container of hand soap. I was mortified. Had I stolen it from the loos?! I told Holly and she checked her bag. 'Oh, Christ, I've got one, too,' she yelped. Oh my God, we'd robbed Nobu. I immediately phoned them to confess. Through their laughter the manager explained that we had both returned from the Gents and the Ladies loudly praising the 'wonderful quality and beautiful smell of the soap' so they had kindly given us both a bottle. Oh, and yes, I had paid the bill.

Holly had come to the conclusion that if you only drink tequila and nothing else on a night out you didn't get a hangover. We decided to try it out on *The Alan Carr Show*, where we were both to be guests. Alan was famous for his 'on show' drinks cabinet, where guests could choose their tipple of choice. We were on first. We told Alan and the audience what our experiment was and all three of us necked shots of tequila as we chatted. By the end of it, we were all plastered. We finished the interview and sat in the make-up room, watching Alan trying to chat to his other guests. With each one, he also had to have a 'social drink'. It was one of the funniest shows I've ever watched – about eighty per cent of it was cut out. As he slurred his way through, his glasses steamed up and he couldn't see a thing. At the end of the recording he rolled into the Green Room and the three of us recklessly had another couple of shots of tequila. All of us staggered off into the night. The next day was a Monday, a *This Morning* Monday!! The alarm went off at 5.30 a.m. and I opened my eyes. Was I okay? Was I hideously hung over? The experiment had worked. I felt fine! I texted Holly on the way into work and we marvelled that we were okay.

Alan Carr woke up and turned on his TV. He had mixed his drinks; we hadn't. He was appallingly hung over and stunned by the two of us, bright and sparkling on the telly. He got up to walk his dog in Hyde Park and, as he bent forward to pick up a ball, he rolled forward and fell into the Serpentine.

Don't try that experiment, by the way. I have no idea how it worked for us, because every friend since who has tried to follow in our footsteps has been horribly sick the next day!

You may wonder if we've ever been told off down our ear-pieces by a boss in the production gallery. Not once in the Fern days or the Holly days has anyone said, 'Pull yourselves together,' or 'Stop it.' Usually, the gallery is laughing, too. We had a lovely director called Martin Lord who was a wonderful audience. Occasionally in our ear we would hear the gallery door slide open and then close as he stood howling helplessly with laughter in the corridor. The worst trigger is looking behind the camera and seeing the operator's shoulders bouncing up and down. That is guaranteed to make it ten times worse. If you make the crew laugh, it really *is* funny!

The job of a vision mixer is to cut between the cameras, effects, slides and graphics. A very good one will also be watching the presenters on the studio floor. Andrew Jennings is one of our vision mixers on *This Morning*, and he is very good. He catches every expression and every sideways glance. He can read my face very well, pissed or sober, and always catches the little looks I make to the camera.

One of the jobs of a production assistant in the gallery is to ensure that everything runs to time. It's the PA who counts down in our ear, and we have some of the best on *This Morning*. Kate Groome was an Australian PA who took no nonsense. Sometimes she could calm us down by just sighing. It was her way of saying, 'You are so over time here with your laughing. You're messing up my timings.' Kate was also a genius at hiding time! She would keep a minute or so secret from us and it would miraculously materialize when needed. We would ask where the time had come from and she'd say, in her Aussie accent, 'I had a minute stashed up my

This Morning away day at Downton Abbey.

knicker leg.' When Kate retired she gave me a bag full of glittery '1's. She said they were all the spare minutes she had found when she shook out her knickers and she hoped they'd come in handy.

Yes, Studio 8 at the London Studios had some magical memories but, if I'm honest, the thing I miss the most is the live view. We took our set with us and recorded the view in all weather states before we left. It looks great on the telly – you can't tell the difference – but I can't gaze out to distract myself. If you get too close, your eyes go blurred! On the other side of the 'view' is the GMB studio. One day, on the show from our new home, all the screens went black. One quick wit tweeted, 'Fuck me, there's been an eclipse!' Recently, a number of Tweets from shocked twits said they were appalled that the people walking outside weren't socially distancing. We informed them that the view was in fact three years old.

The intention was that we would move out of the London Studios and move temporarily to Television Centre. The Southbank would be totally transformed, with an entirely new Daytime collection of purpose-built studios, new offices, a residential area, shops and cafés. When completed, we would move back to our new home. One day at lunch with my boss Kevin Lygo, I said, 'We're not going back, are we?'

'Nope', was his reply.

Moving *This Morning* to TC3 at Television Centre literally messed with my mind. Still does, if I'm honest. You'll understand why because of everything I've told you. To be back there at this stage of my career is the most extraordinary kismet. When BBC Television Centre closed in March 2013 I was invited on to its last-ever programme. I have a picture in my office of me with Noel, Barry Cryer, Brucey and Ronnie

Corbett that was taken that night. When I arrived, I met the producer, who told me what I would be doing and what time I was needed. I had two hours to kill. TV production teams like to know, quite rightly, where the presenters or guests are They worry if you're not where you're supposed to be. I had a word with the producer. I explained my history with the building and that I *had* to have a final look around. I promised I would be in my dressing room in an hour and gave him my phone number in case of emergency. He understood.

I re-created the walk I had taken when I was seventeen, but this time the building was deserted. All the attention was focused on TC1, from where the show was being transmitted. Everywhere else was silent.

I walked through every studio. I stood in an empty TC7 and could hear the echoes of *Going Live*. I walked up to the fourth floor, to the hidden staircase behind the lifts, and to where the Broom Cupboard had been. There had been many alterations in that part of the building, but eventually I found the window that had been behind our board of pictures. Where I used to sit was now just a corridor. I couldn't believe it was closing down. I was heartbroken that this was it. Would they demolish it?

I walked to the studio, did my bit on the show and left.

Standing back there five years later, I was thrilled with how sensitively the adaptation from studio complex to studio/residential complex had been done. The look and feel are the same. There may now only be three studios, TCs 1, 2 and 3, but at least there *are* studios. The main reception may now be the reception for the Helios Hotel and the residents' area, but the Piper mural remains, as do the 'Doughnut' and the Helios statue that Sarah Greene and I used to call Golden Balls. TV sits alongside restaurants, bars and Soho House. TC has been pimped.

In April 2018, TV Centre became our home. We share TC3 with *Good Morning Britain*. Next door, *Lorraine* and *Loose Women* share TC2. After our first show, Holly said, 'Show me where the Broom Cupboard was.' We set off across the 'Doughnut' and up the beautiful suspended staircase to the fourth floor. To the left of the lifts, where the staircase to Presentation used to be, was a white door, I tried the handle. It was unlocked and the door opened. We both stared in disbelief then burst out laughing as we took out our phones to take a picture. The door opened on to a cleaning cupboard, and inside was a mop . . . and a broom.

I suppose it was kismet that the interview that would alter my world the most would be in that building, the very same building where I began working in broadcasting and where my face first appeared on TV screens. This most life-changing interview was not one that I conducted, though, it was one that I would give to Holly a little under two years later.

14

So here we are then. Maybe the only reason you're reading this is because you knew I had to get here eventually. I've seen this part of my story appear over the horizon and get closer and closer as I type. Now we are here, I have no idea how to start. I have stared at the flashing cursor on my laptop screen for most of the morning. I've drunk three mugs of tea and gone for a walk around the garden. You should know that my only concern here is that I don't hurt Steph and the girls any more than I already have. It is not in my nature to hurt people and, as they are the three most important people in my life, I have no wish to wound them further. The mere fact that we all knew I'd have to write this chapter has caused great pain. In an ideal world, I would like to have written, 'And *This Morning* moved to Television Centre. The End.'

But I know you won't accept that. Maybe I'll just jump straight in and see how this goes.

There are twin paths that nearly finished me off: sexuality and reported untruths. Those two paths converged just before Christmas 2019 and brought me to the darkest of places and almost overwhelmed me.

Let me answer the primary questions first. Did I know I was gay when I married Steph? Absolutely, unequivocally not. If I had, I wouldn't have got married. I love her with all my heart. We have had the best marriage, we have travelled the world, laughed our way through life and had two beautiful girls, who we worship. I utterly adore every atom of her being. Everyone loves Steph, and for very good reason: she is one of the world's good guys. Kind in heart, spirit and soul. No one could love me harder than Steph loves me, and no one is more conflicted and confused than I am right now. Do I wish this was different? Yes. As in *The Book of Mormon*, do I wish I could 'turn it off'? Yes. Am I proud of myself? Yes. Does that help? No.

The second headline question. Was I forced out? Categorically not. No one else was involved in the decision other than me and Steph. Only my close friends knew, and only when I told them. None had a clue beforehand. I came out for me and the safety of my head. Anything you may have read, any rumours you may have heard about my hand being forced, are totally untrue.

For the moment, those are the headlines.

I have no idea when my centre of balance shifted. There is no specific day or time that I can pin down, but I would say that I have been 'increasingly aware' for around five years, and even when I realized that I wasn't what I thought I was, I had no idea it would cause such serious issues.

I think Steph would agree that I've had totally unrelated moments in the past when I'm down or 'sad'. Not depressed, just down, when little things seem so much worse. I know I have a habit of seeing a half-empty glass rather than a half-full one. In fact, Steph has helped me to change that perception over the years. I know that in recent years I have developed a habit of catastrophizing – seeing one big unfixable mess, rather than a series of manageable issues. A realization that my sexuality was more complicated than I'd imagined, seriously unseated my head. It was a small atom of an issue that grew to an enormous, all-consuming red giant. I was totally honest with Steph. We talked together, we cried a lot together, mostly because we didn't know where the hell it was going to lead us, or what was happening to me.

For the first time in my life, I was really scared, not TV scared, not nervous scared, but emotionally, fundamentally scared.

I found myself staring into the fire, unable to think of anything else. I would distract my chaotic thoughts by re-reading whole series of books – *Harry Potter*, *The Lord of the Rings* – nothing would calm me. I cried a lot, we cried a lot. I obsessed over how I could make this work for everyone. How we could get through this without anyone getting hurt? I realized it just wasn't possible.

I would walk into work on Monday and everyone would be discussing their weekends. They would ask how mine was. 'It was lovely,' I would answer. The reality was that I would have stared silently into a fireplace watching the flames consume the logs and wishing they were consuming me.

Steph was astonishing, literally, unbelievably incredible! She comforted me, held me tightly, wiped away my tears and listened to my desolate confusion. No matter where I looked, there was no way out. When things got really dark, she reminded me how much they all loved me and that there was nothing that the four of us couldn't cope with. I had grave doubts there. I tried mindfulness apps and meditation, but I found myself existing on two hours' sleep a night, if I was lucky. Constantly tortured by the loops in my head. The loops . . . the bloody loops. I read papers, books and studies in a desperate attempt to pick my way through.

A lot of literature talks about shame. That was not an emotion I felt. My torture was guilt. GUILT in huge red letters, just behind my tired eyelids. I couldn't make it go away. I still can't. I read a paper written by a man around my age who came out later in life. He said he had 'no one in his life', but he 'felt a sense of peace'. That was it! That was what I wanted. I just wanted peace, I wanted the chaos in my head to shut up. But that wasn't going to work. 'No one in his life,' and he found peace? How was that possible? I had to have Steph and the girls in my life or there could never be peace. But that was definitely what I wanted. What I want. Peace.

One day on the show Gino D'Acampo was setting up for his cookery slot. We were in a commercial break. The first I knew that I had caught his attention was when I felt him touch my shoulder. 'What's wrong, my friend?' he said. 'You were just standing totally still in the middle of the studio looking at your feet for two minutes!' I smiled and told him I was fine, and a look of 'I don't believe you' crossed his face. As he walked back to the studio kitchen he turned, looked me dead in the eye and made the universal sign for 'Call me' with his hand.

I didn't.

My spiralling thoughts crossed over into my job twice. On the way to *This Morning* I was writing up an interview with Annie Lennox. As I tried to structure my questions, my head was yelling at me, 'You're fucking up everything and everyone and there's no way to stop it.'

As we got to Wood Lane, I said to Tony that he should carry on to the flat. Without questioning me, he did so. We'd bought a flat in South-east London a few years earlier because, at the time, it was close to ITV if I was working late and needed a place to crash, but more importantly, it would be somewhere for the girls to be safe if they got jobs in London. Steph and I regularly used it if we'd been out with friends and didn't want a long journey home. I texted Steph and Paul that 'I couldn't do the show', and turned my phone off. I sat alone in the flat, staring at the walls, as *This Morning* started on the other side of London. It was a very stupid thing to do. Everyone panicked. All my closest friends knew how ragged my head was, but no one except Steph knew why. Holly had to do the show on her own that day. This frightened me even more. It was the first time my issues had spilled over into my work. Another day I had to leave a fashion item halfway through to be sick. I now knew that I needed professional help.

Being ready to talk out loud to a stranger was a big step. If your head becomes your enemy, you have to talk to someone, even if it's just a friend. You can't sort it out on your own.

I will never, *ever* complain about being recognized. It is part of the job and part of a lucky and charmed life, but there are times, though, when I wish I could turn it off for a couple of hours. I poured my heart out to my therapist and sobbed myself breathless. Then my hour was up and I found myself out on the street with a blotchy face and red eyes. I slipped around a corner into a mews to hide and recover. At that moment, a guy stopped beside me on his bike.

'Hey, Phil! You have to come and see *Kinky Boots*, mate. It's a great show. I'm in it.'

'Okay, great, definitely,' I said as he pedalled off.

On another occasion, I slipped around the corner, closed my eyes. As I looked up to the sunshine and leaned back against a gate, it swung open and, thankfully, I caught the metal railing with my hand before I fell backwards down into someone's basement. That made a friend or two laugh when I told them.

Talking helped, and the pills I was prescribed took away the hard edges without having any other nasty side effects. But I knew what I had to do. I had to come out. If I didn't, the secret was going to give me a total breakdown . . . at best.

I had to confide in some of my friends. Not one single one of them said, 'Ah, that makes sense,' or 'I've always had my suspicions', or 'Yeah, I guessed.' Quite obviously, just as I didn't know, neither did they.

There had been moments when I was very down and Holly

knew something was wrong. A number of times she took me to one side and asked if I was okay. She never pushed, she was always so gentle and caring, but I could tell she was worried about me. 'Please talk to me,' she said. 'I'm always here.'

One day I knew I had to tell her, because I needed her. I needed her advice and her wisdom and I needed her to have my back at work if I faltered. I asked her to come into my dressing room and I told her everything. I knew she would be incredible. She was so much more than that. After I had confided in her and after the hugs, I opened my dressing-room door. Perfectly positioned on the floor outside was a pristine white feather. She picked it up and gave it to me.

'See,' she said. 'It's all going to be okay.' The feather is in my wallet.

Paul and Daz were also unflinching. 'Okay, mate. No problem. Now we understand your head. It'll be okay. We're here for you all.' We talked a lot about what it meant for the family, principally, how were the girls? How was Steph? All they cared about was our wellbeing and how we would pick our way through the uncertainty, confusion and heartache. I spoke to Simon Schofield, because his no-nonsense and pragmatic approach was vital. His words were also perfect. 'Oh, you twat. Why didn't you tell us all this before? Okay, we all have to make sure that Steph and the girls are okay, because that is a good place to start in your head.' We drank a lot of beer that day.

At the same time, home was my sanctuary, and it was Steph, my wife, the person who knew me best, who continually scraped me up.

At work, my make-up and wardrobe team knew something was up. Suzie and David are very dear friends. We've worked on so many shows together and they know me incredibly well. Neither of them knew why, but they could see the weight falling off me. The fun make-up room chats became fewer, as I stared into the mirror, trying to figure out my life.

As well as the love of my wife and my friends, I had my safe place: work. The closeness of the team around me, who were being so kind and caring because they, too, knew something was up. As I walked up the stairs from the production offices to the studio, I felt the distraction kick in.

Apart from home, this was where I was safest, in the studio, with people I adored, safe in the arms of a team and the comforting smell of TC3.

And then that professional rug was ripped from underneath my feet.

I have absolutely no problem with being held to account by newspapers. I know how lucky I am to have the job I have. I also know that in the game we all play, sometimes 'it's your turn'. Just as in *The Lord of the Rings*, where Sauron's all-seeking eye fixes on Frodo, so the ever-searching eye of the press settles on someone in the business and holds us to account, often, quite rightly. It keeps our feet on the ground. We see it happening to our friends and we offer words of sympathy and comfort: 'It'll pass,' or 'It'll be someone else tomorrow,' or 'No one believes it.'

Somewhere towards the end of 2019, Sauron's eye settled on me, but with such severity it stunned me and everyone around me. I couldn't understand what was happening. It felt like that moment between being asleep and being awake. When you wake up blinking and confused and, just for a moment, nothing makes sense. I was *in* that moment, but it lasted for months. Apparently, Holly and I were in the midst of a terrible feud. I was jealous of her success, the atmosphere at *This Morning* was strained, I was difficult to work with. I didn't recognize the man I was being portrayed as or the environment we were apparently working in. I didn't understand and, what's more, neither did my friends or my colleagues. As someone who has always tried to be the most fun to be around and always professional and caring, I was reading about a 'me' who was a total stranger. It felt like death by a thousand cuts, each little wound not serious on its own but, collectively, I felt like I was bleeding out. How many times had we said in interviews that one nasty comment online seems harmless, but the destructive power of many comments can be a mental disaster? I live a lucky life, yes, I've worked hard, but it certainly appears to be charmed. As anyone looking in would rightly say, 'It's just a bit of criticism. Man up. Grow a pair. It's the price you pay for the lovely house you live in, it's part of the job.' And that would have been absolutely true, had it not come on top of the most potentially catastrophic storm already raging in my head.

It went on, week after week, relentlessly feeding on itself and based on not one single truth that I could identify.

I think the most confusing story was my 'continuing' feud with Holly. What no one could possibly know at the time was that we were closer than we'd ever been. Holly knew my truth and was helping me to hold everything together. She was literally one of the friends I was desperately clinging on to. At work, I was constantly asked if I was okay. No, I really was not. I was not okay in any aspect of my life. I had nothing to hold on to. My ship was rudderless and sailing into the darkness. Again and again, Steph saved me. 'It'll pass.' 'It'll be someone else tomorrow.' 'No one believes it.'

By this stage, Molly, who had been employed by James Grant after uni, had worked her way through the ranks to become one of my managers. It was increasingly unbearable for her to juggle between being a reassuring manager and a daughter increasingly deeply worried about her dad. I was also well aware of the fact that, at that time, she only knew half of the turmoil.

Christmas 2019 was difficult in the extreme. To use a quote from *Friends*: 'There was rock bottom, then fifty feet of crap, and then me.'

No matter what, the James Grant mantra has always been, say nothing; no knee-jerk reactions. Keep your dignity. Keep your head down. If you comment, you add oxygen to the fire. Saying nothing starves it, but it's so incredibly painful to stand in the eye of a storm and stay silent as it rages around you.

Steph was extraordinary. She sectioned off the shit in her head and concentrated on family and happiness. I was in total awe at her ability to host Christmas for twenty-two family members while I was in such a state. As I was hurting

With Ruby.

and brooding, the girls, in contrast, were kind and loving. This was all so painful for Molly, because she had to deal with the cruelty on a managerial level and the fall-out at home on a father/daughter level. It was upsetting her to see her dad in so much pain and be powerless to make it stop. The hugs I got from all three of my girls were vital. I was beginning to feel a dawning realization. There was nothing I could do about Sauron's eye, but in the other aspect of my life I had to see if honesty could save me.

All over Christmas and the New Year I was very low and my head was in an extremely dark place. As I watched the fireworks explode over London on the TV on New Year's Eve, taking us into 2020, I sobbed quietly in the dark. The dawn of a New Year, and every bit of it looked terrifying. It's hard to explain how I felt, and to some extent still sometimes feel. It's like being inside the blackest cloud and feeling consumed by crushing, desperate sadness. Nothing and no one can make it better. There's an overpowering feeling of hopelessness that is very hard to shake.

A few years ago, Steph and I had a wonderful holiday in the Hamptons. We'd had our picture taken by a friend and, when I saw it, I was horrified by how chunky I looked. I was probably over twelve stone. I immediately put myself on the 5:2 diet, and it worked, so much so that my weight dropped to just under eleven stone and ITV asked the office if I was okay. I decided that eleven stone was as far as I should go. In the process, I'd shrunk my stomach, so my appetite was much smaller and the weight was easy to maintain. Now, I couldn't eat at all. I was in such a state of turmoil that I had no interest in food. Steph kept trying to get me to eat, but I couldn't face anything. My weight dropped, and as it hit nine stone twelve pounds the *This Morning* viewers started to notice. I was getting Tweets from people asking if I was ill, or saying that if I was on a diet I should stop, because I'd lost too much weight.

Would coming out save me? Would it fix what was wrong in my head? I had absolutely no idea if that level of honesty and immediate, intense public scrutiny would just make it worse. If I thought about what the potential cost would be, it just plunged me further into crisis. One difficult evening when I was talking it all through with Steph, I said that I felt like I'd fallen into the crack between two lives. How could I possibly align the two? How could I understand the implications? I could see no way forward and no way back. It all seemed so huge and so frightening. She continually reassured me that, no matter what, she unconditionally loved me, and so did the girls. As with so many things in my life, I can worry and torture myself but, ultimately, I knew what I had to do. I had to come out. Whatever the cost.

Telling the girls almost made me sick. Steph and I couldn't decide who should drive the car to tell them. Both our legs were like jelly. Steph drove in the end. They were extraordinary. My beautiful, wise, smart girls were suddenly, briefly, the parents as they leapt up to hug me and tell me it was going to be okay. I knew how much it hurt them, and still does, but I'm so bloody proud of them, and I'm so proud of how they have become fierce, protective lionesses around their mum.

Steph and I have always been careful with what we share about our lives. She is much more private than I am. Making this decision would attract a great deal of scrutiny and a great deal of that would be in her direction, and she was a totally innocent party. I couldn't bear that I would hurt her in public.

We had long, painful conversations, kept nothing from each other, approached it from every angle, day after painful day, hour after distraught hour.

There was another person that I had to tell. I had to come

out to my mum. I decided that if I drove to Cornwall, I couldn't guarantee that my concentration levels would be high enough to make driving safe, so I asked Tony to drive me down. He must have wondered what was going on. We stopped in Newquay town centre and Tony picked up fish and chips from Flounders. I couldn't go in, because this was a secret trip. I knocked on my mum's door and walked in with the fish and chips, I'd obviously warned her I was coming, and she was deeply suspicious. She had cornered me earlier in the year and said she knew something was wrong because I wasn't eating. I was so skinny and 'seemed so sad'. I told her, when the time was right, I would tell her, but promised I wasn't ill. We ate the fish and chips and chatted. Fistral Bay was shimmering in the sun. The beach looked beautiful. Out of her window I could see the car park where I had had my personally triumphant moment on the Roadshow all those years ago.

I told her. She looked at me and said:

'Oh.' There was a big pause, and she said, 'I wasn't expecting that. I thought you were going blind.'

'Blind?! Why the hell would you think I was going blind?'

'Your eye floaters bother you so much.'

I have really irritating floaters in each eye. They drive me mad, especially if they settle in the middle of my vision when I'm reading, or on a bright, sunny day. They are annoying, but harmless.

'No, Mum, my eyes are fine.'

'Well, darling, I don't care about your sexuality, as long as the four of you are okay and can work your way through this. I love you no matter what.'

I looked at her and started to cry.

'Would Dad be disappointed in me?'

'Oh my goodness, darling. No, he wouldn't. He would be so proud of you, just as he always was.'

The entire family reacted in the same way. I felt so incredibly lucky to have this support network around me. I know that many who come out are not so fortunate. More importantly, I knew that Steph and the girls would be smothered with love.

At Christmas, Steph's wonderful mum, Gill, had looked at me as I was clearing up and wiping surfaces, and said with a smile, 'You really are perfect, you know.'

I nearly burst into tears, but I just said, 'That's lovely to say, but no, Gill, I'm far from perfect.'

One of my greatest concerns was John, Steph's dad. I adore him, and he's pretty fond of me. I call him Captain because he used to both fly and sail. How does a father react when he finds out that his son-in-law has dropped such a bomb at the centre of his daughter's life? He texted me when Steph told him.

'I may be your pa-in-law, but think of me as your surrogate pa, and long may it continue! Briefed today. That's a big load off your mind. As long as Steph's okay, we don't have a problem.'

I texted back, 'Thank you so much, Captain. I'm so deeply, deeply sorry to disappoint you.'

'Nothing to be sorry for, so cheer up,' he replied.

At the precise moment Steph told her family (she decided that would be the best way), I was filming in Heathrow's Terminal 2. I was recording a summer *How to Spend It Well*. As I delivered my links and conducted my interviews, my phone kept lighting up with the reactions from the family. That was a hard shoot. The programme never went out anyway. You can't transmit a holiday show when everyone is in lockdown.

Paul, Daz and I also had many meetings. We had to decide on some kind of strategy. Unfortunately, something like this doesn't just happen. The right people have to know at the right time. It is testament to all my friends that not one single hint of what was to happen ever got leaked.

There was never any question that I would do this any other way than on the *This Morning* sofa. I had to be among friends for that moment, I had to have Holly opposite me and I owed it to our loyal viewing family that they should be the first to hear me speak. Holly and I had lunch at Mark's Club and sat outside on the terrace. It helped because she knows and cares for both me and Steph. We went through everything. What sort of impact would it have on my job? How would those that followed my career react? What about those who didn't? Would *This Morning* be okay? Would I be damaged? Although all of these things concerned me, I was more concerned for Steph and the girls. The public reaction would be what it would be. Holly spent the afternoon reassuring me that everything would be okay.

It was that afternoon that the date was decided. I suggested a Thursday. We could start the show together and then I could leave and Holly could continue with someone else.

'Absolutely not,' was her adamant response.

She said that there was no chance that I would come out and then she would carry on without me!

'We do this together, then we leave together.' So it had to be a Friday. And the one that worked was Friday, 7 February. I hated that I had to schedule something of this magnitude like a meeting. If only it could be simpler. If only I could run away and not have to face this.

I had started a WhatsApp group called 'The Event'. As it got closer and closer, I hired a PR company. I've never needed PR in my life, but I needed it now.

One of the men I most admire in my career is Martin Frizell, the editor of *This Morning*. He's a gruff Scot but a softie at heart, and I trust him with my life. He is a brilliant editor, maverick but sensible. He's been a journalist and broadcaster himself and he knows the game inside out. *This Morning* has shone under his leadership, as the National Television Awards prove. I called him into my dressing room to tell him. Paul was there and I asked Holly to come in and hold my hand. I told him.

'Oh, thank fuck. Is that it? I thought you were dying.'

The reaction throughout ITV was the same, from our CEO Dame Carolyn McCall, through Head of Studios Kevin Lygo to Managing Director of Daytime Emma Gormley. They all scooped me up and told me they were with me. I began to feel that at least my career would be okay.

My brand partners all said they stood shoulder to shoulder with me. I was so bloody proud of them all and so enormously grateful.

The stage was set. Tomorrow I nuke my life.

On Friday, 7 February 2020, I kissed goodbye to Steph and the girls and got into Tony's car. He was very confused. Why would I be going to Television Centre on a Friday? When I arrived, Paul was there, then Holly arrived. Kevin Lygo was there with the heavyweights of the ITV press department. Martin Frizell and Emma Gormley were there with big hugs of support. I would appear with Holly and then afterwards do one newspaper interview, and that would be it. No other comment. This book wasn't in my head, but then neither was a lockdown. Kevin Lygo looked me in the eye and said:

'Are you sure?'

'I'm absolutely sure.'

'Okay, that's good. We're very proud of you.'

Emily Page is my manager and part of my inner sanctum. She had of course been brought into the loop when I was ready to make my announcement and had been one of the

Us four at FriendsFest.

founder members of 'The Event' WhatsApp group. She is always such a powerful source of kindness and support. As I looked at her smiling face, her eyes willing me on and telling me this was going to be okay, I felt such adoration for my team, always there, always supportive, always utterly loyal. How lucky I am.

Very few of the *This Morning* gang knew why I was there or what was happening. Next to be told were my 'glam squad', my devoted friends David and Suzie. They had known for a long time that I was in a mess and had put it all down to the negative press coverage that I'd received. They, too, were relieved that I wasn't critically ill. Again, big hugs and those important words, 'We're right here with you.' I went in to see Eamonn and Ruth, who made me cry with their hugs and support. Suddenly, it became clear to them why there was a ten-minute 'news' item at the top of their show but they'd had no information as to what it was.

I had written two statements that were sitting in 'Notes' on my phone. At 9 a.m., I sent the first to all my friends, telling them what I was about to do. Andi Peters immediately texted back and made me laugh. He was in New York and asked if I was on *The Michael McIntyre Show*. Was this 'Send to All?' I texted back, saying no, it was real, and if it was 'Send to All', it was a pretty shit joke. The responses were instantly lovely. 'We love you.' 'You have our full support.' 'We're proud of you.'

The second statement was ready to post on Instagram at 9.45 a.m. There was a lot of work going on behind the scenes. A newspaper journalist had been told that she 'might want to come to Television Centre as something big was about to happen'. She was to be brought over to the studio as soon as I posted and could sit in the studio as Holly talked to me. When 9.45 ticked into view I was in a dressing room with

Holly, David and Suzie. We all looked at each other. This was the 'nuke' moment. My right thumb would change my life and the lives of all those around me for ever. They watched my thumb. It pressed send. And that was it. It was done. The result was almost instantaneous. All our phones started pinging with news alerts: 'Phillip Schofield comes out.'

We walked from the production offices up to the studio. By the time we got upstairs, everyone knew. The smiles and the 'well dones' were a huge help and steadied my nerves. Holly and I stood for a moment behind the scenes and had a final hug. 'It will be okay,' she reassured me. I turned to look at Paul and my *This Morning* family. About five minutes before the opening titles rolled we both walked on to the studio floor. Another hug from Eamonn and Ruth, and then the two of us walked over to sit down. I was holding on to Holly like a ship in a tempest needs an anchor. Sitting on the other side of the sofa from my friend was so tough. When we have a nervous guest, I always say, 'Keep looking into my eyes. You'll see all the support you need. Just keep looking at me.' I knew that's what I had to do now. If I needed a handhold to cling on to, I just had to look into Holly's eyes. Eamonn and Ruth explained to the viewers what was happening and handed over to Holly.

Holly was incredible, faultless in every way, journalistically and as a friend. It was a tough line to walk and, as always, she walked it with style, compassion and class.

There is no one else on the planet that I would have trusted with that moment. For me, it was her finest hour and I will never forget it.

The interview ended, Eamonn and Ruth came over for a hug and we went to a break. I walked across the studio floor and the *This Morning* team clapped as I walked past. I loved them so much for that. Downstairs and into my newspaper interview, and then it was done. That interview, which I was very happy with, said two things that were either misunderstood or I wasn't clear about. One of them I have already corrected at the start of this chapter. I absolutely did not know I was gay when I got married, or indeed, for many, many years after that wonderful day in Ackergill Tower. I also appeared to say that in coming out, there was 'no confusion'. I may not have been clear. But for me, there was nothing *but* confusion. Crippling, damaging confusion that still occasionally sits at the head of the table in my head. If you are gay and have no idea what to do, there will be mountains of confusion. It's okay, it gets better. Please talk to someone.

I finished the interview and walked back into the corridor, and there was Tony, with tears in his eyes.

'I'll always be proud to drive you,' he said.

If you call a *This Morning* phone-in and you need extra help, we might say, 'Stay on the phone.' The chances are you will talk to our counsellor, Penny Jordan, who is literally an angel in human form. My dressing room is next to Penny's office. One morning a few weeks before 'The Event', she was lying in wait. As I left my dressing room, she gently held both of my shoulders and looked me in the eye.

'I see you pass my office countless times every day. Every time your head is down as you walk. I want you to tell me what is wrong.'

'There's nothing wrong,' I said.

'*You* are a lying bastard,' said Penny.

Her office was next on my travels. She was in bits. We had a big hug, and after that and until lockdown and the building becoming practically empty, I visited her office a lot.

Back in the days that *This Morning* came from the Southbank, along with the charity CALM (Campaign Against Living Miserably), we launched Project 84, one of our proudest charity involvements. It was an art installation that placed eighty-four life-sized statues of men on the *This Morning* building and the ITV Tower. Every statue represented a man who had taken his own life in a week in the UK. Some of the statues were dressed by families in the clothes of the loved one they had lost. It was a heartbreaking representation of the pain felt by so many, and by the ones left behind. It led to the appointment by then PM Theresa May of the first UK Minister for Suicide Prevention.

Back downstairs in the quiet of the dressing room, and surrounded by my treasured friends and colleagues, I felt that maybe I might have helped advance the LGBTQ+ cause just a little further forward. It absolutely wasn't a flag I ever expected to wave, but I am proud to have picked it up. My friends got in touch in their hundreds, and people who I didn't expect to hear from, people who stunned me with their love and support and words of kindness. From all across the business and all across the world, I felt a very tight hug.

On social media, there were so many words of encouragement, I was a 'legend' and an 'icon'. I felt like neither, but I know that I have helped a lot of other people to take that step and I'm incredibly proud of that.

At the end of that extraordinary day, I was desperate to get home to hug my family, the three people who now had to pick their own way through the debris that I had caused.

It was done. I had opened up Pandora's box. Now I would find out what was inside.

The mainstream press was incredibly supportive. I was pleased across the board with the way they had handled my story, and I'm immensely grateful to them for that. Sauron's eye was again firmly fixed on me, but this time I felt genuine kindness and support. It obviously also focused on Steph, but that was understandable, and we all hunkered down together. This was not the attention that I ever wanted to be fixed on her. I felt such overwhelming love for her. She was still by my side, still my girl.

I had agonized over this decision for a long time. It was vital for me and my family that I was as dignified as I possibly could be, for their sake. Over many, many sleepless nights, I had approached the chaotic loops from every point of view, weighed up every angle and consequence. I knew what to expect and I knew we'd get through it. I also knew that amid the kindness there would also be cruelty. I'd always had a relatively easy ride on social media, but it can occasionally turn against you and the relentless negativity of the professionally outraged can sap your ability to see the good in people.

Twitter, in particular, is a strange beast. I was one of the first telly folk to join, after Stephen Fry and Jonathan Ross. Back then, it was a small and very funny club. You could post an observation or something you found amusing, and the Twitter folk would happily jump in and continue the joke. And then the miserable, perpetually angry keyboard warriors found it. Those who were on the constant look-out to find something that would offend them. I've so often had my finger over the delete button, but then just decided not to look at it for a while. I just stick it in a far-off folder on a distant page on my phone and let it fester for a bit. Years earlier, one set of Tweets had me in that 'hovering delete' mode, until I saw how ludicrous it was.

Me: Oh, great, the Brit Awards are on.
Twitter: They're shit, the music this year has been shit.
Me: Great! Love that Mumford and Sons have won best album.

Twitter: They're a shit band with shit music.

Me (the next day): What a beautiful day.

Twitter: The weather is shit here, stop rubbing it in, just shut up.

Me: I think I'll go for a walk.

Twitter: You're lucky you've got legs.

It had become like the comments section of an online paper. You could post a picture of a basket of kittens and someone would find a way to be offended. I've often said that the comment sections of some online papers is like staring directly up the devil's arse.

The comments section on Instagram is, sadly, going the same way. For the moment, the good folk on Snapchat are still mostly funny.

I expected a wave of hatred. It didn't come, and on the whole people were very kind and supportive. Some attacked on behalf of Steph. I understood that and, although it really stung, I was glad for her that people were so kind. A few accused me of 'lying to her for twenty-seven years'. That is absolutely not the case. When I eventually knew, so did she. It was, however, lovely, on the whole, to see a kinder, more inclusive side to the online comments.

What I didn't expect was the Wild West cesspit of fake-news websites online. Unregulated and able to concoct any story they cared to invent. Family friends and valued work colleagues plus their friends and families were dragged into vile lies and wicked innuendo. It was the very last thing I expected to happen, and it stunned me. The saddest thing is how many people are happy to lap it up and repeat it back to me. Like sheep being led, bleating from one story to another, happy to believe anything. Apparently, there were super injunctions in place. Apparently, a national newspaper was bribing me to come out (which is illegal on so many levels). All total bollocks.

There is still, sadly, a seething pit of homophobia in our country and, just as I was happy to pick up the rainbow flag, I'm also happy to point a finger at the unregulated filth that pollutes our online news.

Make sure you get your news from reliable sources. Don't be a sheep, obediently following where you are led and bleating your beliefs online. Give people the benefit of the doubt and above all else . . . be kind.

I felt like I was wearing new clothes and now I had to go out to see how people felt to see me wearing them. The first test after that Friday was *Dancing on Ice* on the Sunday. Our production meeting was loving and supportive. The faces of the people I loved working with so much still smiled, they still cracked jokes. It was still them. I was still me.

Rehearsing in the studio was odd, though. I said to Holly, 'It doesn't feel right.' She said, 'They probably don't know how to react.' Halfway through the rehearsal, mid-link, I stopped and said to everyone at the rink, 'I know there is a massive elephant in the room, but if you want to give me a hug, I'd really appreciate it.'

The atmosphere in the room changed. It was as if everyone just needed permission to acknowledge what they knew. There was a collective sigh of relief. I got a lot of hugs that day. I wondered how the audience would react when I was introduced to them just before the show went live. The applause as I walked out with Holly was loud and sustained, and so needed. It was a very emotional show. But not as emotional as the one we would present a week later, when it was announced that our friend Caroline Flack had taken her life. Another lost soul who fell through the net.

15

I came out on 7 February and my phone went into melt-down. My friends were anxious to check in on me.

'We need to check you're okay.'

'Come out to dinner.'

'You're amazing, and so brave.'

My family were astonishingly supportive, constantly texting to see if I was all right.

Suddenly, I was being asked for advice and guidance from people, young and old, who saw me as some kind of torch-bearer. They felt trapped; could I help them? How had I got the guts? How should they come out to their families? I'm very careful to explain that I'm not a professional therapist or qualified adviser, but I help where I can, and it's been deeply heartening to hear back from people who took a brave step forward because of me and who found family and friends to be sensitive, loving and supportive. I had a message from a guy who was married with a child and realized he was gay. He had come out a few years ago but it had been very difficult. He said to me:

'Up until this year I struggled with it and wanted to end my life as a result. You changed that and changed my mind-set. Thanks to you, I have never been more proud, and I look at you and you continue to inspire me every day. Thank you for changing my life for the better, you rock.'

That meant the world to me. It's moments like that I cling to if the clouds roll in.

I'm also very aware that understanding and sensitivity is

not always the outcome in many families and that the struggle goes on. I have had some desperately sad conversations on social media and have had to come to the conclusion that the best help would be in the comforting arms of the Samaritans. If you are one of those people I spoke to, I hope you're okay.

I have also had people stop me to confide in me. I've been told extraordinary secrets in confidence by people who felt that because I had been so honest, I could obviously be trusted. As I've said before, I'm the best secret-keeper!

My world was new and different. I stopped to buy a card in a card shop; it was the first time I'd ventured out to the shops. The lady behind the counter looked at me and asked if I was all right. I said yes, I thought I was. As I got to the door of the shop, a well-spoken and elegant elderly lady grabbed my arm.

'It's you!' she said. I braced myself for a negative reaction.

'You have no idea the good you have done, you have no idea the lives you have saved and I am so very proud of you.' I felt the tears well up in my eyes as I thanked her for her kindness.

People were kind in the street, too, coming up to me and offering hugs, which I accepted. Complete strangers just walked up to me, looked me in the eye and asked if I was okay. They told me I was brave. Straight or gay, they told me how much I had helped move the country forward a step or two and then they put their arms around me and gave me a hug. One of the things I miss the most in lockdown and with social distancing are hugs. It has been made very clear to me just how much we humans need physical contact. A reassuring touch of the hand, a hug when you most need it. For many, it is what changes us from a lonely island into a loved village.

Two of our experienced female team members on *Dancing on Ice* called me into their office and told me that because of what I'd done, they had finally decided to declare their love to one another publicly and set a date for their wedding. A journalist who had been part of Sauron's machinery texted me to say that she thought I'd advanced the cause by ten years.

Maybe things might be okay. There is a red-flag emoji on my phone and I have a code with my family and my closest friends. If I send the red flag, I'm in trouble. I've been close, but I haven't yet had to fly it.

I was beginning to feel happy in the warmth of the people I was meeting. The kind words and unexpected hugs were beginning to make me feel better about myself.

Then along came 23 March 2020 and Covid-19 put the UK into lockdown.

No friends to meet, no dinners, no plans.

I came out and the world went in.

Holly and I were given key-worker status, so we could travel from work and home. In case Television Centre was closed at short notice, all of the Daytime presenters had mini studios installed in their homes so that we could work remotely. The wifi at home is too weak to broadcast, so the studio has been built in our flat in London. So far, it hasn't been needed.

And so, it is today.

We are, miraculously, still on air with *This Morning* from TC3, sharing our limited facilities with *Good Morning Britain* and *Lorraine*. No guests are allowed into the studio and so everyone is 'down the line'. I counted the staff in our studio at *This Morning*. It's usually heaving. If you include me and Holly, today there were eight people. The team spirit is remarkable and we're all holding each other together. We often look at each other as we wait to go on air with expressions of 'what the hell has happened here?'

I think our viewers are finding some comfort in the 'normality' of us being there each morning. We just got our highest viewing figures for seventeen years. I know without a doubt that presenting the show each day during lockdown has been my saviour; it's given a sense of normality in my head in a suddenly very different world.

So, what happens now for me? What am I supposed to do next? There's no rule book here, no roadmap. Holly has continued to be my daily therapist each morning in the make-up room. It's just the two of us getting ready these days, but although we both desperately miss our 'glam squad' friends, I'm loving the one-to-one time we get with each other. I'm lucky to have such a wise, kind and loving friend. I said to her today that she has a calming, spiritual aura around her that is so soothing. She said she wished she could really hug me rather than send virtual, socially distanced hugs from two metres away. I'd like that. I'm really ready for it.

I'm not fixed, though, not yet. I wouldn't want you to go away thinking that I am.

In so many of the texts and messages I've been sent, people have said I can now 'live my best life'. I wish it was as simple as that. For a very long time, I thought I was! I wish I had the vaguest notion of what 'my best life' actually could be. I will always be aware that each step I take, in any direction, will have consequences. I seem to be walking through a bizarre minefield. Wherever I step, I blow someone else up. My mental health is still a work in progress. I talk regularly to a professional team who tell me that everything will be okay. Sometimes I have my doubts. If I'm totally honest with you, as I've said before, it's not in my nature to hurt people and so, with that in mind, I'm finding it hard to pick my way through the debris. Is there a way to reveal a secret like this to the world and not hurt your wife or your family? The answer is obviously not. But we are close and loving. We'll get through. Am I struggling with it all? Very much. I'm wearing new clothes, but they don't quite fit. Maybe I'll grow into them.

I still have dark days full of confusion, days when wading

through life would be easier if the water wasn't at chest height. The overriding question has always been 'How do I make this work?' The dominant emotion is still guilt – I've found out I'm really good at guilt. I would go so far as to admit that I am now a guilt ninja. I should have realized that, though. When I was about seven, my mum lovingly made me some fish-paste sarnies for me to take to school for lunch. I hated them and threw them in the bin. I still feel guilty about that even now. Yes, I'm good at guilt. I like to think that I've always been sensitive and empathic towards others, but maybe now I'll be on higher alert for those who run up their own red flag. I know that I am profoundly changed as a man. I think I'll properly find out how changed I am when my head isn't so bloody exhausted from all the self-analysis and worry. How can you think about moving forward if the entire world is paused?

Life at home is as loving as it has always been. The girls are here in lockdown with us, as is Ruby's boyfriend, Will, who, right from the lockdown announcement, chose to be here with us and is great company. It's a tight family unit. We wish Molly's boyfriend, who is also called Will, could be here, too. It's a great feeling to know that both of my girls have their own wonderful support. It's like a thriving office with so many people working from home, but there's also lots of baking and lots of puzzles and, thankfully, lots of sunshine and laughter. The girls don't talk about it very much. I guess they are at the start of their own long healing process.

I talk a lot with Steph, though. She continues to be the most incredibly understanding foundation to my head, spirit and soul. She's very good at guiding me through the bleak moments when they wash over me. She is kinder to me and more understanding than I deserve. Am I a good support for her? Again, how does that work? What is my role? For the

moment, our best currency is hugs. She knows how much I love her. I'm glad that 'The Event' has enabled her to talk this through with her friends, because for so long she didn't have anyone to talk to, and I hated that. I want to make good on my promise to her dad, John. I will always make sure she is safe and secure and I will love her for ever. She is constantly loving and thoughtful. The other day she gave me a wrapped gift. I opened it and it was Charlie Mackesy's *The Boy, The Mole, The Fox and the Horse*. She said it might help my head. When I read it, it made me cry. So much of it was what I felt, and it was immensely comforting. If you're struggling with heavy thoughts, I highly recommend it. It was such a typically beautiful thing for her to do for me.

I was right in one respect. Pressing the 'nuke' button released a lot of pressure. It's certainly not sunny with blue skies in my head at the moment – it may never be – but the sky isn't always as black as it was and there are fewer hurricanes.

I know for a fact that, no matter what, I love the three most important women in my life, and I know they love me. All three of my girls have read this book and have given their approval. We all know that releasing it will open everything up to scrutiny again and that Sauron will once more look in our direction, I hope kindly, at least for them.

Work is my enduring foundation. My life in television remains as exciting and fulfilling as it was when I first looked into a camera in the *Shazam!* audition. It is where I want to be, it is everything I had hoped it would be and more and it has given me some of the greatest moments of my life. It is also where I intend to stay for as long as it will have me. I think *it* will decide when it is bored of me, long before I am bored of it. There is constant speculation that Holly and I are leaving *This Morning*. As I type these words, that is most definitely not the case. We have travelled with the show through the uncertainty of lockdown and we intend to be there when the world walks blinking into the sunshine again and then to continue with it into the future. Beyond that, I'll be honest with you, I don't know. Which of us can map out their future with confidence? Let's just see what happens, eh? And 2021 will mark forty years in television for me, so I'll stick around for the party.

There have been many times when I've thought how lucky the kid from Newquay has been. There are moments when I've pinched myself and thought, 'How did this ever happen? How did you do this? How did you get here?' Sometimes, when people ask me how I am, I'll reply, 'Still getting away with it.' I never forget how lucky I am.

When I served that explosive can of Coke to the bright-red man at the end of Fistral beach, I could have no idea that this was where my life would take me. In a way, I'm thankful to lockdown for giving me the time to tell it. I've interviewed so many people who have written their autobiographies, many of whom say it was a cathartic experience. I think it's been cathartic. Most of it has been great fun to remember and to discuss with everyone. I'm just not sure yet how much the final couple of chapters have helped. Maybe they helped you? If that happens to be the case, then it was worth it.

As I said in my statement, released on Instagram: 'You never know what is going on in someone's seemingly perfect life, what issues they are struggling with, or the state of their wellbeing.' I hope I have now explained a little more than I wrote in that brief statement. I went on to say: 'My inner conflict contrasts with an outside world that has changed so very much for the better. Today, quite rightly, being gay is a reason to celebrate and be proud.' I am immensely proud of myself. I'm not sure about the celebration, though. Maybe that will come in time. Besides, the pubs are shut anyway.

We are all walking our own paths through life, sometimes alone, sometimes with company. Some of us on that path have a clear, determined view of the destination, some are stumbling and lost. Some smile as they walk, others walk with their heads down. The path can be joyful and fulfilling or it can be chaotic, confusing and frightening. Whatever path we walk, we have to take comfort and support from those we find walking beside us. We should not be embarrassed to hold out our hand for help and allow others to show us the way forward. If we see someone stumble and fall, we should be there to offer our hand to help them back up because, no matter who we are, we all walk together.

Talk openly to the people around you, they may surprise you with their understanding. Above all . . . be kind.

What on earth am I going to do now? Maybe I'll buy a bike.

Thank You

To my gorgeous Stephie. Literally, no words will ever suffice. I love you.

To Molly and Ruby, for loving me so much. No man could wish for two more perfect daughters.

To you all . . . Us 4, for ever. The same, but different.

To my incredible, understanding, endlessly loving and, as it turns out, very modern mum, thank you for being there and for the calming chats.

To my dad, the kindest man in the world and who gave me my sense of humour. I hope I still make you proud.

To my brother, Tim, you mean the absolute world to me, but you know that.

To my incredible family for not wavering for a second.

To my wonderful network of friends, who have made me and us feel so supported.

To my teams past and present at YMU (James Grant), who, over the years, have always been there for me 24/7.

To Pete, Paul, Daz, Russ and Simon, you know how important you are to me, my besties.

To darling Mish, 'lil sis', for her diligent checking.

To Amanda at YMU, for teasing this book out of me.

To my manager, Emily Page, always by my side in waters calm or stormy.

To Martin Frizell and Emma Gormley, I couldn't be in more caring, gentle and calming hands.

To Kevin Lygo, Carolyn McCall, Peter Bazalgette and the

entire ITV family, for your support, kindness and for making me feel safe.

To the ever loyal *This Morning* team, who I totally adore and of whom I'm so proud.

To everyone I have worked with over the years. Each of you has individually added all the layers and wonderful colour to my career. Thank you for adding your memories and some of the details for this book.

To Phil, Jill and Emma, who take care of my head when the storm rages.

Thank you to Holly, for listening, hugging (when we were allowed), reassurance, love and wisdom. The sister I never had, I love you so much.

To Louise, Charlotte, Clare and the team at Michael Joseph, my publishers (how grown-up!). I couldn't have met a kinder and more thoughtful new literary family, not just for me, but also for Steph.

Thank you to Lisa, Jo, Anne, Lesley, Amanda, Grainne, Ellen, Jan, Julie, Grace and Michelle. I'm immensely lucky to have such incredibly loyal fans, but you win the prize for being there the longest.

To Charlie Mackesy, whose book helped me so much when I needed it. I'm immensely grateful that you have done an illustration for me.

Thank you to Joss for being so caring and kind as I recorded the audiobook.

And thank you . . . to you, for reading and for sticking with me through the years x